CONTEMPORARY ARCHITECTURE IN CHINA

Towards A Critical Pragmatism

Edited by Li Xiangning   Translated by He Yanfei

CONTEMPORARY ARCHITECTURE IN CHINA

Towards A Critical Pragmatism

images
Publishing

Contents

Foreword

Li Xiangning

Architectural exhibition is an important aspect in the study and transmission of architectural culture. Throughout Western architecture, we find that the academic thoughts and design styles that influence the trends of global architecture are all established through important architectural exhibitions, such as the 'International Style Exhibition' (1932) and 'Deconstructivism Exhibition' (1988) of the Museum of Modern Art in New York (MOMA). The rapid development of Chinese modern cities and large quantities of architectural design practices have been winning unprecedented attention to modern Chinese architecture and opportunities for its development. Exhibitions featured with the theme in modern Chinese architecture are staged in important international academic conferences and exhibitions held by Venice Biennale of Architecture, the Culture Center of Ponpieer in Paris, Nederlands Architectuurinstituut (NAI), and so on.

This book is also schemed with the inspiration from an exhibition. I was invited by Harvard Graduate School of Design (GSD) in 2016 to be a visiting professor on contemporary Chinese architecture and cities. I took this opportunity to hold the main exhibition of the GSD Autumn 2016: 'Towards a Critical Pragmatism: Contemporary Architecture in China.' The exhibition, presenting 60 works of 60 contemporary Chinese architects, revealed the features of contemporary Chinese architecture from a unique perspective. It is the first large-scale collective appearance of contemporary Chinese architecture in North America. Interestingly, it coincided with the 60th birthday of Yongho Chang—the oldest architect in the exhibition, so the exhibition was also a gift to him and the generation of architects after him.

When I returned to China from Harvard, Images Publishing Group contacted me in the hope of collecting these works from the exhibition in a book. I think contemporary Chinese architecture is constantly developing and growing, and what is recorded in the book may be a section or specimen of the age. Maybe when we look back upon this golden time of contemporary Chinese architecture several decades later, we will sigh with emotion. As a record of the time, the collection of works naturally has its own value. Due to considerations on the themes, types, and occasion of the exhibition, some works and architects were not selected in the exhibition. We hope there are other opportunities for them to be presented in larger-scale retrospective exhibitions.

I will give my appreciation to Mohsen Mostafavi, professor and Dean of the Harvard Graduate School of Design, who is responsible for arranging the exhibitions; Inaki Abalos, professor and Dean of architecture at Harvard University; Michael Hays and Antonie Picon, professors who attended the dialogue with Chinese architects in the opening forum; Kenneth Frampton, a professor who commented on the exhibition in the subsequent speech; Dan Borelli, who worked hard for the exhibition; and SO-IL office in New York, which provided brilliant exhibition design.

Thanks for Chen Ciliang and Liu Guanghan from Images Publishing Group who kept encouraging and pushing me to publish the exhibition works. I also want to express my gratitude to my students, including Gao Changjun, Yao Weiwei, Jiang Jiawei, Wu Yuhe, Chen Jiadi, and so on, who made huge contributions to the exhibition and the book. Without their efforts, the exhibition and the book would have been impossible.

Heartfelt thanks for those architects who have made constant contributions to contemporary Chinese architecture. They are good teachers and helpful friends who have enthusiastically supported my exhibitions and the publication of this book and painstakingly prepared all the materials. Lastly, I would also like to thank the age that we shall all feel grateful: it has helped foster Chinese contemporary architecture and architects.

From 'experimental architecture' to 'critical pragmatism': Practice of contemporary individual architects in China

Li Xiangning

In March 2010, an exhibition themed 'Projects across China: architecture stories of three studios from 1999 to 2010' and a symposium were held in Beijing. It was a joint exhibition on the works of Atelier Liu Jiakun, Mada Spam, and Urbanus—the three very active and representative architectural firms in contemporary Chinese architecture. All the three firms were established in 1999, the same year that the UIA World Congress of Architecture was held in Beijing. The decade had witnessed the growth and expansion of Chinese privately operated architectural firms and their competing with state-owned design institutes. The exhibition symbolized the particular voice gradually heard from this unique group in contemporary Chinese architectural practice. Encountering similar dilemmas of contemporary artists,[1] private architectural firms were nearly excluded from all official design awards (including the National Survey and Design Awards and the Architectural Society of China's Design Awards) because they were outside the state-owned institute system. However, they dominated the international and domestic exhibitions and media reports, and even become idols of the mass media and architecture students.

According to a research study about leading Chinese architectural journals,[2] among the top 40 architects whose works were reported and commented on the most since 2000, individual architectural practices accounted for 60 percent, the architects who taught in architecture schools and owned relatively independent studios in medium and large design institutes account for 27.5 percent, while the full-time architects from the state-owned design institutes account for only 12.5 percent.

Since the establishment of the people's republic of China, the key player in Chinese architectural practices has been the state-owned design institutes. Privately-operated architectural firms began to emerge in 1980s and, arguably, they started to draw public attention since Yungho Chang founded Atelier FCJZ (Fei Chang Jian Zhu) in 1993 after he returned to China from the United States. The discussion about experimental architecture among architectural journals like The Architect and World Architecture Review was mostly about the practice of the budding individual architects then, like Yungho Chang, Liu Jiakun, Wang Shu, Zhao Bing, Tang Hua, and so on. And an experimental paradigm, different from that of the mainstream state-owned architecture institutes, emerged from the practices of these rising stars architects. Their 'experiments,' in some way, threw a challenge to the mainstream model, and gained steam for the architecture culture with the latest Western architecture theory and practice as reference. A new movement finally took place and

architecture, as a new contemporary culture public, attracted more and more public attention and enthusiasm.

Encouraged by the success of the predecessor individual architects, more and more graduated architecture students decided to establish their own architectural firms to conduct independent architectural practice, most of which are based in major cities of China. Many of these architects have overseas study experience, and some even worked in Western architectural firms for several years. Most of them are base in China's major cities. By the virtue of the urbanism and culture there, they are frequently seen at architectural exhibitions and reported by mass media. In the 2013 Shanghai's Westbund Biennale of Architecture and Contemporary Art, which gave a comprehensive and complete review of China's contemporary architecture since the year of 2000, nearly 70 Chinese architects, mainly individual architects, were selected to participate in the exhibition. Among them, about 35 percent were from Beijing, 30 percent from Shanghai, and the remaining 35 percent from all the other regions of China.

Different from the experimental architectural practices in the 1990s, there were a large number of younger individual architects with more diversified patterns of practice. Without a definite common guiding principles or revolutionary commitment, they worked for the government, private developers, small private owners, and other different kinds of clients. More flexible and adaptive strategies have been evolved. 'Critical pragmatism' may be an appropriate term to describe the collective practices of contemporary Chinese individual architects of the new millennium.

This chapter tries to sort out the practices of individual architects in China from 1990s 'experimental architecture' to a contemporary approach of 'critical pragmatism' A shift of practical strategies, as a response to changing social reality and a spatial production system, will be discussed. Current opportunities and challenges brought about by the latest new technology and social transformation will also be examined.

I. Experimental architecture as resistance

No matter if the term 'experimental architecture' is agreed upon or not, it is indisputable that in 1990s a kind of 'new' architectural practice 'different' from the past practice appeared in China. Such new and different aspects are not only reflected in the architecture image, but also in the more independent way of thinking and manner of working. Many scholars in China described this new architectural practice as experimental architecture, and accordingly the designers were tagged as experimental architects, most of whom were the emerging individual architects. Over 10 years, these experimental architects turned into a group of star architects with vigorous creativity and outstanding works executed now and then in contemporary China.

1   Today, Chinese art academy system and official artists and painters' association develop in a totally different direction from the practices of so-called 'independent contemporary art artists.'
2   The study and report conducted for 2013 Westbund Biennale of Architecture and Contemporary Art, by Wang Kai, Zeng Qiaoqiao, and Li Xiangning. It was based on publications of China's five leading architecture magazines, including Architectural Journal, Time+Architecture, World Architecture, The Architect, and New Architecture.

As a matter of fact, the so-called experimental architecture and experimental architects were closely bound with the specific social economy and cultural backdrop of China in the late 1980s and early 1990s. At the time, a new trend was surging—in both contemporary art and in architecture—in the desire to break through tradition and communicate with the world. The development of contemporary art (the '85 New Tide' art movement as an important node) and introduction and translation of foreign architectural theories set the stage for Chinese experimental architecture. If the 10 years between mid-1980s and mid-1990s, can be thought of as the 'preparation period'[3] of Chinese experimental architecture, another decade, starting from the mid-1990s, is when Chinese experimental architecture boomed, witnessing a number of emerging architects, buildings, and architecture events, and recording the development trajectory of Chinese experimental architecture—the phenomenon coming into being as response to the social transition period of China.

Chang Yungho, Ma Qingyun, Wang Shu, Liu Jiakun, and Tang Hua were definitely the leading figures of Chinese 'experimental architects.' Chang Yungho and Ma Qingyun were educated abroad and established their own architectural firms. In 1993, Chang Yungho established Atelier FCJZ and two years later, Ma Qingyun founded his Mada Spam. In 1996, Chang Yungho completed the reconstruction project for Xishu Bookstore in Beijing, which is arguably known as the first and famous example in Chinese experimental architecture. Chang's other project—the Split House of the commune by the Great Wall—puts forth efforts in addressing the issues of material and structure. Chang also discussed the relationship between Chinese tradition and modern urbanism through installation works such as 'Bamboo City.'

Tianyi Square of Ningbo and the reconstruction of the entrance of Garden of Winding Water (Qu Shui Yuan) in Qingpu district of Shanghai designed by Ma Qingyun both illustrate his reflection of China's current urbanism. Irony and banter that are often found in his works have fully replied to the rapidly growing new urban fabric and declination, death and renewal of the old urban quarters. He borrowed this idea and used it as the theme of the 2005 Shenzhen Biennale, of which he was the chief curator.

Different from Chang Yungho and Ma Qingyun, Wang Shu and Liu Jiakun were homegrown architects. Wang Shu's thorough comprehension of and strong interest in Chinese traditional culture had made him a traditional cultural man, who is persistent in reference of traditional cultural artistic conceptions in his architectural design. His early work, Wenzheng Library of Suzhou University, was designed as pure white and simple modern volumes, which implied

the special reference to Chinese traditional gardens. Although he read Western authors like Roland Barthes and Jaque Derrida, Wang Shu insisted on using traditional Chinese materials like dark blue brick, wood, ceramic tile, and rammed earth and applied traditional construction technology in his buildings or art installations.

Such exploration in 'Chineseness' was perfectly demonstrated in Xiangshan Campus of China Academy of Art and Ningbo History Museum. Liu Jiakun used to work for a state-owned design institute. He showed his interest in humanity and literature from the early stage of his career and even published his own novel. Like the term he used to describe his career, 'designing in the west of China,' he set up his firm in Chengdu. His designing works Mrgadava Museum of Stone Sculpture and the faculty building of Sculpture Department in Sichuan Academy of Fine Arts applied regional materials and construction, revealing his unique understanding of China's architecture in the western region and local cultural characteristics. Public attention to Tang Hua has resulted from his proficient command of modernistic form, which was very rare in Chinese architects at that time. He is the first among all Chinese architects to have a solo exhibition in the Shanghai Art Museum. On the list of experimental architects, we can also find younger architects like Dong Yugan, Zhu Jinxiang, Zhang Lei, Urbanus, Wang Yun, Zhu Pei, Atelier Deshaus, Standard Architecture, and so on.

Apart from architects and their works, there were a series of architecture events (exhibitions, forums, and so on) evolved around Chinese experimental architecture. In the 'experiment and dialogue,' a symposium on Chinese young architects and artists, held in Guangzhou in May 1996, was where the term 'experimental architecture' was put forward. In 1998, two Chinese scholars, Wang Mingxian and Shi Jian, published an article in *Literature & Art Studies* titled 'Chinese experimental architecture in 1990s.' In 1999, Wang Mingxian curated an exhibition titled 'Chinese Young Architects' Experimental Architecture,' during the 20th UIA World Congress of Architecture, and Yungho Chang, Zhao Bing, Tang Hua, Wang Shu, Liu Jiakun, Zhu Wenyi, Xu Weiguo, and Dong Yugan participated in the exhibition.

In 2000, a documentary exhibition of five architects (namely, Yungho Chang, Wang Shu, Ma Qingyun, Dong Yugan, and Zhu Jinxiang) was held in the Shanghai Topart Gallery designed by Wang Shu. In 2001, the 'Tu Mu—Young Architecture of China' exhibition was held in Berlin Aedes East gallery with the participation of Ai Weiwei, Yungho Chang, Liu Jiakun, Ma Qingyun, Wang Shu, and Zhang. This exhibition marked the first appearance of Chinese architects as a group on international stage. In 2002, *Time+Architecture* magazine published a special issue on 'Chinese experimental architecture,' which reviewed the works of the architects under the umbrella of 'experimental architecture.' One year later, the 'Extraordinary 10

3   Shi Jian, 'Transformation of Experimental Architecture: The Contemporary Chinese Architecture in Post-experimental Age,' *Sixty Years of Chinese Architecture (1949–2009): History, Theory and Criticism*, Zhu Jianfei (ed.), Beijing, China Architecture & Building Press, 2012, p. 296.

years in Chinese architecture' exhibition conducted by Atelier FCJZ in Beijing was taken as another landmark in Chinese experimental architecture, which also highlighted the practice of Chang Yungho as an individual architect and inspired more young architects and architectural students to explore thoughtful and independent architectural practice beyond the mainstream official architecture design institute system.

Although it might be difficult to clearly define 'experimental architecture' in China, a rough list of related key words will help people understand this concept: young architects, individual practice, privately-operated architectural firms, avant-garde, marginality, contemporariness, Chineseness, and so on. Some of these words indicate the age of the architects; as Rao Xiaojun pointed out in his article, some expressed a strong questioning attitude and challenging gesture towards orthodox or mainstream architecture trends and ideas from the very beginning.[4] As Wang Mingxian put it in his article, "since the 1980s, the Chinese architects have broken the limitation set by the pure architecture tradition, and attempted to draw and extract the internal essence of the Eastern architecture from classical art. The experimental architecture of 1990s has proved the young architects' efforts in mastering traditional spirit more broadly and thoroughly. They are not content with the extraction of traditional cultural details any more, but try to establish a new evaluation system under the condition of cultural exchange at present times, to seek and interpret an eastern culture that can counterweigh the Western culture."[5]

Another writer, Li Wuying, points out more clearly that the new architects (mainly referring to Wang Shu, Liu Jiakun, and Yungho Chang) are apt to be "right-leaning, conservative, personal, narrowly-narrative, emphasizing autonomous issues of architecture itself, tectonics, light and personal aesthetic experience; but the architecture before 1976 are almost completely opposite: left-leaning, (politically) radical, collective, broadly-narrative, irrespective of architecture itself."[6] I myself would rather use the term 'resistance' or 'refusal' to describe the attitudes of the independent individual architects, to use architecture as vehicle to challenge the Western and Chinese mainstream architectural discourse and ideology, with or without consciousness in their pursuit of avant-gardism.[7]

II. Diversified architectural practice and critical pragmatism

Circling back to the 10-year exhibition 'Projects across China: architecture stories of three studios from 1999 to 2010' by Liu

Jiakun, Mada Spam, and Urbanus, the exhibition title geographically summarizes the cities (Beijing, Shanghai, Shenzhen, Xi'an, and Chengdu) where the three firms and their branches are located, but we can also find such information delivered: compared with the 1990s' experimental architecture movement with only several representative architects, today's China has witnessed individual architects establishing their own tribes and clusters in several important cities. Most of them are the main force between their 40s and 50s, such as: Yungho Chang, Ma Yansong, Wang Hui, Zhu Pei, Zhang Ke, Hua Li, Li Hu, Dong Gong, Li Xinggang, Li Xiaodong, Wang Yun, Wu Gang, Dong Yugan, Xu Tiantian in Beijing, Ma Qingyun, Liu Yichun, Chen Yifeng, Zhuang Shen, Yuan Feng, Zhang Ming, Zhang Bin, Rossana Hu, Liu Yuyang, Zhu Xiaofeng, Tong Ming, Li Li, Li Linxue, Yu Ting, Zhang Jiajing, Bu Bing in Shanghai, Zhang Lei, Ge Ming, Fu Xiao, Zhou Ling in Nanjing, Liu Xiaodu, Meng Yan, Liu Heng in Shenzhen, Liu Kecheng in Xi'an, Wei Chunyu in Changsha, Liu Jiakun in Chengdu, Wang Shu in Hangzhou, Wang Weiren, Zhu Jingxiang, John Lin in Hong Kong, as well as Huang Shengyuan and Xie Yingjun in Taiwan. There are also some young architects in their 30s emerging with talents demonstrated, such as Han Tao, Tao Lei, Wang Shuo, Feng Guochuan, Fan Ling, Wang Yan, and so on.

These individual architects meet and communicate in various publications, exhibitions, collective design activities, and seminars, revealing different subpopulation characteristics of different cities. In addition, they participate in the architectural education of well-known Chinese architectural schools in small groups. Recently, Tongji University in Shanghai and Tsinghua University in Beijing successively invited more than 10 individual architects to teach as visiting professors. With a focus on architectural practice, these architects also develop their career in multi-dimensions, including exhibitions, writing, teaching, academic research, and cultural communication. Such a state is quite different from that of Western architects and also their predecessor Chinese architects, and even those in the contemporary state-owned design institutes. Confronting the complex social and cultural environment and featuring different living conditions and practice strategies, they are seeking their personal positions in such an intricate relationship network of different poles, such as architectural autonomy versus social reality, globalization versus localization, and politics versus form.

Firstly, they are confronted with the relationship between architectural autonomy and social reality. The 'post-critical' architectural theory in American developed in the last decade advocates a kind of 'reflective' architectural practice, which can reflect the reality. Rather than a mere avant-garde resistance or simple refusal, it identifies an approach compromising with the capital and social reality. Representatives of this theory—Sarah Whiting and Robert Somol—have participated more than once in Chinese architectural symposiums

4 Rao Xiaojun, 'Experimental Architecture: A Conceptual Exploration,' *Time + Architecture*, 2000 (02), p. 13.
5 Wang Mingxian and Shi, Jian, 'Chinese Experimental Architecture in 1990s,' *Literature and Art Studies*, 1998 (01), p. 121.
6 Li Wuying, 'Anti Tradition Rather Than Avant-garde—Notes of "Tu Mu Back Home" Exhibition,' *Construction Time*, 2002, pp. 8–20.
7 See Li Xiangning, 'Architecture as Resistance: Wang Shu and his Architecture,' *World Architecture*, 2012 (05), pp. 30–33.

and discussion in 'critical/post-critical' featured an issue of *Time+ Architecture* magazine, exerting impact on Chinese architectural practice and theory.

For Chinese architects, the chances to build their designs will bring them the greatest benefit for living in the world's biggest building factory, and also win them more attention and more say on the international stage. Architecture has always been struggling between its autonomy and reliance on the capital and politics. The contemporary architecture discipline is unable to ignore the social economy and political culture to realize its pure autonomy. Therefore, the majority of current individual architects now face up to the reality and try to achieve a critical position through cooperation with reality and to make the most of it.[8]

Diversity in client types, such as the government, real-estate developers, cultural institutes, and individual proprietors, and constant variability in project nature and scale may explain why few architects maintain a complete and persistent architecture language, but constantly change strategies. After all, there are few architects that enjoy the right to pick their clients as Wang Shu does. It might also be reflected by the critical realism that to survive and develop in the market, some individual architectural firms would resort to some short-term expedited commercial and mass residential design projects with quick returns to support the production of more interesting public cultural buildings that are also more time and energy consuming. They are clearly aware of the difference between the two types of design, so those 'cash dispenser projects' would never be shown in publications or exhibitions. Such survival guidance, more or less coming out of passive choice, might have promulgated the reality that many contemporary individual architects have to be confronted with.

Secondly, they are confronted with the relationship between globalization and localization. Thanks to the international experience and vision brought by their overseas education, many contemporary young Chinese architects are sensitive enough to take the initiative to think over the position of architectural practice in the binary opposition of globalization and localization, as well as how to interpret issues of 'Chineseness' in a contemporary manner. To respond to the local conditions with a global modern form may be a result of negotiation and makeshift action, but it has commendably presented the balance between the architects' design ideal and the complicated social reality.

Among Chinese individual architects, we can find those who preside over the international architectural education as deans and heads of architecture schools with their overseas education background and architectural practice at home, such as Yungho Chang and Ma

Qingyun,[9] those who win international building projects by constant participation in international competitions like Ma Yansong, and those who are educated in China but internationally accredited through persistent exploration of 'Chinese contemporary' architectural identity like Wang Shu. The dual practice formulated by real construction in China and exposure in international architectural exhibitions and professional media publications enables each individual architect to find his or her own position in between two poles of globalization and localization.

Another figure worth mentioning is Ma Yansong and his design firm MAD. His few built-up works have maintained consistent formal identity and design quality. His recent work Erdos Museum is a perfect combination of cutting edge concept and nonlinear form. His Absolute World Towers accomplished in 2012 in Canada and the Lucas Museum of Narrative Art in Chicago, which he recently won through competition with Zaha Hadid, UNStudio and several other European firms, have made him the first contemporary Chinese architect who has built important public architecture in the West. His recent practice tries to transplant the nonlinear form architecture onto traditional Chinese Shan Shui (Mountain and River, or Scenery) city concept.

Finally, they have to achieve the balance between politics and form. Form, as a matter of fact, is an important part of the core of the architecture discipline. No matter how an architect claims his or her works is divorced from formalism, form has taken root in the architecture. The larger system of the contemporary Chinese architecture has developed competition evaluation criteria based on judgment of form in most competitions and tendering. Whatever approaches the evaluation takes, what is to be resolved in the end is a proposition of form. The trajectory of contemporary Chinese politics has inevitable influence on architectural form.

City policy makers with obscure political desire and aesthetic taste may eventually decide the formal criteria of architecture and urban design. However, politics can also have a positive influence on architecture and urban design by providing proper guidance. The 'Qingpu-Jiading' effect is an exemplary case. Dr. Sun Jiwei, the key figure of the district government, meticulously selected from a name list of best contemporary individual architects to design projects in the district. Some young and talented individual architects seized the opportunity and started their career there. These two suburb districts of Shanghai serve as an experimental field for young architects, to make a figure and gradually step onto the contemporary Chinese architecture stage, such as Liu Yichun, Zhuang Shen, and Zhu Xiaofeng, among others. Most of their early architectural works were executed there and at the same time, these works took on certain special features because of the provincial characteristics of the two

8   See Li Xiangning, 'Make-the-Most-of-It: Architecture and Chinese Young Architects,' *City*, Routledge, July 2008, pp. 226–236.

9   Yungho Chang used to be the head of MIT Department of Architecture, and Ma Qingyun is the current dean of USC School of Architecture and Planning.

districts famous for their beautiful traditional water towns. As Dr. Sun takes his post in Xuhui district and Pudong new district, a group of high-quality buildings will be erected there designed by leading contemporary individual architects invited by him. The Long Museum designed by Liu Yichun is one of the exemplary buildings with very high overall construction quality that deserves the sensational design deliberation of the architect.

III. Opportunities and challenges

For more than two decades—and still today—China has embraced rapid social, economic, and cultural change. Discussion of contemporary Chinese architecture typically involves complaints about limits and restrictions, while much of the construction activity in China is described negatively as shortsighted operations impelled by expedient value judgments. In contrast, positive expositions identify individual Chinese architects whose works stand as manifestoes of resistance to the existing attitudes of society and also of mainstream professional architects, both Chinese and international. A gap becomes apparent between good taste and neat architectural articulation of the buildings selected and exhibited worldwide, and the mass construction that permeates everywhere in China. What will be the prospects for Chinese architecture in the near future? Is there an opportunity for better Chinese architecture as a whole, rather than just a matter of exemplary but dispersed works? Will there be an approach to Chinese architecture that positively represents an urban transformation that could not be fitted into any of the social-urban paradigms that the West has experienced?

It is true that most new Chinese architecture may be considered to be some kind of makeshift or temporary solution. But confronting a society marked by uncertainty and now inhabiting an instant urban environment that could be thoroughly reconfigured within a few years, what is the point of imagining monuments? The pursuit of quantity, speed, efficiency, ephemerality has been, for many years, seen to be lacking in quality, deliberation, eternity, and so on. However, might we not take those characteristics of the contemporary Chinese ethos as stimulating challenges? Instead of retreating to Chinese cultural tradition and finding nostalgic motifs for design, we might seek architectural positions responsive to massive change at the urban scale. If we could develop a Chinese model of urban development that is a new proposition—an alternative to the models pursued and propagated by the West, could we not develop a new value system in making judgments about contemporary Chinese architecture?

Interaction between the traditional core of architecture discipline and the new technological innovation has provided new chances to review the practice of individual contemporary Chinese architects and therefore looking for the way for future development and the possibility of making special contribution to architecture. What we now observe from contemporary Chinese architecture is mostly variations of typical Western modernism architecture, regarding space, dimension, structure, material, function, or—if going a little further—light, poetics, and tectonics. From the practice of these individual architects, it is hard to find an independent and insistent architectural language (which Wang Shu's works may have), or mature strategies that are responsive to the rapid transformation taking place in contemporary Chinese cities, as well as continued attempts in architecture innovation and industrialization. But still some trends could be noticed in the practice of individual architects and these may become driving factors for the future Chinese architectural evolution in China.

Digital building technologies (including 3D printing, kinetic architecture, and BIM system) and international waves of parametric architecture brought by today's digital innovation have greatly influenced the practice of Chinese individual architects. Xu Guowei, Yuan Feng, Song Gang and Wang Zhenfei are China's representational pioneers in this direction. They have organized a series of international digital architecture workshops during the recent three years. Apart from inviting leading architects and theorists in international digital architecture for discussion on Chinese architecture practice, they also developed a new direction for digital design and construction through their own built works.

Xu Weiguo, from Tsinghua University, was the first to introduce digital approaches into architecture teaching and practice at the beginning of the 21st century. And the completion of some parametric buildings by those architects in recent years, such as the 'silk wall' and teahouse project built by Yuan Feng in Shanghai for his workshop, and Yujiabao Engineering Command Center by Wang Zhenfei, has demonstrated the possibility that the digital building technology takes its root and develops in China. Such an innovation does not only mean creative changes in fancy forms, but also changes in the architectural culture and way of space production. If we take Lanxi Court in Chengdu designed by Yuan Feng as an example, the architect adopted the digital construction technology and combined traditional Chinese material (brick in this case) and way of construction. Recent development in 3D-printed concrete houses in China also reveals a chance of industrialization and mass production in the near future. At the same time, the digital architecture practice by individual architects also begins to influence the architects of state-owned institutes. The practice combining parametric and BIM construction technologies may change the production model of future Chinese architecture. A recent example is the headquarters of Phoenix Publishing & Media Group designed by Shao Weiping, chief architect of the biggest state-owned design institute BIAD.

Another trend developing simultaneously with the digital architecture is the increasing concern about social justice and building ethics in the practice of individual architects. One symbolic event is the appraisal of China Architecture Media Awards since 2006 that exerts an influence on the public and professional field. Advocating 'civil architecture,' this award places the architectures' common and social character and contribution to society at a more important position than architecture aesthetics and designs itself. Award-winning projects as the Gehua Youth and Cultural Center by Li Hu's Open Architecture studio, Maosi Ecological Experimental Primary School by Wu Enrong and Cultural Center by Fu Xiao, and the Xinya Primary Schools by Zhu Jingxiang have all pushed forward a kind of public culture value. The award, forum, and related media report greatly improved the social impact of a group of young and middle-aged individual architects. Due to recent occurrences of several natural disasters, the public participation and social ethic values are highlighted during spontaneous public relief. The design and construction activities for public welfare with architects and artists involved, like post-earthquake reconstruction, bring to the contemporary young architects more concern about people's livelihood, social equity, and justice. More projects appear with a higher sense of social responsibility like the Tulou Commune—affordable apartments for low-income groups in cities designed by Urbanus adopts the form of traditional southern Hakka dwellings—ring-shaped earthen buildings. Inspiration from regional architectural style and user-friendly design approach are both mobilized to create nice form.

A new trend correlative to the increasing social responsibility and equity in architecture is that more individual architects turn their eyes to the countryside, design and construct country buildings and even take part in its social reconstruction. Until nearly 10 years ago, architects concentrated on the architecture design and construction in cities, ignoring the countryside because of its unfavorable economies and cultural conditions. While in recent years, the crowded streets and industrial pollution in cities have lost attraction to architects, who then turn to the countryside where the idyllic pastoral dreams can still be realized.

Additionally, the Chinese government has begun to pay attention to countryside development during the new urbanization progress, which began with the design and construction of a number of Hope Primary Schools. The School Bridge project in Fujian province designed by Li Xiaodong won the 2012 Aga Khan Award for Architecture, and serial rural construction including House for All Seasons designed by the Hong Kong architect John Lin made him the winner of the 2013 Ralph Erskine Award from the Swedish Association of Architects. As some artists, designers and social workers are stationed in the countryside and participate in community reconstruction there, some individual architects also persevere in building the countryside even further out from the cities to become a member of the local community, such as Huang Shengyuan and his Fieldoffice Architects in Taiwan Yilan, and Wang Hao, Zhao Yang, Huang Yingwu, Chen Haoru, who have attracted a lot attention for their architecture activities in mainland China's countryside.

Among the rural architectural practices, there is an individual architect who deserves special attention: Xie Yingjun from Taiwan. He conducts low-cost residence projects simultaneously in Taiwan and the mainland. The combined application of lightweight steel frame systems and local building-material techniques greatly reduce the construction cost. Unlike most architects, who are building neat projects while pursuing design quality as first priority, Xie Yingjun pays more attention to the possibility of a low-cost industrial system. He himself has invested in a factory to research and develop new structural and building system that can be mass produced and industrialized. With local villagers taking part in his construction practice, he created an opportunity for social mobilization. He is clearly aware of the contrast between China's abundant mass production of buildings and the lack of industrial system. Subconsciously, we are drifting away from the architectural revolution that the Deutscher Werkbund and even Le Corbusier's own dream of housing industrialization. More often than not, the architectural experiment of mass construction and designing industrial system that Xie Yingjun really focuses on is ignored and he would be taken easily as another example of an architect who uses his architecture as a vehicle for social care only.

IV. Conclusion

Nowadays, the external environment for Chinese architects has been greatly improved from 10 years ago. Young architects are even able to complete large-scale buildings with high construction quality. At the same time, the main challenge confronting them is how to choose among an ocean of styles, to hold their own positions, and to keep the continuity of their formal identity and design strategy, in an ever-changing social and political environment. We cannot deny that the flooding of Western architecture makes a total or partial copy of the architectural form and design concept from Switzerland, Netherlands, Spain, or Japan, a shortcut that saves time and money. This pragmatist approach lacking in self-consciousness introspection and critique will eventually result in a failure to balance. Therefore, pragmatic or expedited operations will outweigh social consciousness and self-criticality.

Although contemporary Chinese architectural practices have drawn international attention and Chinese architects have entered the spotlight of the international stage, the theory and criticism of contemporary Chinese architecture is indeed an alarming concern. We only see either superficial architectural criticism published by Western journalists and researchers, or Chinese scholar's research following popular Western theories and discourses. What we are truly lacking is the specific critical discourses that not only recognize complicated cultural context and social reality in China, but are also comprehensible and meaningful to the Western audience. However, if we look at the discourses and theories that have greatly influenced the contemporary individual Chinese architects in the last two decades, it is quite disappointing that we end up with Western theories and methodology, with rare exception.

Although the individual architects have contributed a large number of quality works over decades, they have not responded forcefully to the distinctive characteristics of the contemporary Chinese urbanism such as bigness, swiftness, cheapness, uncertainty and so on. As a result, subconsciously, people could take Chinese architects as not proficient enough to counterweigh Western architects, both in the eyes of the general public and the professional. In my own experience, I often ask my architectural students about their favorite contemporary architects. Among various answers they gave, I. M. Pei was generally the only Chinese architect. Wang Shu started to enter the list only after he received the Pritzker Architecture Prize. Even so, voices questioning the impartiality of the award are often heard among Chinese architects. The lack of self-confidence is another reason why most landmarks in China's big cities are designed by international architectural firms.

Therefore, as we rejoice in the quality buildings springing up designed by Chinese architects, we have to be aware that the improvement of design and construction quality also relies on the independent critical consciousness. Reflecting the ethos of our society and demonstrating it in built forms, paying more attention to the social connotation of architecture and exploring the latent influence of new technological innovation might be the impetus for individual Chinese architects to step further with greater expectations.

Bibliography

Chang, Yung Ho, *Pingchang Jianzhu*, China Architecture & Building Press, Beijing, 2002.

LI Xiangning, *Mapping China: Construction and Deliberation in Chinese Metropolis*, Barcelona, Actar, 2014.

Li Xiangning, '"Make-the-Most-of-It:" Architecture and Chinese Young Architects,' *City*, Routledge, July 2008.

LI Xiangning (ed.), *Contemporary Chinese Architecture Reader*, China Architecture & Building Press, Beijing, 2017.

Liu Jiakun, *Ci Shi Ci Di*, China Architecture & Building Press, Beijing, 2002.

Qin Lei, Zhongguo Dangdai Jianzhu Zai Haiwai de Zhanlan (Overseas Exhibitions of Contemporary China's Architecture), *Time + Architecture*, 2010 (01).

Rao Xiaojun, 'Shiyan Jianzhu: Yizhong Guannianxing de Tansuo' (Experimental Architecture: A Conceptual Exploration), *Time + Architecture*, 2000 (02).

Wang Mingxian, Shi Jian, 'Jiushi Niandai Zhongguo Shiyanxinxing Jianzhu' (Chinese Experimental Architecture in 1990s), *Literature and Art Studies*, 1998 (01).

Wang Shu, *Sheji de Kaishi*, China Architecture & Building Press, Beijing, 2002.

Wang Ying, Wang Kai, Zitai, 'Gestures, Perspectives and Positions: Notes on Overseas Reportage and Studies on Contemporary Chinese Architecture and Urbanism in Recent 10 Years,' *Time + Architecture*, 2010 (04).

Xu Weiguo, Digital Avant-Garde: Emerging Architects in China, *Time + Architecture*, 2011 (01).

Xue, Charlie Q. L., *Building a Revolution: Chinese Architecture Since 1980*, Hong Kong University Press, Hong Kong, 2005.

Zhu Jianfei, *Architecture of Modern China: A Historical Critique*, Routledge, London and New York, 2009.

Zhu Jianfei (ed.), *Zhongguo Jianzhu 60nian (1949–2009): Lishi, Lilun he Piping (Sixty Years of Chinese Architecture (1949–2009): History, Theory and Criticism*, China Architecture & Building Press, Beijing, 2012.

Zhu Tao, Zhao lei, One Supports Another: Architecture, Media and Civilian Society Construction, *New Architecture*, 2009 (03).

Cultural ▶

The rise of 'experimental architecture' in China was closely tied to the social and cultural transitions that took place during the late 1980s and early 1990s. Within the last few decades, major Chinese cities witnessed the building of an unprecedented number of new museums, libraries, and cultural centers. In order to focus their time and energy on designing public cultural buildings, many Chinese architects turned to expeditious commercial and residential projects to financially support their practices.

If the short-term real-estate projects were largely ignored in media coverage, photographic and video documentation of cultural buildings deliberating on issues of space, light, and material quickly captured the attention of international and national audiences, generating widespread enthusiasm for a new mode of Chinese architectural production attuned to contemporaneous cultural needs. Up until today, the search for criticality and a desire to experiment with the Chinese tradition continues to characterize the design of buildings associated with the production of knowledge and culture.

Novartis Shanghai campus laboratory building

Yung Ho Chang
Atelier FCJZ

Location Shanghai, China
Gross building area 151,297 ft²
(14,056 m²)
Site area 873,695 ft² (81,619 m²)
Completion 2016

Master plan

The project is located at the headquarters campus of Novartis Shanghai. The design starts from the combination of architecture and landscape with the main entrance leading to the courtyard. Though the office space and laboratories admit only scientific researchers and work staff, the courtyard is open to the whole community. The design of the laboratories was based on a flexible and open concept—the laboratories and non-laboratory spaces are connected with a series of 'living rooms' (public spaces): the reinforced concrete structure was cut open in the center to build an open staircase in the atrium. The atrium staircase is both a traffic space and a leisure and exchange center with a library.

Garden

Although the project site is within a science and technology park, Atelier FCJZ proposed from the very beginning that rather than suburban mentality, the project should achieve urbanity through density, cultural continuity, and clearly-defined public spaces. The heritage of garden-making tradition in the Yangtze River Delta region (Jiangnan region), where the project is located, inspired the design in two distinct aspects: on the one hand, in the overall planning of the park, the architects organized the public spaces as architecturally defined outdoor areas with connecting paths like in the Jiangnan gardens; on the other hand, as the architect of one of the two laboratory complexes, they mixed the tones of the contemporary terracotta products on the building exteriors to simulate the qualities of the old Jiangnan clay tiles.

Courtyard

Based on the campus master planning design FCJZ put together, each building complex was asked to specifically have its own courtyard. For the laboratory building designed by FCJZ, the singular courtyard was conceived as a room without a roof, meaning a place for people to be in, not a place only for enjoying the view. One enters the complex through the courtyard surrounded by covered walkways on four sides, which makes it the center of all the activities around the complex. On the opposite side of the laboratory building, a restaurant is located, which invites everyone on the campus to come to dine but also to enjoy the courtyard. For the Novartis Shanghai campus, the diverse courtyard designs could be the reasons why people may want to walk about and explore the campus. In other

words, a series of interconnected courtyards constitutes an important part of the public space system for this project.

The tea house concept

Traditionally, a tea house is public living room, social space, or salon for human interaction, with or without a cup of tea. In the center of the FCJZ laboratory building, open rooms of different sizes stacked on top of each other and connected by stairways function conceptually as tea houses or salons within the lab. Scientists may come to one of such spaces to take a break, have a tea or coffee, or run into a colleague or two and brainstorm some ideas. In the contemporary terminology, the conceptual 'tea house' on the stairs is designed for spontaneous collaboration. This tower of communicators—a term the client used to suggest public staircases, also encourages people to walk and climb rather than taking the elevator and thus promote a healthy lifestyle as well.

South elevation

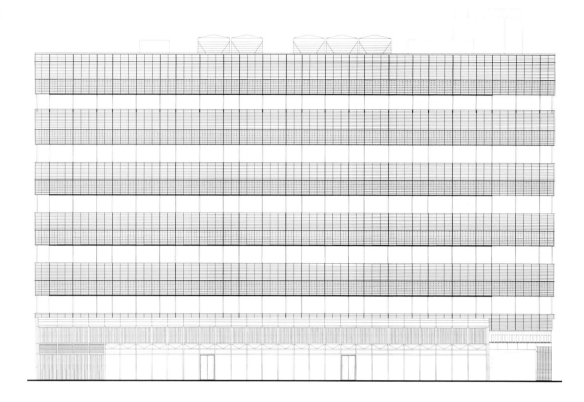

North elevation

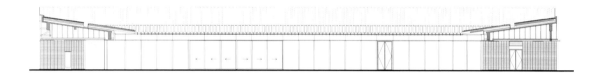

Section

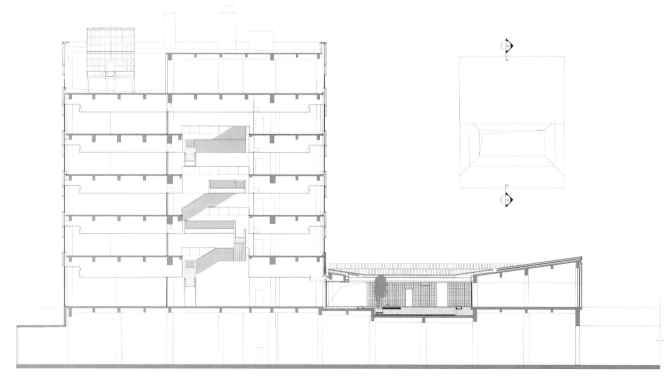

First floor plan

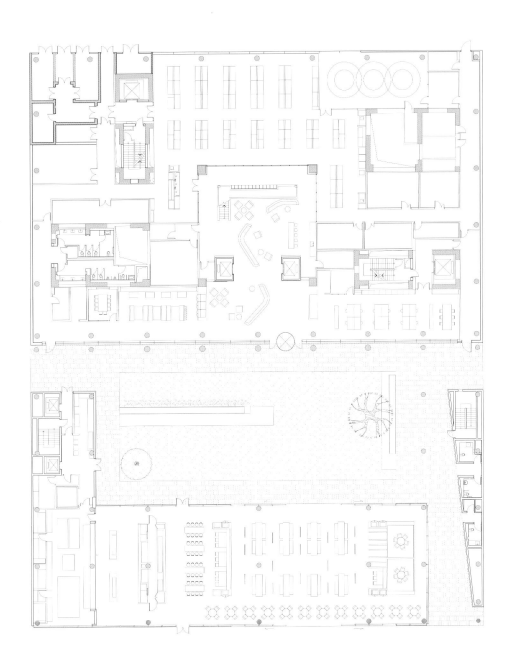

Typical floor plan

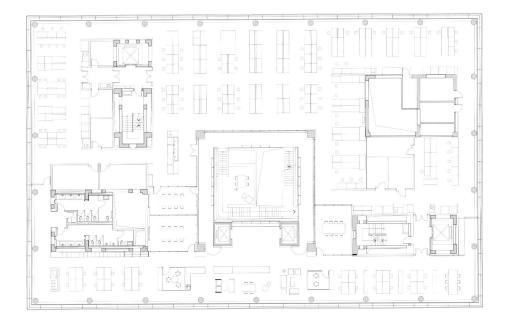

Yushu Khamba Arts Center

Cui Kai
Cui Kai Studio

Location Yushu, China
Gross building area 219,583 ft²
(20,400 m²)
Site area 26,3715 ft² (24,500 m²)
Completion 2013

Axonometric

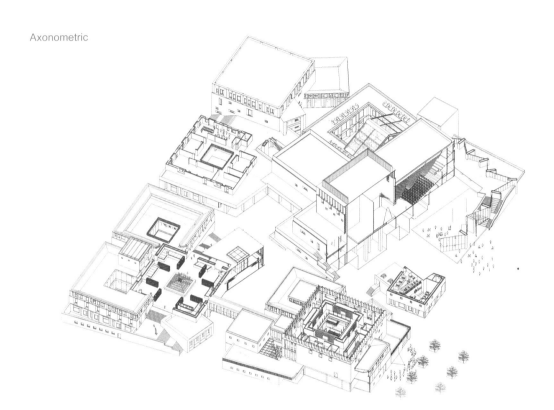

Located in Yushu in the province of Qinghai, this project is a post-disaster reconstruction structure built with social-aid funding. It mainly consists of Yushu State Theater, Yushu Prefecture Theater, Yushu State Theatrical Troupe, Yushu State Cultural Center, and Yushu State Library. The general architectural layout is loose but well-arranged, and its density respects traditional urban texture. The scale of pedestrian street goes well with Tang-Tibet Ancient Road shopping street. The center creates rich spatial layers through the organization of courtyards, and reproduces the surface texture of Tibet architecture by means of materials and colors.

Fit in

As one of the important projects for reconstructing Yushu, the architects wanted to establish a settlement that fits in the block, rather than a landmark isolated from the surrounding. Two internal roads crossing each other divide the lot into four parts, which separately corresponds four buildings with different functions. The organization of unit-courtyards further integrates each building with its surrounding. It obscures their volume while enriching its internal space, providing more possibilities for citizens participating in public activities.

White

White is a sacred and sublime color in Tibetans' minds as it is the color of a snowy mountain, clouds, and milk. On the other hand, white becomes a representative color of modernist architecture due to its abstract nature. The white color of Khamba Arts Center possesses both of these characters. The white paint doesn't conceal the block's texture; instead, it acquires an abstract sense on the whole and retains the natural and simple aspects of the building, thus smartly integrating the simplicity and abstraction of modern architecture with Tibet colors.

Piling

Tibetan structures such as Ta'er Lamasery and Mani Stone Pile express a sense of architecture. The construction technique of adding-up allow people to learn the central spirit of Tibetan architecture. Compared with hanging boards and veneering, piling can present its own characters and construction logic in a truer way. For the convenience of construction in Tibet, the architects chose concrete hollow blocks, a most common material. Regular blocks themselves can ensure accuracy and efficiency of construction, while flexible and variable construction technique give walls a lively and natural appearance.

Elevation of theater

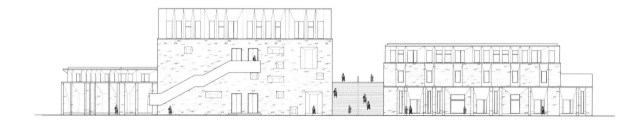

Section of library and cultural center

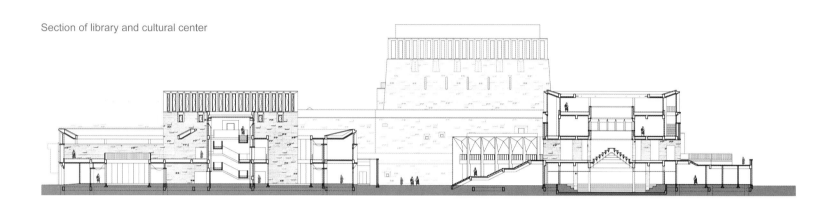

Third floor plan

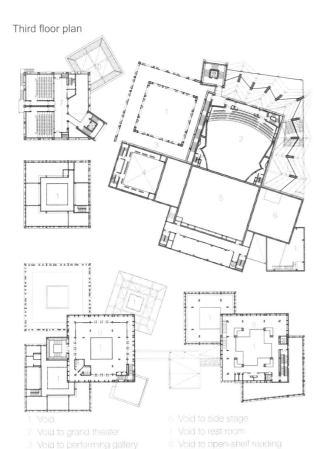

1 Void
2 Void to grand theater
3 Void to performing gallery
4 Void to multi-function theater
5 Void to main stage
6 Void to side stage
7 Void to rest room
8 Void to open-shelf reading
9 Gesar cultural research center
10 Roof

Fourth floor plan

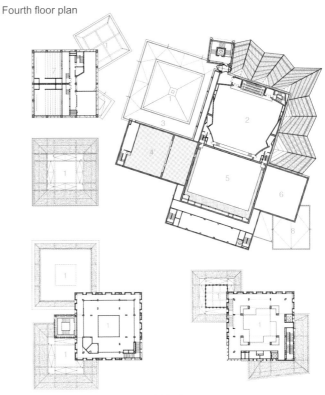

1 Void
2 Void to audience hall
3 Gallery
4 Grid top
5 Void to main stage
6 Void to stage
7 Void to side stage
8 Void to cinema hall
9 Roof

First floor plan

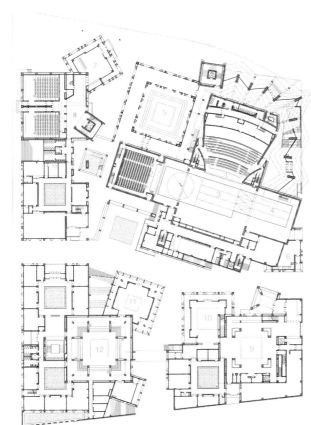

1 Grand theater
2 Multi-function theater
3 Main stage
4 Side stage
5 Semi-outdoor
6 Performing gallery
7 Ticket hall
8 Cinema hall
9 Periodical reading area
10 Children's reading room
11 Exhibition hall
12 Shared lobby

Second floor plan

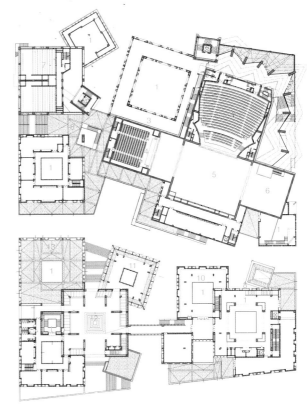

1 Void
2 Grand theater seating area
3 Semi-outdoor performing gallery
4 Void to multi-function theater
5 Void to main stage
6 Void to side stage
7 Void to cinema hall
8 Terrace
9 Open-shelf reading
10 Children's reading room
11 Semi-outdoor exhibition
12 Public activity platform
13 Outdoor exhibition

Details of construction

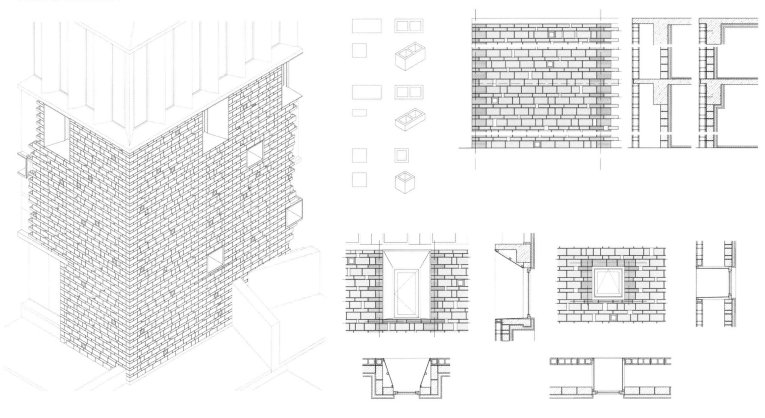

Tree Art Museum

Dai Pu
Daipu Architects

Location Beijing, China
Gross building area 34,444 ft² (3200 m²)
Site area 29,008 ft² (2695 m²)
Completion 2012

Sketch

Urban fabric

Tree Art Museum is located at the roadside of a local trunk road in the Song Village of Beijing. The initial design concept was to organically combine the arts show space with the natural environment to the best advantage, yet the result is actually somewhat conservative by today's view. It simplifies and abstracts the natural environment, and integrates it with an extremely simple interior in a super luminous way. This response was greatly influenced by traditional Chinese courtyard culture.

Hybrid

Whether confronting each other in European classic traditions or enclosing each other, alternatively, in some South-Asian traditions, the relationship between artificial structures and the natural environment is based on the idea of an either-or question. Today, although architecture has already recognized the value of diffusing the boundaries between inside and outside, artificial and natural, how far will this awareness be extended? Can the either-or relationship be changed? Besides using glass curtains and planting trees on high floors, is there any possibility to build a closer relationship between artificial structures and nature (although real nature, in fact, is not very inhabitable)?

Ruins

The temple surrounded by banyan trees in Angkor Wat brings the original temple closer to its initial divine pursuit. While this is an

invasion of one power into another, it is also integration. The original forms of nature could be simulated with artificial construction logic, or the natural codes (such as DNS project) could be partially changed to adapt to human needs. Of course, the later poses great dangers in a large extent because many believe it is against God. Some knowledge could be accumulated about the balance of artificial structures and the natural environment through analysis of the ruins.

Features of time

When architecture stops being worshiped as a long-lasting permanent structure or being injected with traditional emotions by people wishfully, it is able to be appreciated and discussed in a more relaxing way in regard to the dimension of time. For example, a part of a structure takes root through the banyan trees, giving birth to more lives; another part of it dies naturally and supports the structure, embodying the history, somewhat like the Venetians sculpture series by Pawel Althamer. A building may be like a healthy city with a part of it as a new life and a part of it as history or nature.

Section 1-1

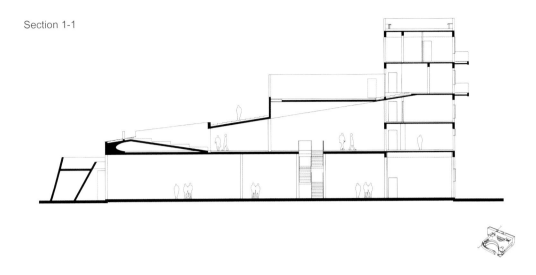

Section 2-2

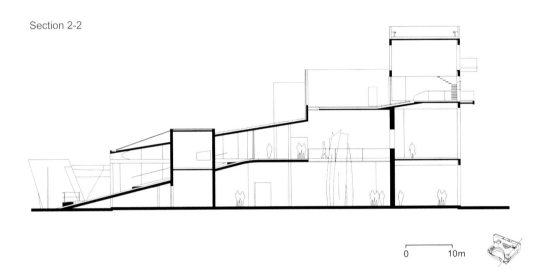

0   10m

Top / fourth / fifth floor plan

First floor plan

Second / third floor plan

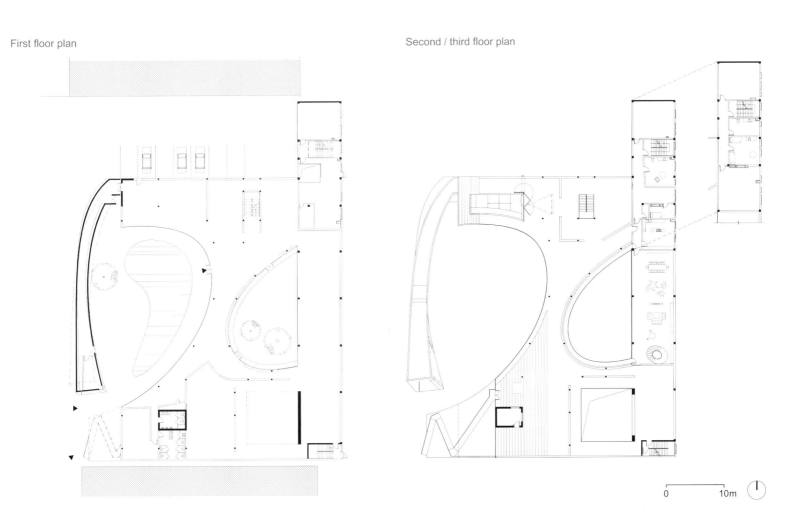

0   10m

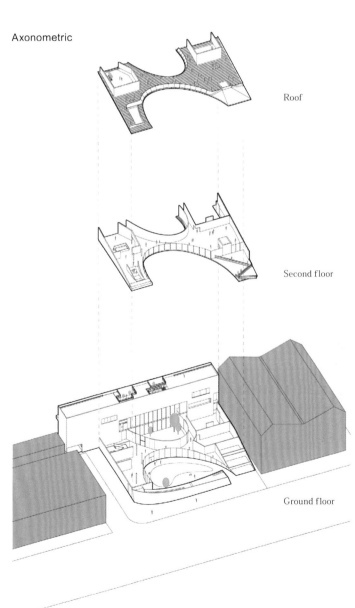

Axonometric

Roof

Second floor

Ground floor

Seashore Library

Gong Dong
Vector Architects

Location Qinhuangdao, China
Gross building area 4844 ft² (450 m²)
Site area 4090 ft² (380 m²)
Completion 2014

Site plan

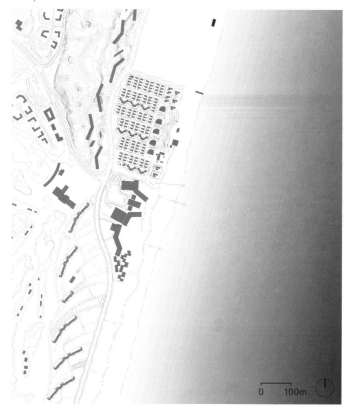

The site is located at the coastline of China's Bohai Gulf. Its main design concept is to explore the co-existing relationships between spatial boundaries, physical activities, variations of light, flow of air, and ocean views. The library faces the sea to the east, serves community residents to the west in spring, summer and autumn, and is open to the public.

Community spirits

Modern communities can provide a high-quality living environment with improved privacy and livability, but they generally overlook the relationships between individual families while protecting the independence of them. In this design, active and high-quality community public spaces can provide places for daily socializing, gathering, and recreation. The architects attempted to break this isolation status of individual families in the community with the intervention of public activities, gradually increase community cohesion, wake up people's acknowledgement of and yearning for close neighbor relationships, and finally change the indifferent status ubiquitous in today's community.

Sketch

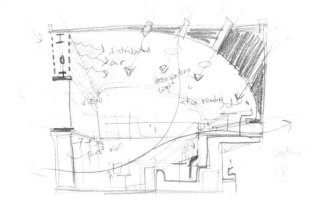

Body and boundary

The territorial sense of space usually comes from the establishment of a clear physical boundary, but it is not necessarily and absolutely equal to the psychological boundary of people's understanding of space. In this project, due to the uniqueness of the site itself, the creation of architectural perception was not limited to the walls and the structure, but also related to the boundless and abstract beach and sea. The bodily perception of structures and the site acquired a psychological extension because of the insertion of tangible artifacts into an endless site. Tangible and defined physical boundaries precisely offer possibilities for expanding the intangible psychological boundary.

Light and wind

Each site has its own unique light and wind. They have a certain potential power that allows buildings to connect with a more expansive space-time system. In this project, the light and wind environment are very important in view of the requirements of the project functions and the uniqueness of the site environment. The expression of architectural material texture and the creation of whole atmosphere are closely related with the capture, use, and expression of these elements. The strong natural light at the seashore provides unique conditions for shaping the architectural visual volume and creating an internal light environment, while the study of the wind environment further establishes more private and closer relationships between the architecture and the site from the sense of perception. The light and wind in the site are intangible site conditions, while the introduction of spaces reveals their particularities and eventually transforms them into perceivable experiences and living elements.

Second floor plan

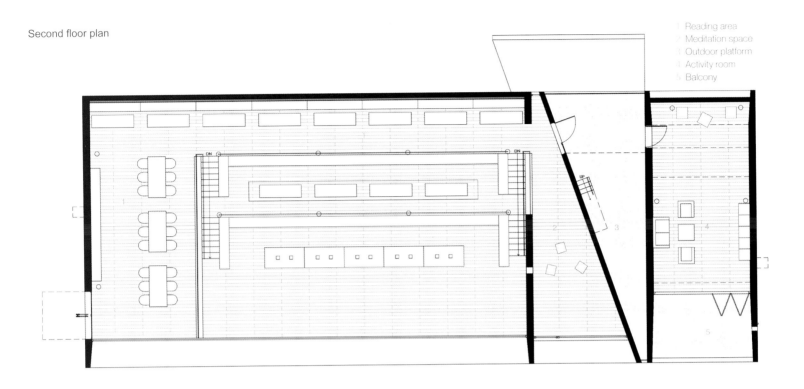

First floor plan

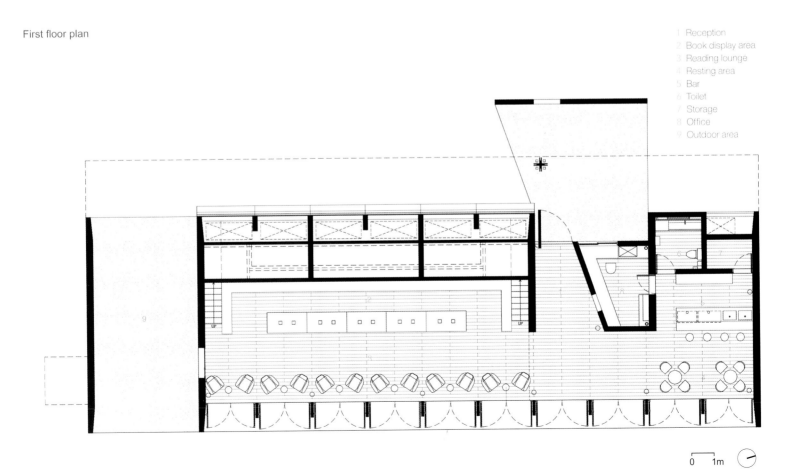

0   1m

West elevation

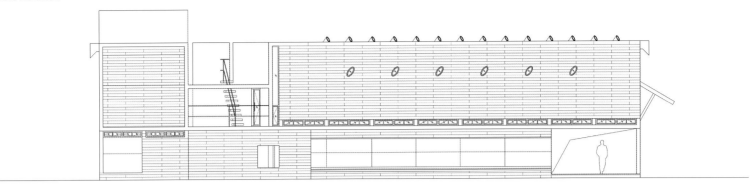

East elevation

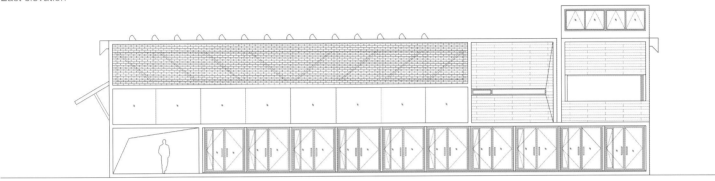

0   1m

Sections

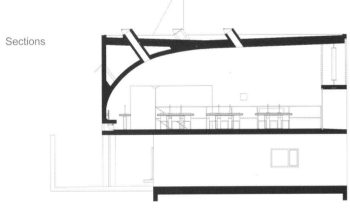

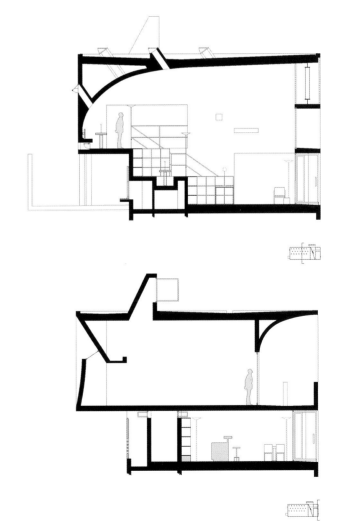

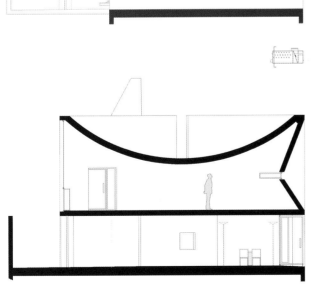

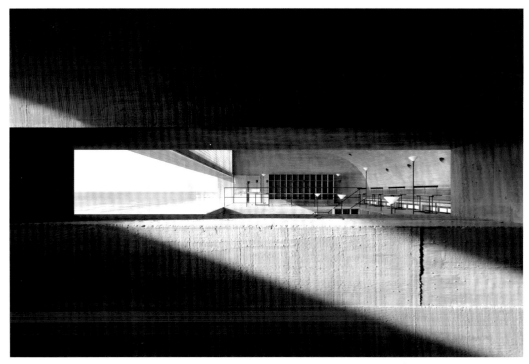

Pavilion of Science and Technology at the International Horticultural Exposition 2014 Qingdao

Fu Xiao
School of Architecture and Urban
Planning, Nanjing University

Location Qingdao, China
Gross building area 34,444 ft² (3200 m²)
Site area 77,553 ft² (7205 m²)
Completion 2014

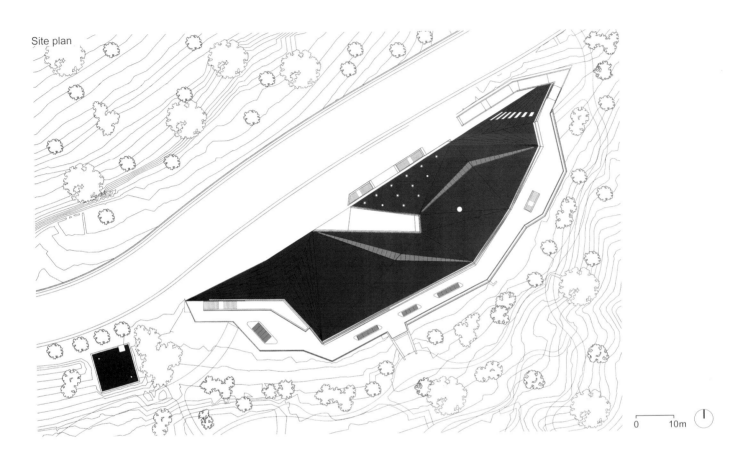

Site plan

0   10m

The project is an exhibition structure at the International Horticultural Exposition 2014 Qingdao. As the exposition is sited at a hilly area and the project is perched at the highest point of the site, the major conception of the design was how to unveil it from the mountain woods to attract visitors as well as integrate it with the surrounding to create a tranquil atmosphere. The architects designed an earth-sheltered building, making it coordinate with the whole through a rolling form.

Hidden in nature

The pavilion looks down at the whole site with a landscape view of green mountains that stretches several miles. It serves as the science and technology building, allowing people to experience the changes of nature through high-tech means. Taking full advantage of the elevation differences of the topography, the design lowered the architectural height and reduced the volume so as to create an earth-covered building that connects well with the natural mountains. Though the building is named Pavilion of Science and Technology, it was not designed to epitomize an image of science and technology; the

architects held that 'complying with nature' was the most paramount.

Energy-saving

The project undertook a lot of experiments in construction techniques. Following the basic principle of sustainability, the design makes full use of passive energy-saving measures to reduce energy consumption. These measures include a green roof, ventilated patios, light collection and ventilation system, light pipes, rainwater collection system, and so on.

Bright and dim

The project utilized the differences of elevation to form an impeccable visiting route, which combines the architecture with nature by changing spaces from bright to dim and back to bright. The detailed route started at the outdoor square, went through the underground path, then entered the Dream Pavilion of Science and Technology and 4D Hall, finally climbed up the exit passage and returned to the ground, where the open and whole view of the Expo could be enjoyed.

Section

0   10m

First floor plan

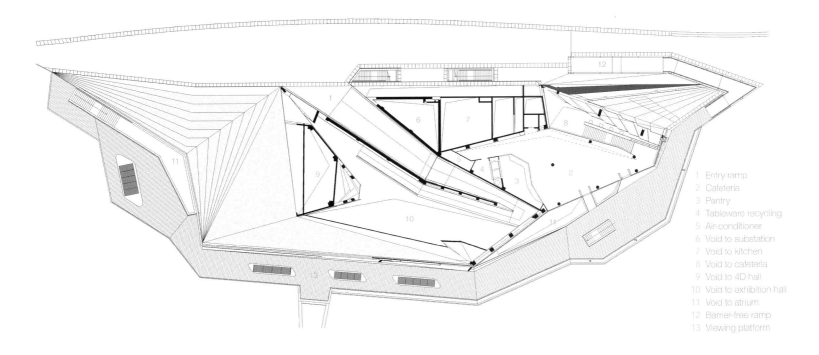

1 Entry ramp
2 Cafeteria
3 Pantry
4 Tableware recycling
5 Air-conditioner
6 Void to substation
7 Void to kitchen
8 Void to cafeteria
9 Void to 4D hall
10 Void to exhibition hall
11 Void to atrium
12 Barrier-free ramp
13 Viewing platform

Underground first floor

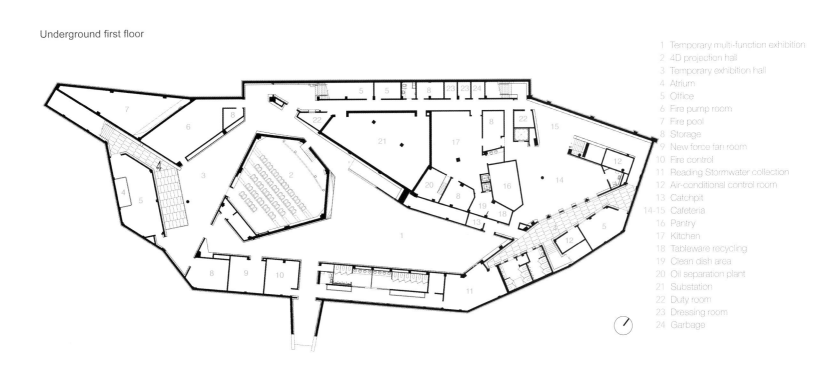

1 Temporary multi-function exhibition
2 4D projection hall
3 Temporary exhibition hall
4 Atrium
5 Office
6 Fire pump room
7 Fire pool
8 Storage
9 New force fan room
10 Fire control
11 Reading Stormwater collection
12 Air-conditional control room
13 Catchpit
14-15 Cafeteria
16 Pantry
17 Kitchen
18 Tableware recycling
19 Clean dish area
20 Oil separation plant
21 Substation
22 Duty room
23 Dressing room
24 Garbage

Chinese Academy of Oil Painting

Han Tao, He Ziming
ThanLab Office

Location Beijing, China
Gross building area 142,043 ft²
(13,200 m²)
Site area 53,819 ft² (5000 m²)
Completion 2016

Site plan

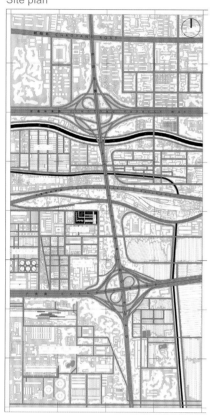

Masterplan

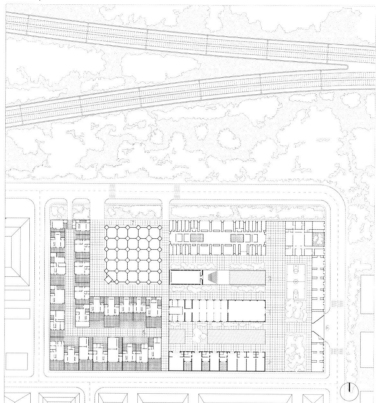

1 Phase one factory building renovation
2 Phase one art studio
3 Phase two lecture hall
4 Phase two teaching building
5 Phase two art studio
6 Annex building along the street
7 Museum

The project was a design experiment in Gaobeidian, Beijing, and the effort of an individual artist, rather than an investment by the government or a real-estate company.

Commune

The architects' perspective was that the Chinese Academy of Oil Painting was not a society but a commune. The academy spent 10 years conducting a sociological experiment rather than an architectural one. The questions it raised were: 30 years after the break down of unit-courtyards, could we build a new 'commune' that combines work, living, and belief under the new free market framework during the urbanization that constantly produces social separation? In this 'commune,' artists become the subject of non-material production, the artist group becomes a common part of contemporary intellectuals and new working class, and the artistic area becomes an early paradigm of future communes.

Type

The integration of factories and human settlements produced the architectural type of future communes. Once being devoid of production activities, a settlement will become a false real estate with only living functions; while if being divorced from living function, factories will turn into a pure division form of labor. Together with factories and settlements comes the architectural type in Post-Fordism mode of production. In the Academy of Oil Painting, the renovated structure, with the factory as the main body, includes the settlement into the factory; the teaching building, with the settlement as the main body, organize the factory into the settlement; the office structure attaches equal importance to the factory and the settlement and arrange them closely shoulder to shoulder.

Space production

The Academy of Oil Painting is a site for production of three types of space. First, the academy is an unregistered structure; it's a temporary building but may become permanent in the future. Second, the academy could be understood as a production process in which intellectuals transform the commune into a series of spaces at a separated joint area of city and countryside. Here, separation becomes a starting point of creating a commune. Iterative updating in the continuous daily use is the basic logic of the academy.

Research process of studio sectional structure

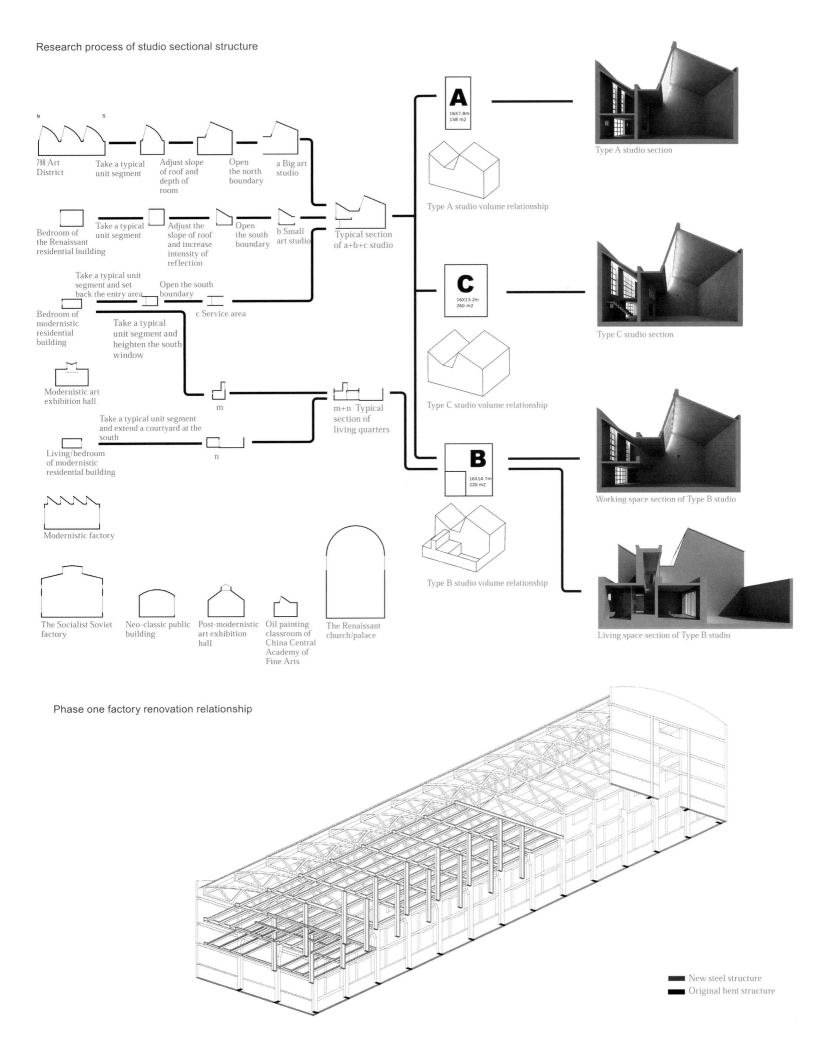

N   S

798 Art District

Take a typical unit segment

Adjust slope of roof and depth of room

Open the north boundary

a Big art studio

Bedroom of the Renaissant residential building

Take a typical unit segment

Adjust the slope of roof and increase intensity of reflection

Open the south boundary

b Small art studio

Typical section of a+b+c studio

Bedroom of modernistic residential building

Take a typical unit segment and set back the entry area

Open the south boundary

c Service area

Take a typical unit segment and heighten the south window

Modernistic art exhibition hall

m

Living/bedroom of modernistic residential building

Take a typical unit segment and extend a courtyard at the south

n

m+n Typical section of living quarters

Modernistic factory

The Socialist Soviet factory

Neo-classic public building

Post-modernistic art exhibition hall

Oil painting classroom of China Central Academy of Fine Arts

The Renaissant church/palace

A
16X7.8m
158 m2

Type A studio volume relationship

Type A studio section

C
16X13.2m
260 m2

Type C studio volume relationship

Type C studio section

B
16X14.7m
220 m2

Type B studio volume relationship

Working space section of Type B studio

Living space section of Type B studio

Phase one factory renovation relationship

New steel structure
Original bent structure

61

Tiens Tiens

Hua Li
Trace Architecture Office

Location Beijing, China
Gross building area 1464 ft² (136 m²)
Site area 646 ft² (60 m²)
Completion 2015

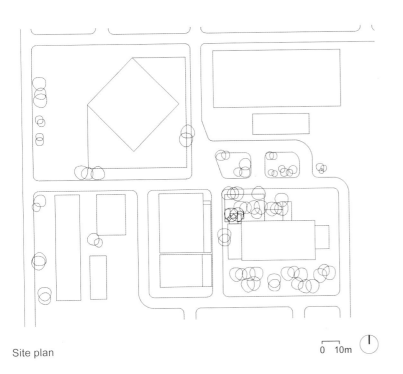

Site plan

0 10m

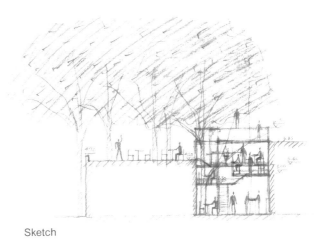

Sketch

The project, located at Sanlitun village, was built around big trees. Within the small site of 646 square feet (60 square meters), the architecture was designed into several platforms at different heights around two big trees. The spaces at varied height allow people to create close relationships with trees from different angles, while the spiral staircase travels through the green leaves and twigs.

Decomposing

Due to the limitations of the site, the architect divided the whole second floor into three platforms at varied heights. The gaps between them provided many possibilities for the passage of visual lines. The traditional spatial layers were decomposed by separate platforms and gaps. Upon the decomposition of the single perspective, an obscure and flowing spatial overlaying gets away from the mode that architectural spaces start from wall structure, and then establishes a new spatial order in a more flowing form. The lightness of the structure creates possibilities for the spatial fluidity. The architect created a much richer experience between people and architecture inside a limited space of the little dessert shop through decomposition and reorganization of space and the use of a glass curtain.

Spatial order

Generally speaking, the architect first dismantled some elements in the structure and used another component—trees—to reorganize these elements. The architectural belief was that the dismantlement of traditional spatial form doesn't mean the loss of order. Therefore, the existing trees in the site were well protected while the spaces at different layers, visual lines, and behavioral lines were developed around the trees. The potential spatial guide with the trees reorganized these fragmented spaces. The basic units for building spatial order, thus, were transformed from a single wall into a spatial sense guided by trees, and the spatial order became richer and more changeable. The relationships between people and the trees are consequently much closer.

Site specific

Besides the spatial guiding function, the architect kept the trees to reconsider the relationship between significance of place and people. As the project is located at a high-consumption area of Sanlitun village with high land cost, the action of keeping the trees was an attempt to return to nature under the background of consumerism, which was an approach that would not threaten the business of the dessert shop. The unique spatial experience of the structure is designed to attract more people to participate in a series of activities inside the building. The vitality brought about by the Canadian poplar trees in the site awakens people's respect to and thirst for nature, integrating people, space, and nature into the whole building and environment in more constrained way.

Section 1

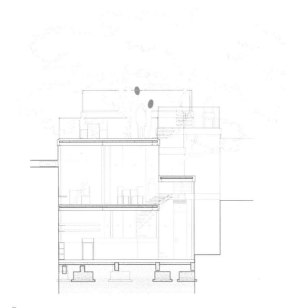

Section 2

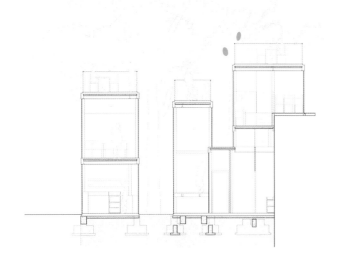

Section 3

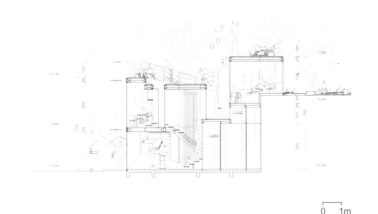

0   1m

Roof floor plan

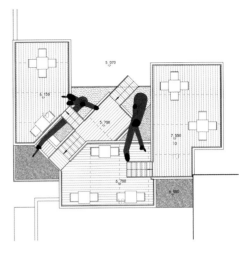

Second floor plan

First floor plan

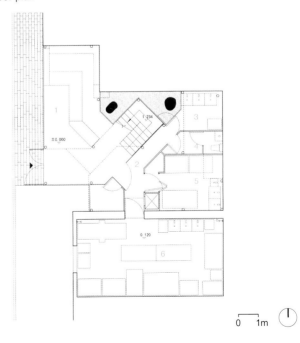

0   1m

1 Take-out area   6 Baking room
2 Staff corridor   7 Dine-in area
3 Disinfection room   8 Drinks bar
4 Staff washroom   9 Customer washroom
5 Decorating room   10 Roof terrace dine-in area

Luoyang Museum

Li Li
Tongji Architectural Design (Group) Co., Ltd.

Location Luoyang, China
Gross building area 10.7 acres (4.4 hectares)
Site area 49 acres (20 hectares)
Completion 2009

Site plan

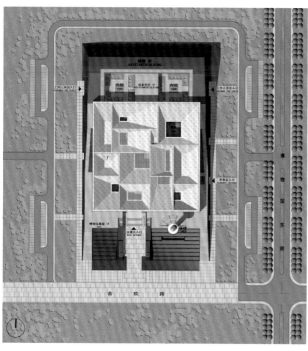

Sketch

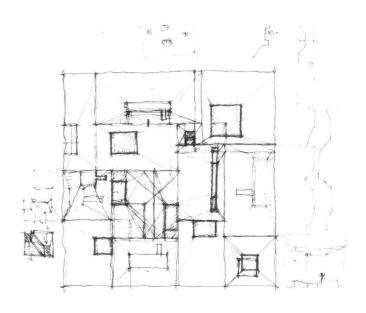

The project is located at South Bund of Luo River, a transition zone between the old town and the new area south of Luoyang. Bordering on Luoyang Sui and Tang Dynasties Relics, the project is a very important landmark on the central axis in Luoyang city. The design concept took the asymmetric spatial structure as supports and created courtyards and skylights in turning points of the square layout with landscaping methods and, finally, realized a dynamic balance in its spatial layout.

History

Luoyang is the birthplace of ancient Chinese civilization and the capital city for 13 dynasties in China's history. The architects encapsulated the whole perception of history, not limited by the architectural form of a specific dynasty. Instead, they regarded the remains of different dynasties as common parts of Luoyang's long history. Therefore, the museum's expression of history was eventually realized by constructing a horizontally extending spatial layout.

Space

The supersize horizontal spatial layout was established in regard to whether there was an effective spatial connection. The public space is located on one side of the square volume, while the L-shaped hallways at both sides of the central hall extend the space. To improve the visitor's path-recognition, the four turning points of the square were designed with courtyards and skylights; meanwhile, at the diagnose line of the square, a clear visual passage was built to stress the vertical sense of the space. The asymmetric layout reaches a dynamic balance, establishing a relationship seemingly disordered but harmonious and compatible in the whole.

Fusion

Luoyang museum integrates manifestation of forms with tranquil spaces and allows coexistence of external heaviness with internal hollowness. It combines classic axes and asymmetric spatial organization, interweaving light and spaces into an internal landscaping atmosphere. It fuses and enclosed appearance with an open topographic shaping, creating both memorial meaning and publicity.

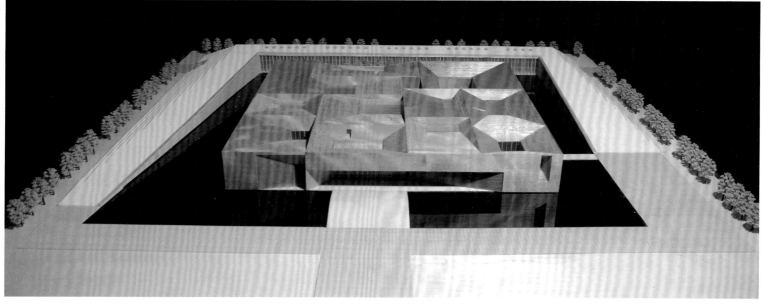

Section 1

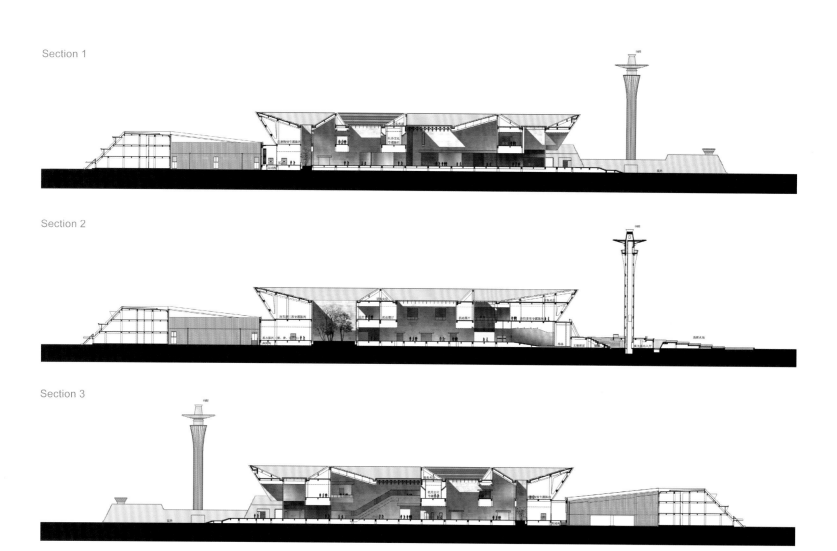

Section 2

Section 3

Jinnan Campus Student Center of Nankai University

Li Linxue
Atelier L+

Location Tianjin, China
Gross building area 117,833 ft²
(10,947 m²)
Site area 791,179 ft² (73,503 m²)
Completion 2015

Site plan

Sketch

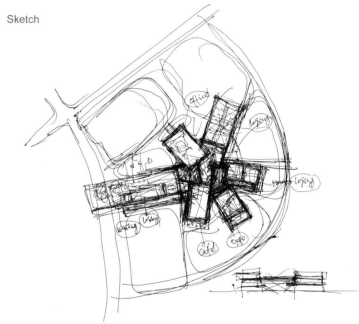

The project, located to the east of the campus axis and the west of Nankai Lake, is a 49-feet (15-meter) high white building with a unique form at the waterside. It includes six structures of different sizes and a radial layout, which looks like a full-bloom begonia. The center consists of an 880-seat theater, a 290-seat concert, and a large terrace at the roof floor for students to hold various outdoor activities.

Nature

A university town, which represents the construction of a university campus in China, usually features large dimensions, fast-built modes, and a lack of diversity. Facing this fact, the designer of Jinan Campus Student Center of Nankai University attempted to create a utopia integrated with nature, while allowing the memories of the original site and place to be recognized from the design. The site is surrounded by a lake and low woods, the flat and spacious natural landscape of which contrasts strongly with the surrounding built environment. The building purposely highlights this contrast through a deep response to the existing natural environment.

Light

Cubic volumes in different sizes were organized into a radial layout around the atrium, creating an integral form of architectural cluster connected by a ring corridor. A porous GRC curtain that covers the architectural volume was adopted to remove the 'orientation characters' and 'vertical characters' set up according to the solar trace, thus maximizing natural lighting. Students can freely move around in all kinds of functional rooms, wander in the architectural public spaces, or have random interactions. They also gain different experiences of the interior light and shadow throughout their day.

Techtonic

The double skins of the GRC curtain wall and perforated aluminum boards of the exterior walls became an architectural base for integrating nature and creating light. They formed textural units through the control of mathematical parameters, and considering the different functional spaces of meeting centers, activity rooms, concert, and other rooms, they can freely impose control over the quantity of light entering the rooms, thus become a 'filtration net' of maximum optimal light and natural landscape. The white texture unit grows from the ground and extends to the sky, continually and completely penetrating the whole building. It obscures the differences between architecture and the nature environment and further stresses the senses of lightness and floating between them.

East elevation

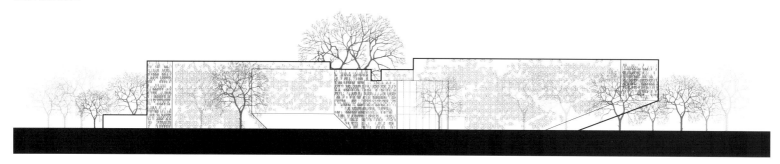

West elevation

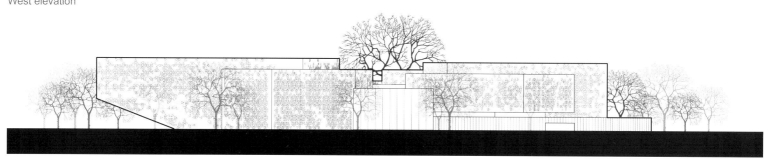

Section 1-1

1 Rehearsal hall
2 Service hall
3 Courtyard
4 Performing arts center

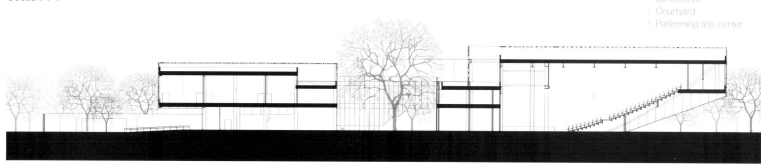

Section 2-2

1 Activity room
2 Office
3 Courtyard
4 Small concert hall

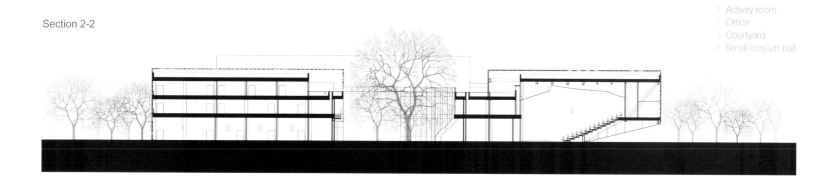

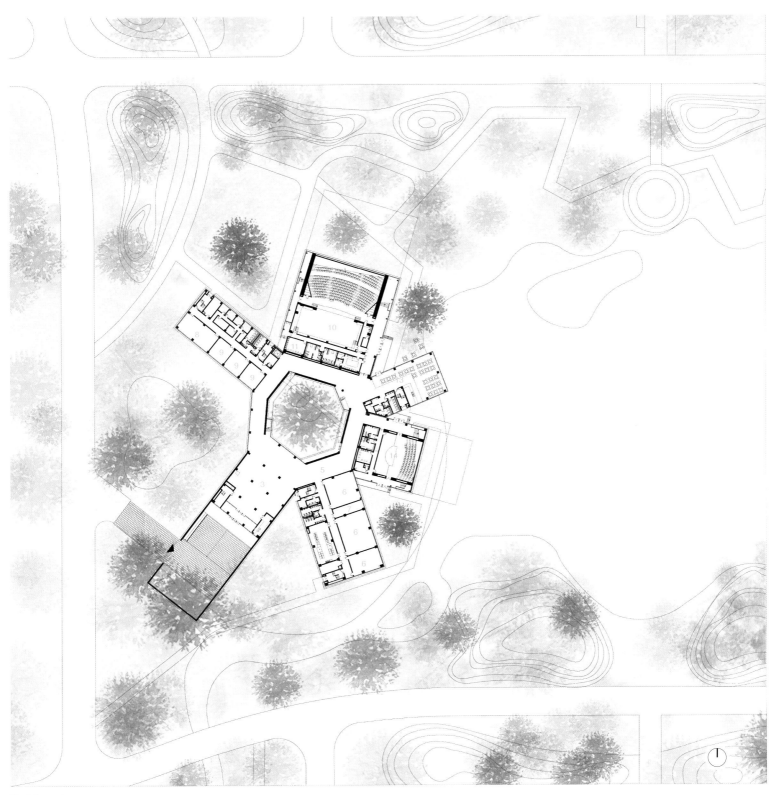

First floor plan

1 Main entrance
2 Entrance courtyard
3 Service hall
4 Central courtyard
5 Gallery
6 Rehearsal hall
7 Storage
8 Activity room
9 Office
10 Performing Arts Center
11 Dressing room
12 VIP
13 Café
14 Small concert hall

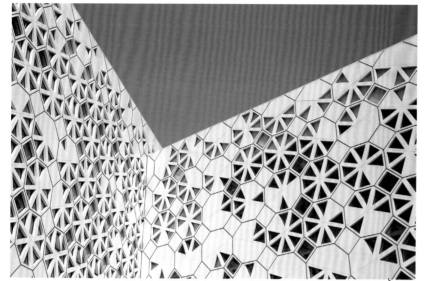

Diagram of façade element

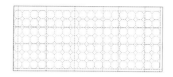

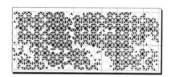

Diagram of form and façade

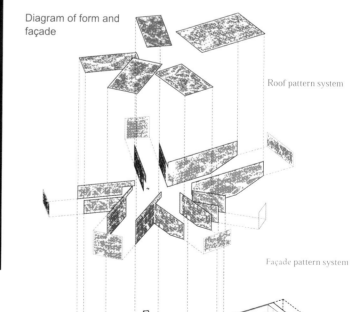

Roof pattern system

Façade pattern system

Function organization

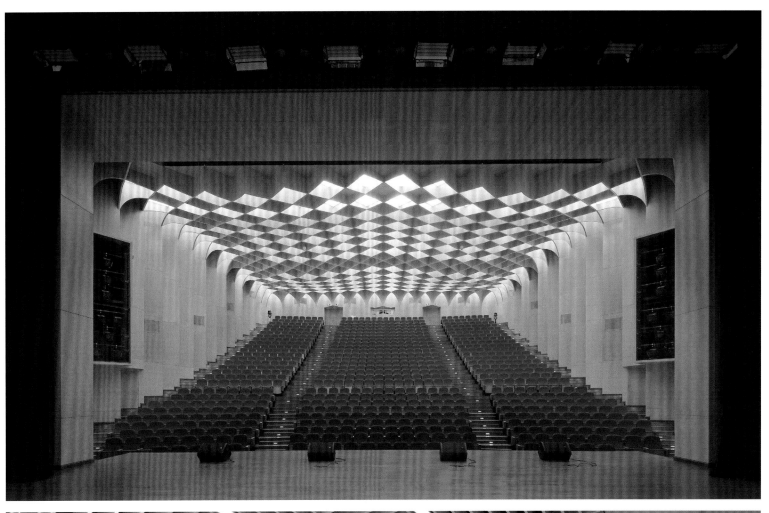

Entrance for Site of Xanadu

Li Xinggang
Li Xinggang Studio

Location Inner Mongolia Autonomous
Region, China
Gross building area 4413 ft² (410 m²)
Site area 179,251 ft² (16,653 m²)
Completion 2011

Site plan

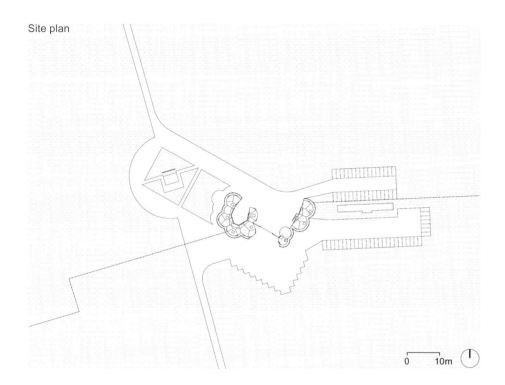

0   10m

Sketch

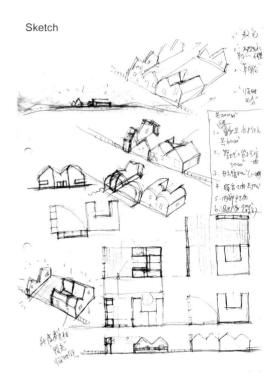

The project, located south of the Site of Xanadu, is an accessory structure of the scenic spot. The pair of little round and eclipse white structures are organized into two courtyards separately open to the outside and the inside for the use of staff and visitors. These little buildings of different sizes at higher and lower sites build an interesting dialogue between themselves.

Scenery and geometry

The Site of Xanadu workstation is sited in a natural environment of the inner Mongolia steppe and cultural environment of the relics site. With interactive and derivative of architectural elements such as structures, spaces, forms, and so forth, it builds spatial poetic qualities closely related with nature and creates supplemental relationships between the artificial and nature. Through careful planning and arrangement of location, organization, and superposition of the structures and space units, it realizes a natural and spiritual scenery (spatial poetic atmosphere) by man-made and materialized geometry (the architectural body).

Spatial units

The architects articulated a rich space in the workstation with spatial units that could be infinitely repeated and organized. The space is defined by simple geometrical and structural characters, including dimensional creation and adjustment closely related with the body and visual picture. It is also combined with the architectural space, form, material, and construction. The unit of structure and space is a round or eclipse slope-crest mixed structure of concrete plus membrane, which is cut into sectional elevations continuously. These spatial units are organized horizontally.

Narrative

One of key elements for creating 'scenery' is to create and stress the sense of expectation and drama in the experiencing process through a dynamic viewing of introduction, elucidation, transition, and summary. The narrative method of the workstation was to create drama in its architectural form. When people recognize this group of little white 'tents' in the distance, they find that they are visually similar to the neighboring traditional Mongol yurts in the grassland. It's only when people walk closer to them that they discover these 'tents' are different. For the part facing the grasslands, the stay bars supporting the exterior white membrane become supporting points in the membrane surface and create a unique surface effect. The parts facing the courtyard are continuous curved walls and eaves with their arcs formed by constant cutting or unfolded architectural sections, bringing the view of the grassland and the site scenery into sight.

West elevation

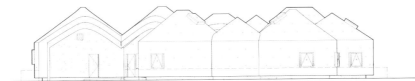

East elevation

South elevation

North elevation

Section B-B

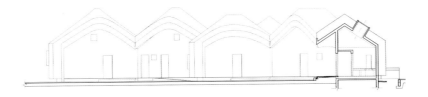

Section C-C

Section A-A

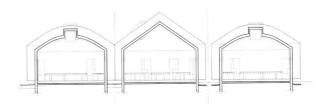

0   5m

First floor plan

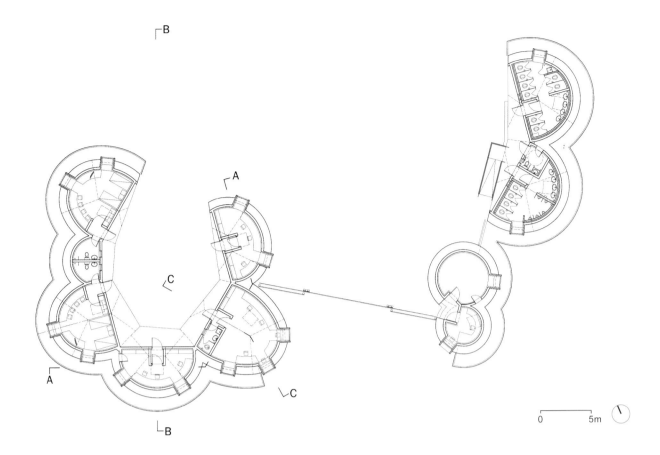

0   5m

Chinese Imperial Examinations Museum

Liu Kecheng
Liu Kecheng Studio

Location Nanjing, China
Gross building area 199,918 ft² (18,573 m²)
Site area 81,806 ft² (7600 m²)
Completion 2016

Neighborhood figure-ground relation

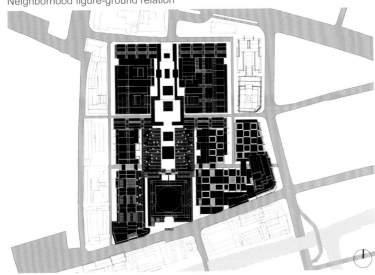

Art work by Wu Guanzhong

The project is situated at the core area of the scenery belt around the Confucius Temple of Qinhuai in Nanjing. It is the center of Chinese Imperial Examination System, Chinese Imperial Examination Culture, and Chinese Cultural Relics of Imperial Examination. The building is a renovation and expansion of the Jiangnan Examination Hall. Besides the above-ground part, the main body also includes an underground structure of several floors. The roof of the sunken structure is a reflecting pool.

History

Imperial examinations were held for selecting officials in ancient China and the examinations halls were the product of imperial examinations system. Jiangnan Imperial Examinations Hall was initially built in 1168 and supplied numerous talents for the country in 737 years in its history.

After the foundation of People's Republic of China, the environment of the historical street of Jiangnan Examinations Hall became deteriorated, the historical memories faded away, and the cultural industry gradually went downhill. There was an urgent need for renovation.

During the re-organization of the whole historical street, the architects primarily had four considerations. First, to protect the cultural relics—put in order the surrounding environment of the Mingyuan Pavilion of Jiangnan Examinations Hall. Second, recover the historical memories—restore its historical layout and build a

Chinese Imperial Examinations Museum. Third, improve the city—open up the north-south axis in Jiangnan Examinations Hall to create a new urban public space. Lastly, recover cultural industry—push the development of traditional Chinese cultural.

Confucius Temple, Jiangnan Examinations Hall, and Qinhuai River are closely bound and have been neighbors since ancient times. Therefore, the design of the museum sought to retain this historical relationship.

Blanking

With modesty and respect to history, the architects endeavored to carry on the historical spirit with modern language to create dialogues with history. The museum is located to the east of the Confucius Temple and in front of the Mingyuan Pavilion. The designers compared the examinations system and culture of Jiang Examinations Hall to a treasury box deeply buried in the ground or an unknown story of the past, waiting for people to discover and explore.

There is a pond on the roof of the museum, which separates it with the surrounding antique buildings. The water reflects the quiet Mingyuan Pavilion like a mirror, which passes the implications of drawing lessons. By concealing the museum underground, the design not only increases a sense of ritual for the relic site, but also reduces the impact of the new building upon the historical axis and urban culture line as much as possible.

Reconstruction

The architects referred to traditional courtyards and streets in the detailed design of the museum. They borrowed architectural words from traditional architecture in Jiangnan regions (south of the Yangtze River). White walls and black tiles were selected for the construction materials. They attempted to reconstruct traditional spaces and elements with modern language, following the cultural line of the city and allowing a dialogue with the history in a modern way.

The main structure of the museum is surrounded by three layers of walls: tiled walls enclosing the outer space of the museum and the bamboo slip wall surrounding the center space. The middle white wall is a guiding wall, which supports the ramp, leading visitors from noisy Confucius Temple Street into the underground space of the museum. Several corridors penetrate the three layers of walls and connect the outer space with the center space, and establish visual relationships between the three walls through the openings.

Underground second floor

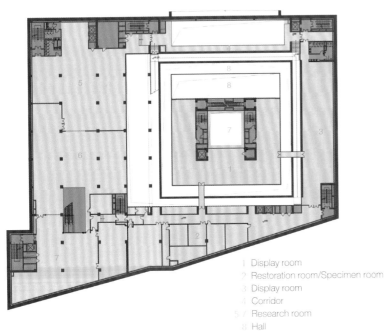

1 Display room
2 Restoration room/Specimen room
3 Display room
4 Corridor
5 / Research room
8 Hall

Underground first floor

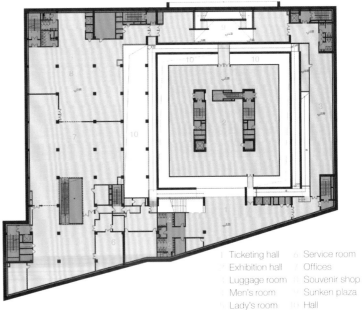

1 Ticketing hall   6 Service room
 Exhibition hall   7 Offices
 Luggage room   8 Souvenir shop
 Men's room   9 Sunken plaza
 Lady's room   10 Hall

Underground fourth floor

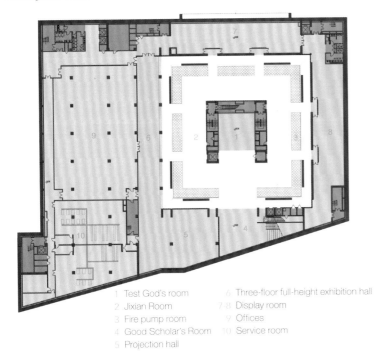

1 Test God's room   6 Three-floor full-height exhibition hall
2 Jixian Room   7-8 Display room
3 Fire pump room   9 Offices
4 Good Scholar's Room   10 Service room
5 Projection hall

Underground third floor

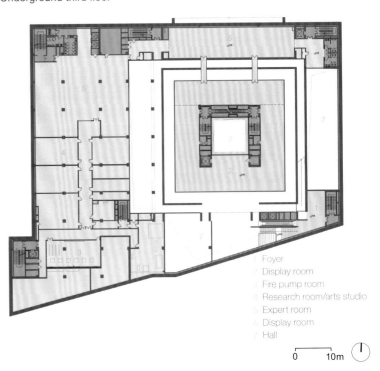

1 Foyer
 Display room
 Fire pump room
 Research room/arts studio
 Expert room
 Display room
7 Hall

0   10m

Expanded view of the section

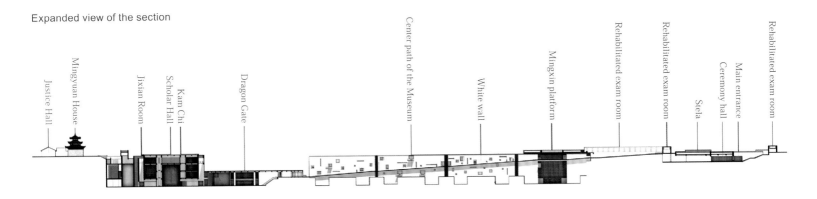

Justice Hall · Mingyuan House · Jixian Room · Scholar Hall · Kam Chi · Dragon Gate · Center path of the Museum · White wall · Mingxin platform · Rehabilitated exam room · Rehabilitated exam room · Stela · Main entrance · Ceremony hall · Rehabilitated exam room

Axonometric sequence

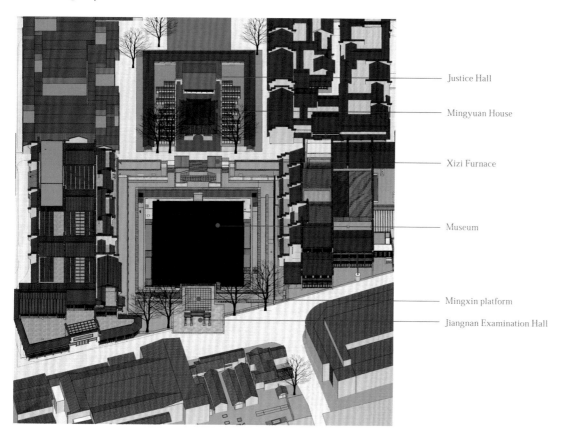

Justice Hall

Mingyuan House

Xizi Furnace

Museum

Mingxin platform

Jiangnan Examination Hall

Sectional view of the Museum and the Qinhuai River

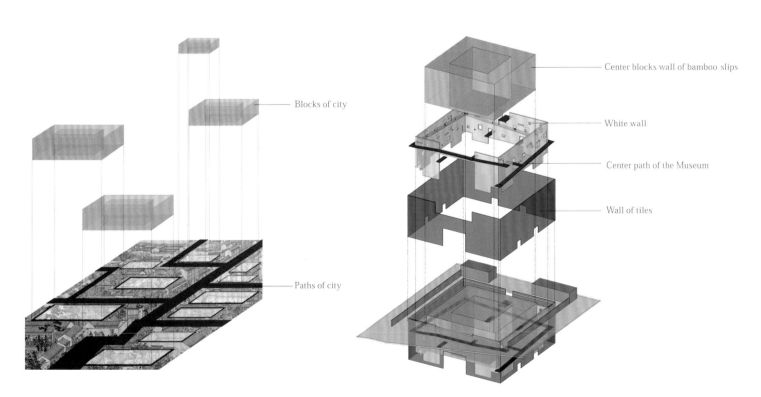

Blocks of city

Paths of city

Center blocks wall of bamboo slips

White wall

Center path of the Museum

Wall of tiles

'Two-dimensional' structure of ancient Chinese city in the regions south of the Yangtze River and 'three-dimensional' structure of the Museum

Long Museum West Bund

Liu Yichun+ Chen Yifeng
Atelier Deshaus

Location Shanghai, China
Gross building area 355,284 ft²
(33,007 m²)
Site area 208,141 ft² (19,337 m²)
Completion 2014

Site plan

0   50m

Section model—old and new structure

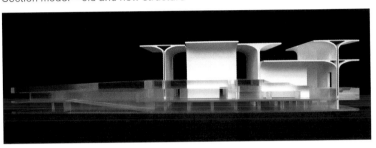

is also distinctively readable and plays a major role in a space, this is what Deshaus refers to as 'architecture.' The 'umbrella arch' designed and introduced by the designers incorporated the frame structure of the original underground garage and also actively adapted to the displaying function of the space, attempting to create free exhibition spaces. In built structures, considerations on many aspects must be clearly presented and understood; therefore, it has obvious Jiagou features.

Root metaphor

Traditionally referring to the images, narratives, or facts that help a person shape the basic cognition of the world and reality, root metaphor in architecture is more about transcending cultures and national characters. The 'umbrella arch' in Long Museum is a tree-form structure. A tree-form space is trans-cultural. It has a root relationship with people, which will not be subjected to limitations of regional culture and is easy to understand for people from any region. Walking between these structures, one has a sense of wandering in the woods. This sense transcends nationalities and regions, so Deshaus sees the structure as a space with root metaphor.

Bodily space

For a body, spatiality not only refers to spatial orientation, but also a status of body in an external environment; thus, bodily space is not a simple physical concept, but an abstract concept of political and cultural properties. It is the starting point of human social attributes.

The umbrella arches in Long Museum are connected not to form a complete arch, but separate ones. They appear as spaces while the space is vaguely and freely enclosed. Without fixed flow lines and boundaries, an obscure relationship is established between tangible structures and intangible spaces. With the huge, massive and heavy concrete structure, the light horizontal flowing spaces, and the anti-gravitational status of flying upward, together they create a body space filled with conflicts and tension. The nervous body may regain its subjectivity in the space.

The site is situated at the bank of Huangpu River in Xuhui, Shanghai. Its four-floor main structure is featured by a unique 'umbrella arch.' Previously a coal transportation quay, the site had an existing protected unloading bridge for coal hoppers, as well as an underground garage, which had been recently built.

Framework

Framework can help people understand the structures from an architect's view. The architect not only needed to consider whether the structure was sound from the view of structural engineers, but also whether it could adapt to specific functions and the site. Therefore, comprehensive thinking was involved. When the structure

Southwest elevation

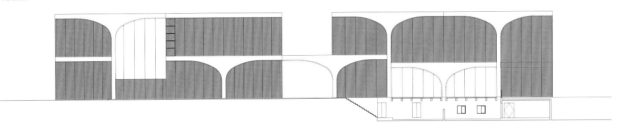

Northeast elevation

Northwest elevation

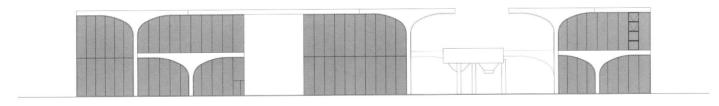

Southeast elevation

0   10m

First floor plan

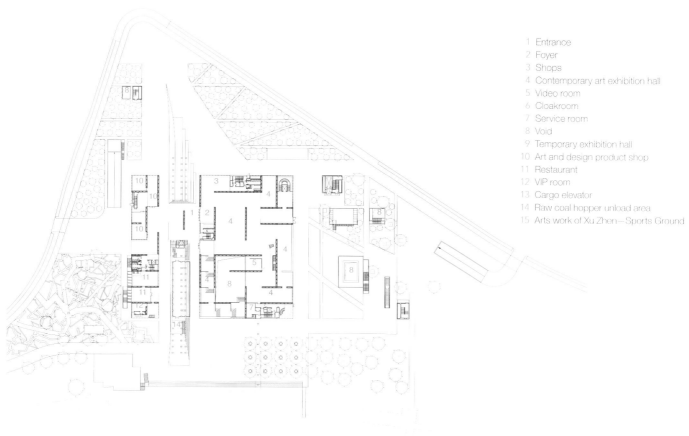

1 Entrance
2 Foyer
3 Shops
4 Contemporary art exhibition hall
5 Video room
6 Cloakroom
7 Service room
8 Void
9 Temporary exhibition hall
10 Art and design product shop
11 Restaurant
12 VIP room
13 Cargo elevator
14 Raw coal hopper unload area
15 Arts work of Xu Zhen—Sports Ground

Underground floor plans

Underground second floor

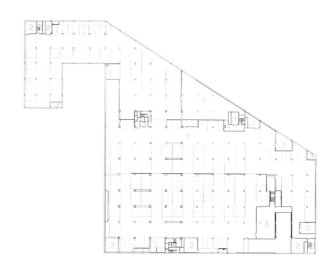

1 Contemporary art hall
2 Ancient art hall
3 Ancient/contemporary art
4 Modern art hall
5 Children's art hall
6 Gallery
7 Restroom
8 Storage for collections
9 Temporary storage
10 Unloading area
11 Reading room
12 Offices
13 Office for curator
14 Meeting room
15 photographic studio
16 Library and archives
17 Tool room
18 Storage
19 Sunken courtyard
20 Security/fire control room
21 Car parking lot
22 Bicycle parking lot
23 Air-conditioning control room
24 Electrical substation
25 Equipment

1 Car parking lot
2 Air-conditioning control room/ventilator room
3 Equipment room

0   10m

Southwest-Northeast section

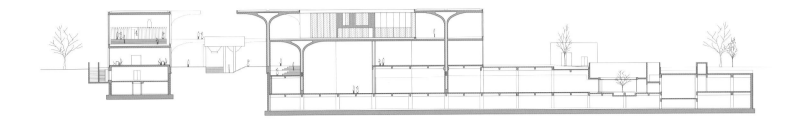

Southeast-Northwest section

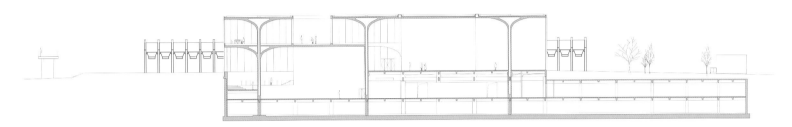

0   10m

China Pavilion for Expo Milano 2015

Lu Yichen
Tsinghua University+Studio Link-Arc

Location Milan, Italy
Gross building area 37,673 ft² (3500 m²)
Site area 49,406 ft² (4590 m²)
Completion 2015

Site plan

1 Water feature
2 East-west public path
3 China Pavilion

0   100m

The inspiration for the project came from a floating cloud over the 'field of hope.' It aspired to create an experience of a public square that is covered by a floating roof and integrated with architectural culture and exhibition units. The unique roof creates an icon image for the project, generating beautiful scenery in the expo site. Its wave-like roof merges the city skyline to the north and landscape to the south, indicating harmonious coexistence of nature and the city, embodying the theme of 'Country of Hope.'

Field and objects

The architects sought to describe the China pavilion as a 'field' in a space instead of another large iconic 'subject' in the Expo. Though different, the 'field' and 'subject' are not clearly demarcated by boundaries, rather they present an attitude of active participation in and response to the surrounding. The visit route of the China pavilion was a process of compliment after criticism. All vertical transportation elements (ramps and stairs) were designed as gently as possible, thus the visiting process is transformed into an act of measuring the architectural space by walking. The architecture further reduces the sense of enclosure and creates an image of 'filed' for visitors wandering inside and outside.

Wood and steel

To construct the large span required inside, the architects used plywood, semi-transparent PVC waterproof layering, and sun-shading bamboo sheets to build an open architectural system for the roof. The plywood beams in the roof correspond to a series of south–north parallel sections in the roof form and each beam is a little varied in its outline. Inserted between these irregular beams are purlins, which follow the curves of the roof. In the intersections of beams and purlins are more than 1400 different 3D joints. Each joint needed to be reinforced by an embedded structural steel plate, which meant that each section of the purlin had to have a prefabricated slot precisely cut by a CNC machine tool. The plywood beams and embedding plates were prefabricated and assembled in the factory so that they could be hoisted quickly to their position.

Light and shadow

The 1059 pieces of roof bamboo tiles are 'written' by parametric design. They express the exterior image of the architecture and provide shade for the interior space. Each bamboo tile is a clear structural unit. It also meets the requirements for 75 percent shading and structural stability and wind loads. Bamboo tiles leave varying shades on the semi-transparent waterproofing under different lighting conditions. This light-and-shadow effect in a thick and layered manner obscures the gaps between bamboo tiles and creates a unified and homogeneous background for recording the passage of time inside the architecture. The architects hoped to produce a deeper relationship with nature through this 'emptiness,' which creates the nature and reminds people of a unique spatial quality of China.

Elevation

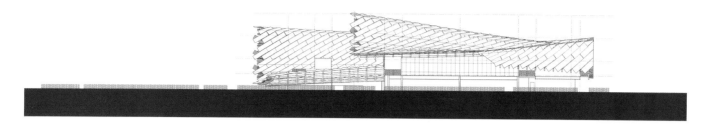

Section

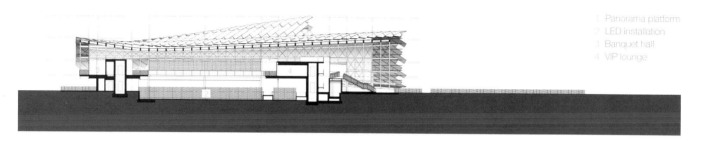

1 Panorama platform
2 LED installation
3 Banquet hall
4 VIP lounge

0   10m

Section 1

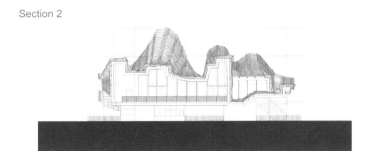

Section 2

Southeast roof plan details

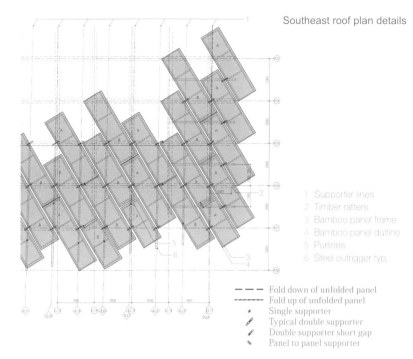

1 Supporter lines
2 Timber rafters
3 Bamboo panel frame
4 Bamboo panel outline
5 Purlines
6 Steel outrigger typ.

– – – Fold down of unfolded panel
········· Fold up of unfolded panel

   Single supporter
   Typical double supporter
   Double supporter short gap
   Panel to panel supporter

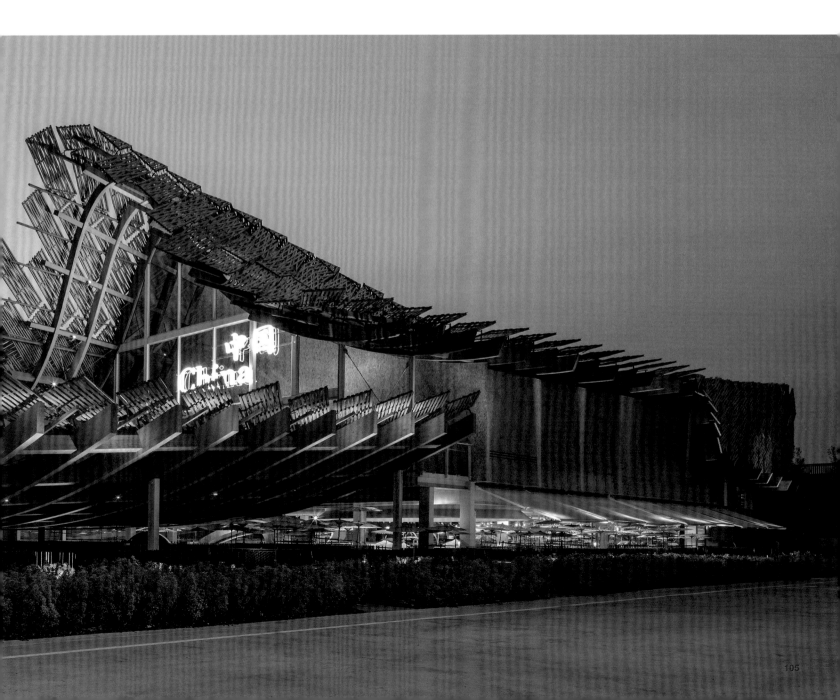

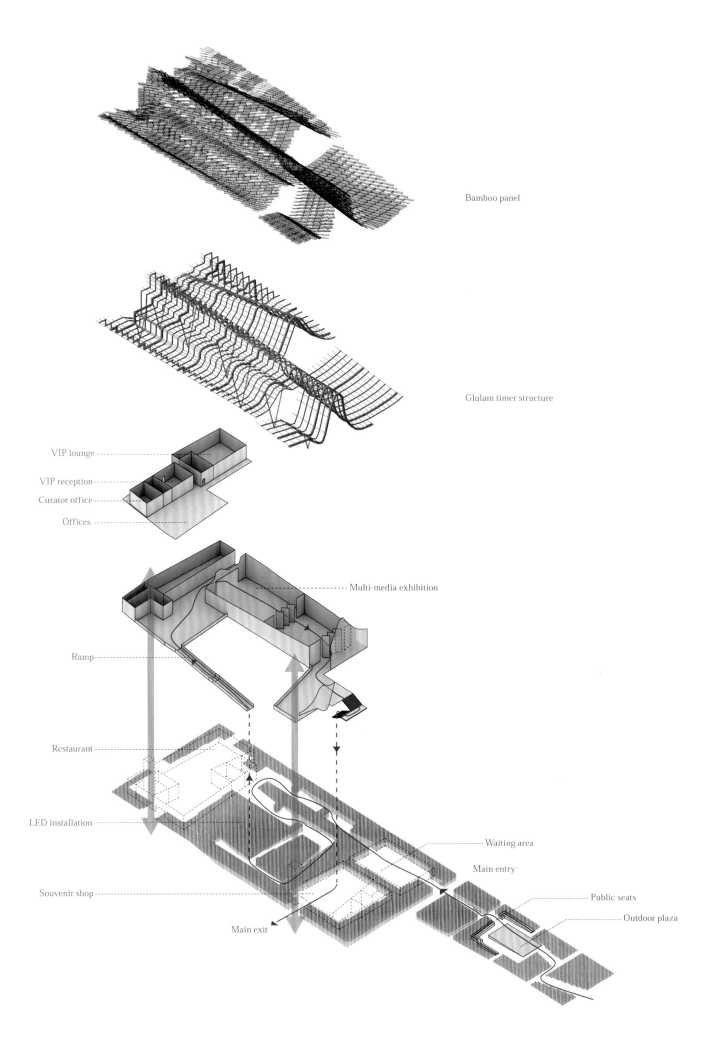

Bamboo panel

Glulam timer structure

VIP lounge

VIP reception

Curator office

Offices

Multi-media exhibition

Ramp

Restaurant

LED installation

Souvenir shop

Waiting area

Main entry

Public seats

Outdoor plaza

Main exit

Roof plan

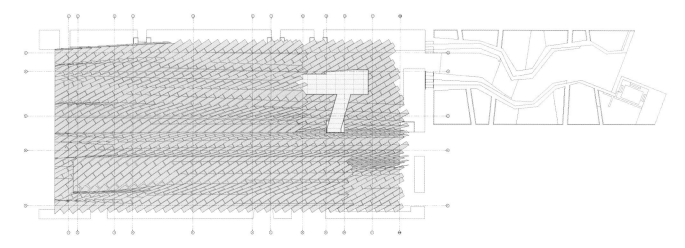

Second floor plan

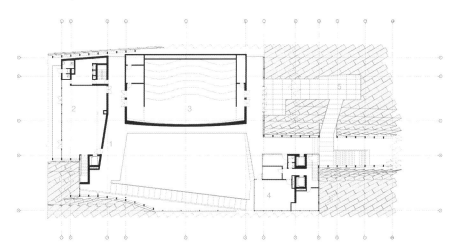

1 Panorama platform
2 Banquet hall
3 Multimedia space
4 VIP lounge
5 Bridge

First floor plan

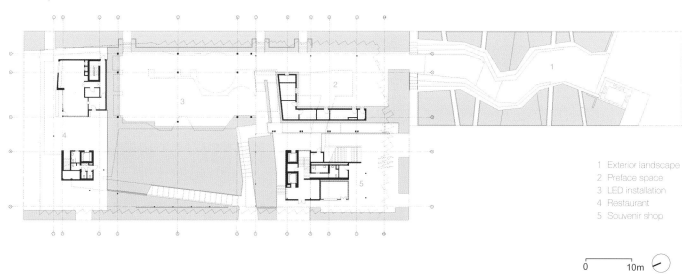

1 Exterior landscape
2 Preface space
3 LED installation
4 Restaurant
5 Souvenir shop

0   10m

107

Details

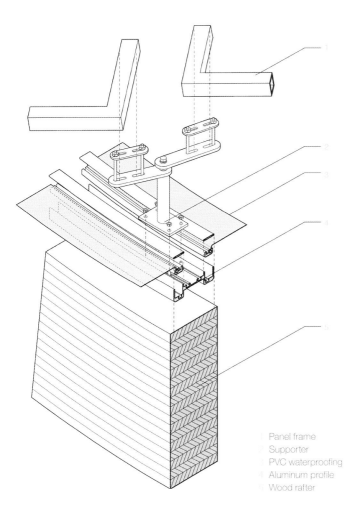

1 Panel frame
2 Supporter
3 PVC waterproofing
4 Aluminum profile
5 Wood rafter

'Chinese seed'— China Corporate United Pavilion of Expo 2015 Milan

Ren Lizhi
Tongji Architectural Design (Group)
Co., Ltd.

Location Milan, Italy
Gross building area 21,527 ft²
(2000 m²)
Site area 13,670 ft² (1270 m²)
Completion April 2015

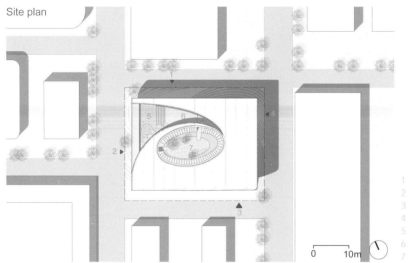

Site plan

1 Restaurant and exhibition hall entrance
2 VIP entrance
3 Main entrance
4 Logistic entrance
5 Roof observation platform
6 Ramp
7 Central garden

Sketch

0   10m

Located at Plot NE.6 in the east part of the Expo Milano 2015 site in Italy, the project was a response to the Expo theme of 'Feeding the Planet, Energy for Life,' taking 'Seeds of China' as the premise conception. The design uses relatively square volumes and sits as open and inclusive through a combination of spaces and the use of materials, and also builds a coordinated relationship with surrounding structures.

Conversion of contradictions

The theme of the Expo Milano 2015—Feeding the Planet, Energy for Life—revealed the conflicting relationship between people and nature; soliciting and back-feeding. 'Reversing is the movement of Tao' illustrates the wisdom of balancing of ancient Chinese people in dealing with conflict relations. The design expanded a series of antagonistic relationships that were inter-convertible—such as square and round, inside and outside, empty and full, hard and soft—to build the basic from of the pavilion, the exterior and interior spaces, and architectural details.

It further explained the architectural ideas based on the theme of the expo. The building inserts an eclipse 'green core' into a square volume to present the concept of square and round; it opens the 'curtain' hanging at the entrance, obscuring the boundaries of exterior and interior architectural spaces. The ring ramp of the green core connects visiting paths while the artificial and natural scenery complement each other. The membrane and steel are turned-up and connected to reflect the coexistent status of hardness and softness.

Blurry dimensions

For exhibition buildings that are subjected to limitations in the height and volume, it is rather challenging to control the dimensions of the entrance. The designers left an entrance space with a 24.6-foot

(7.5-meter) clear height at the southeast corner of the 39.4-foot (12-meter) high building and integrated the entrance with the exterior environment. Ramps at different levels are all revealed here. This multi-sharing of space produces an effect of 'seeing big in small,' like in Chinese traditional gardens. Meanwhile, the interior was decorated with large areas of white-painted ceiling and natural-wood veneer walls, while utmost simplicity and abstractionism was achieved in the details to blur the sense of spatial dimension. Inside the forest-like dendritic column casing there is a movie hall with vertical greening, making people feel like they are in a miniature natural world.

System integration

In this project, the main vertical bearing components in the structural system were integrated with architectural elements—the tree-like column casing in the inner ring and the concealed elevation truss. The spatial form of elevation truss answered architectural aesthetics and mechanic logic. The interior dendritic column is both the formal element of space and an indication of the growth of trees. Inside the pavilion, other than movement space and exhibition walls, which divided the show areas, structural members were integrated with the architecture in a vanishing way. The surface of the steel structural façade truss was covered by membrane. The natural tension of the membrane made it possible for the transmission of surface force of the structure.

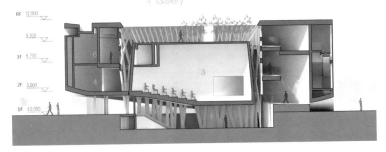

1 Themed activity center   5 Themed discussion area
2 Lobby of VIP room   6 VIP reception
3 Screening room   7 Garden
4 Gallery

Section a-a

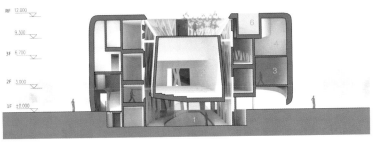

1 Barrier-free entry   4 VIP reception
2 Screening room   5 Garden
3 Waiting area   6 Ramp to the roof terrace

Section b-b

0   5m

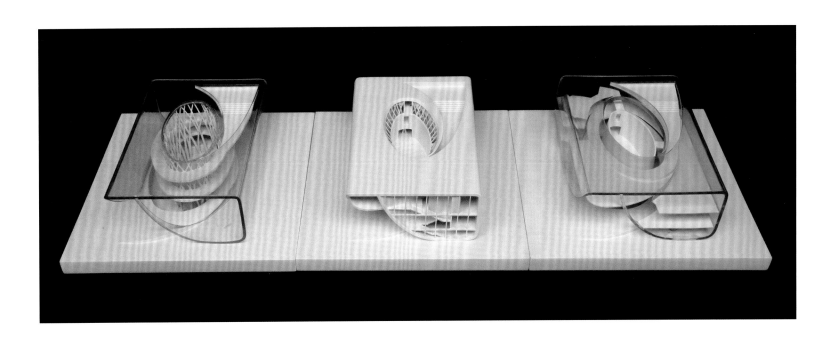

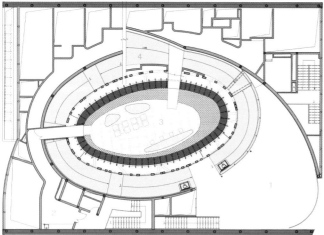

1 Themed discussion area
2 Elevator hall and corridor
3 Garden
4 Ramp to the roof terrace

30.5 feet (9.3 meters) elevation plan

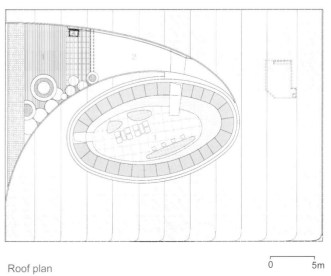

Roof plan

1 Garden
2 Ramp to the roof terrace

0   5m

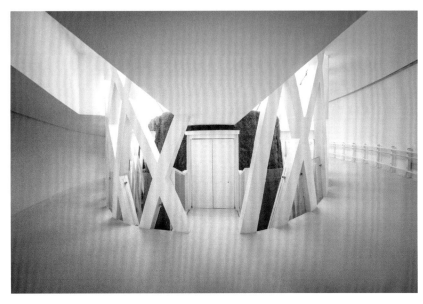

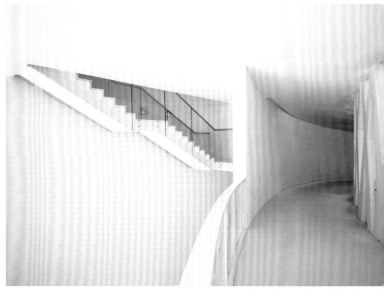

1　Themed activity center
2　Restaurant
3　Lobby of VIP room
4　Preface hall
5　Kitchen
6　Up-ramps
7　Down-ramps
8　Screening room
9　Gallery
10　Waiting area
11　Elevator hall
12　Refrigerator room
13　Themed discussion area
14　VIP reception
15　Curator office
16　Staff offices
17　Meeting room

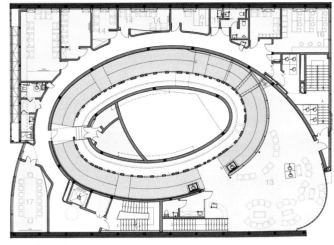

Third floor plan

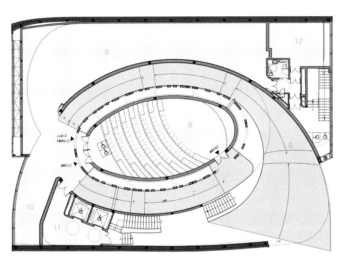

Second floor plan

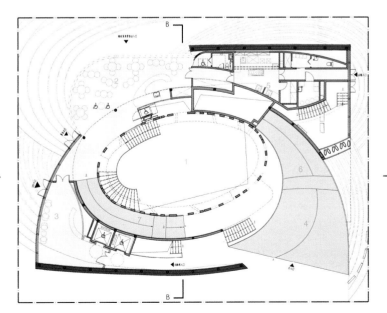

First floor plan

0　　　5m

Tiantai No.2 Primary School

Ruan Hao
LYCS Architecture

Location Tiantai, Taizhou, China
Gross building area 109,684 ft²
(10,190 m²)
Site area 77,608 ft² (7210 m²)
Completion 2014

Site plan

Situated at Chicheng Street, Tiantai County in Zhejiang Province, the project features a distinctive 656-foot (200-meter) long ring lane on the roof. Due to an extremely limited site area, the architects put the ring track on the roof, so as to acquire an extra 32,292-square-feet (3000-square-meters) of public space for the school. The roof track was not only installed with sufficient safeguard facilities to ensure the safety of students, but was also equipped with spring shock absorbers to provide a second absorber system to reduce noises.

Urban renewal

Nowadays, cities in China are no longer a blank canvas like in the large-scale construction period. Urbanization is slowing down, turning gradually from large-scale construction to small-scale regeneration. During this process, architects will often come across insolvable problems when a design brief that is applicable to construction in an open ground is required to be applied to a renewal urban site. How do designers challenge the common practice under such limitations and explore new architectural modes in cities? Architects had to initiate a new reform to change the current status of Chinese architecture.

Rooftop running track

For this project, as the land was extremely limited, the track and suitable teaching buildings required by the school were not achievable under the existing conditions. Therefore, to provide a place for children to run, the architects placed the 656-foot (200-meter) track on the roof and design this concentric school building based on its form. Students running on the roof can feel closer to the sky; thus, this design creates a unique experience on an elevated ground and acquires 32,292 square feet (3000 square meters) of extra ground activity space for the school.

Duplicable mode

Many Chinese cities now face problems such as high density and complicated land conditions. The No.2 Primary School in Tiantai had a very special limited site and reflected many typical characteristics of Chinese cities. It is this coexistence of specialty and typicality that offers an opportunity for the architects to think about the problems in the urbanization, and motivates them to break down barriers and create new modes in the regeneration of cities.

Design process diagram

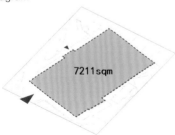

1 Site area and boundary

2 Area of sports facilities

3 Extrusion of massing

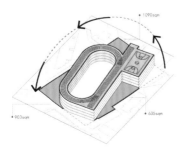

4 Fotation of massing

5 Ground space continuity

6 Vertical circulations

119

Section b-b

1 Classrooms
2 Offices
3 Restaurant
4 Music room
5 Auditorium
6 Lounge

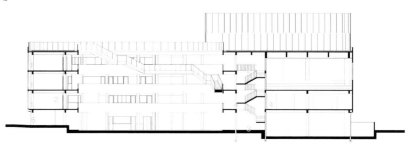

Section c-c

1 Corridor
2 Offices
3 Doorman

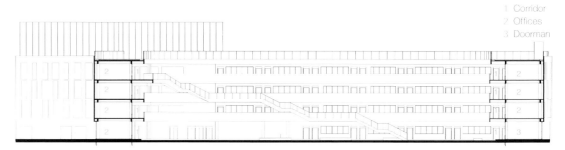

First floor plan

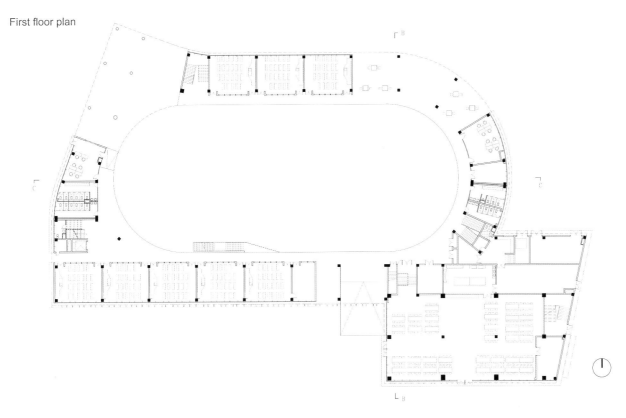

TM Studio [West Bund Office]

Tong Ming
TM Studio

Location Shanghai, China
Gross building area 1937 ft²
(180 m²)
Site area 2153 ft² (200 m²)
Completion 2015

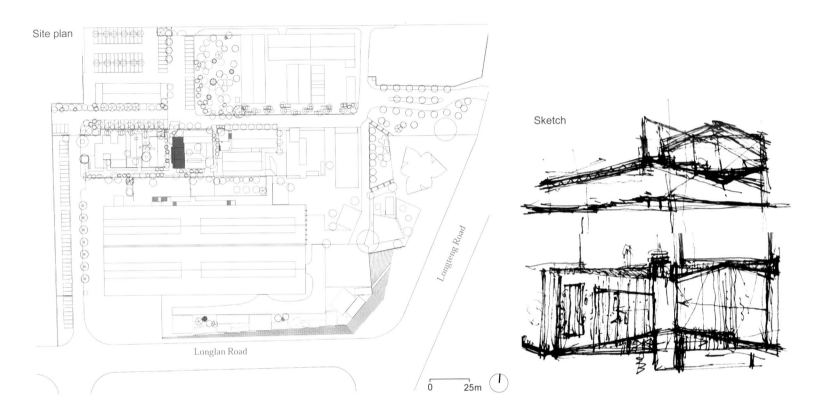

Site plan

Sketch

Longteng Road

Longlan Road

0   25m

Close to architectural offices and arts studios, this project is located at the north of West Bund Art Center at the riverside in Xuhui, Shanghai. The building was constructed with cost-effective, light-weight, and convenient light steel structure and spread in a north–south layout, with two floors at the south and one floor at the north. In the design, some vertical turns were created on the first floor, along with some twists on the ceiling and the floor, which creates a changing effect of turns and twists in the internal area that can also serve as an auxiliary space.

Structure

The structure here refers not only to physical structure, but also linguistic structure. Therefore, architectural design could be understood as a narrative. The structure is not merely important in presenting construction techniques, but also in its explanation of possibilities, because it attempts to organize various segments into a whole. Reconstruction is a process: it is about innovations and traditions, protection and renovation, transformation and continuation, keeping to the beaten track while keeping special.

Experiencing

Architecture is not only about the reproduction of styles or ideas, but about life experience with thoughts about sites and types. It

presents the contrasts between light and heavy, wide and narrow, and high and low by constructing materialism. When the body moves around the rolling ground surface and walks through the endless 3D space, one's spirit can enjoy extreme joy and happiness. With full cooperation of body and spirit, the human experience of reality would surpass their perception of aesthetics and functions.

Fabricating

Fabricating is a skill of reorganizing meaningless fragments into a meaningful whole by flexible and smart use of related principles and gained knowledge. During construction, it requires the accumulation of architectural elements and construction techniques plus occasional innovations. From this sense, architectural design is also a kind of fabricating. The relative elements are already there in its early from but the actual meaning is obscure, while the perfect scene could be finally presented through fabricating.

Section perspective

West elevation

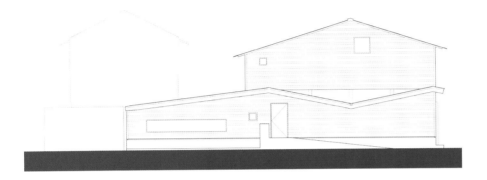

0   5m

Models

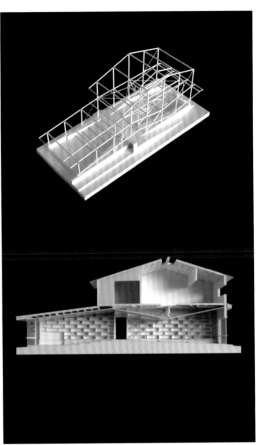

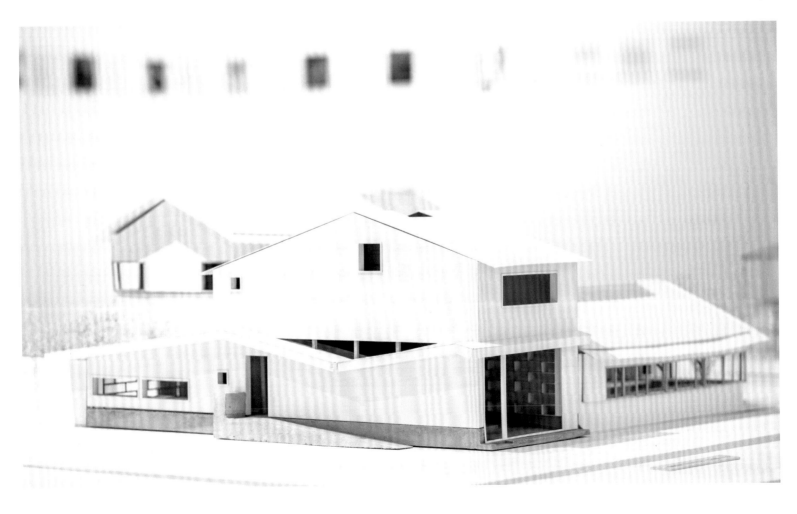

North elevation

South elevation

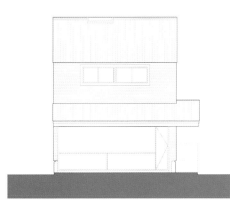

0   5m

Roof plan

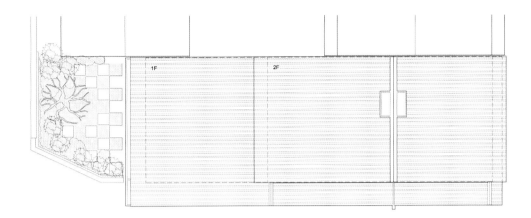

Second floor plan

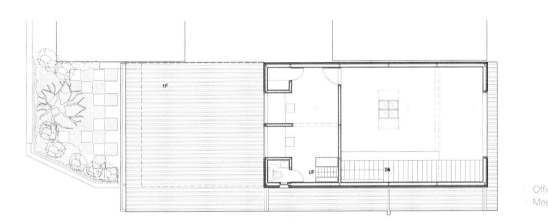

1 Office
2 Meeting

First floor plan

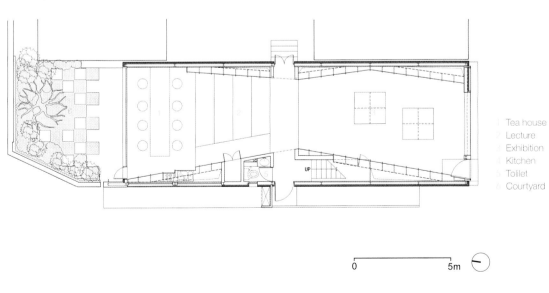

1 Tea house
2 Lecture
3 Exhibition
4 Kitchen
5 Toilet
6 Courtyard

0　　　　　　5m

The ZS Hope Primary School

Wang Lu
School of Architecture, Tsinghua University / In+of
Location Maoping Village, Leiyang, China
Gross building area 12,572 ft² (1168 m²)
Site area 56,758 ft² (5273 m²)
Completion 2007

Site plan

Scale

0   18m

The project was built with ¥500,000, which was urgently raised by Zhejiang Chamber of Commerce in Hunan province in 2006 after the original Maoping village primary school was destroyed by a typhoon. The site is at a sloping ground in the northeast of Maoping village, while the two-floor school building is located at a platform in the slope. Its outlines, sections, materials, and colors are almost the same as local residential buildings, and its gable walls are also identical with its neighboring dwellings. It was a low-cost rural build, constructed with local materials and with help from the villagers.

Low cost

The overall floorage of the hope school is 12,572 square feet (1168 square meters). The actual cost of construction was ¥300,000, which is ¥300 per square meter. To control the cost and adapt to local construction techniques, the architects used small red bricks as the main material for the structure, which create a better dialogue with the surrounding dwellings. Big black bricks were used in small stock to pave roads and the square.

Local conditions

The two-floor school building stands at a platform in the slope. Its outlines, sections, materials, and colors are similar to the local residential buildings. The building is divided east–west by a small

patio corresponding to the teachers' offices and staircase, making the whole structure an assembly of several dwellings. By this method, the school buildings are harmoniously blended into the environment. There are several hollowed-out brick lattices on the north elevation, which was inspired by local dwellings. The south elevation of wood grill, like a long unfolding bamboo script, adds a scroll-like effect to the school buildings.

Participation of local residents

The ZS Hope Primary School project not only expresses local characters and cultural elements, but is also enriches the spirit of times. The design practice used an exploration of architects to build in this poverty-stricken area while retaining the local character. The process of building a study place for children itself is a valuable learning experience. It contains not only conflicts and contradictions that need to be solved, but also solutions to them.

Details

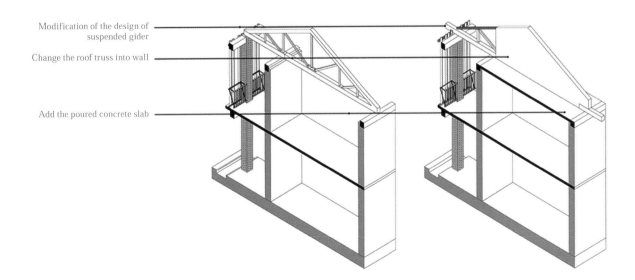

Modification of the design of
suspended gider

Change the roof truss into wall

Add the poured concrete slab

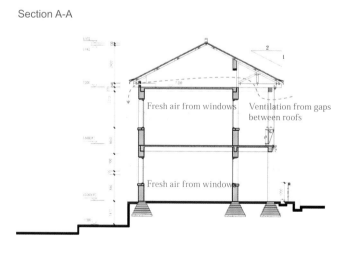

Section A-A

Fresh air from windows

Ventilation from gaps between roofs

Fresh air from windows

Second floor plan

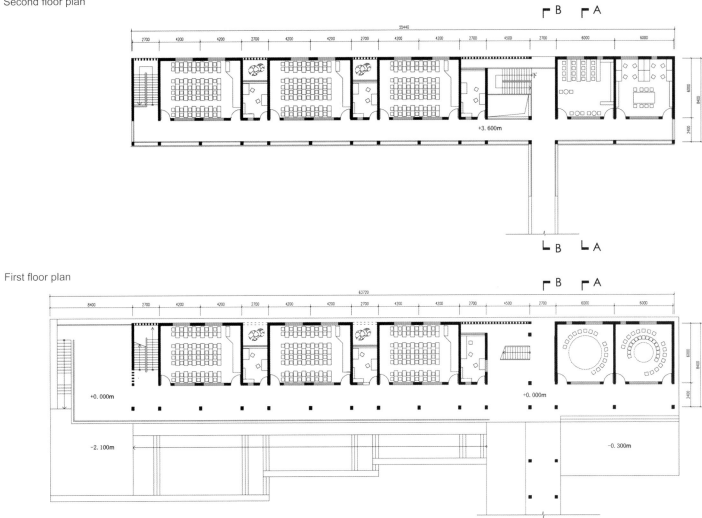

First floor plan

+0. 000m

-2. 100m

+0. 000m

-0. 300m

+3. 600m

Xixi Wetland Artist Village (N site)

Wang Weizhen
Wang Weizhen Architecture

Location Hangzhou, China
Gross building area 48,438 ft²
(4500 m²)
Completion 2011

Bird's view

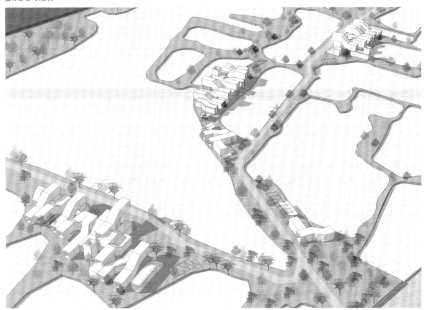

Models

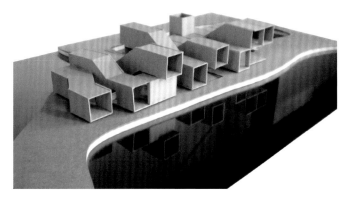

The project, located at Plot N in Hangzhou Xixi Wetland Artist Village, is one of 10 buildings in the third phase of the Xixi Wetland project. Plot N consists of three long, narrow building sites in the north, middle, and south, respectively. The landscape consists of hills and sand dunes, each with water features, in the front and back of the three sites. Visitors can walk along the main paths and enjoy different views of hills, waters, sky, and earth.

Moving view reframing

The architects sought to re-frame the landscape by encouraging visitors to intentionally change their sight and play a subjective role. Western paintings and perspectives are featured by planarization in the 3D space between visitors and the scenery, while the narrative space of Chinese traditional gardening design—'framed scenery'—seeks to establish a space–time relationship between visitors and the scenery, which creates visual variation as one walks. The design sought to explore new possible relationships between time, space, and views by means of movie-reproduction. In this group of narrow sites, the design underlines the varied framed views when one moves. By re-framing, the original landscape is reorganized; meanwhile, the concept and experience of the site scenery are also reorganized through new functions and spaces, forming a series of 'moving scenery.'

Fabrication

Fabrication describes the process of expanding components and parts into a continual, open whole. It also expresses an ability of

procession and transformation. With the reproduction of components and several configurations, it provides people with multidimensional and multi-directional architectural landscape and urban spaces. Rather than the unit modules and sequential relationships between architectural and landscaping textures, fabrication expresses an organic body of constant development of architecture and landscape. Through fabrication and re-fabrication, the design develops into an organic strategy that makes architecture and landscape sustainable and transformable.

Fabricating mountains and waters

Different from Chinese urban block courtyards whose fabrication form is inward, the linear fabrication form of water towns in southern Yangtze River is outward. The waterways and lakes in the settlement are a functional connection system, and the architectural units are also outward, highlighting the relationship between architecture and water. The buildings in Xixi, like the building texture of water towns, start from the relationships between linear series of architectural units and water and sand dunes. All sites in this narrow building plot face the hills and sand dune with their water features, in front and back sides, revealing intersecting series of distant and deep views. Visitors can stroll along the main paths and explore the possibilities of the linear scenery.

North elevation

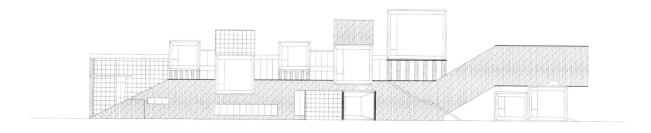

South elevation

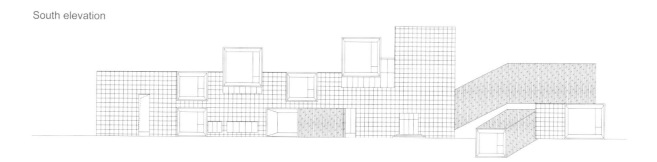

Six frame views of river

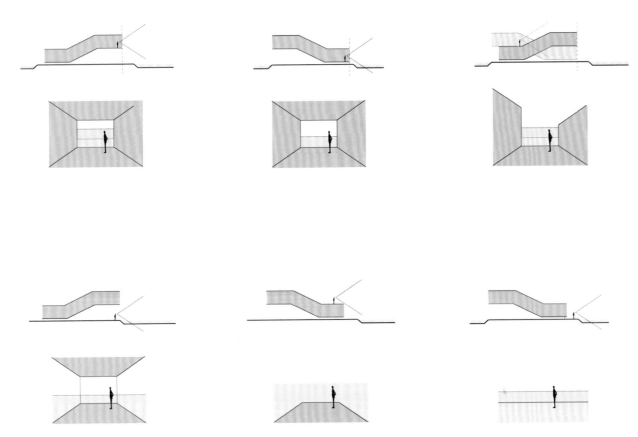

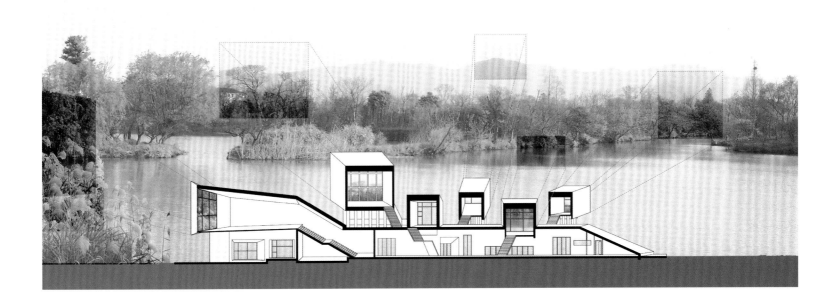

View reframing

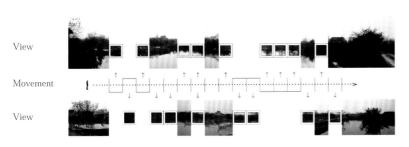

View

Movement

View

I. Frame view

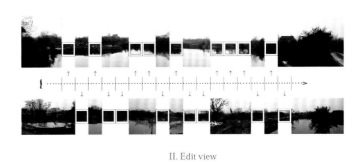

View

Movement

View

II. Edit view

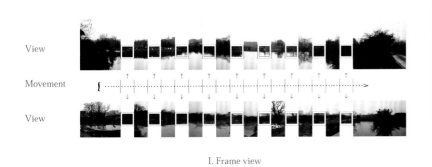

View

Movement

View

III. Cut view

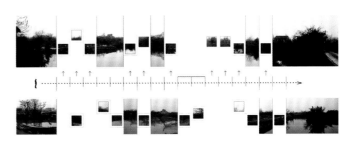

View

Movement

View

IV. Adjust view leveling

First floor plan of the club
in the southern area

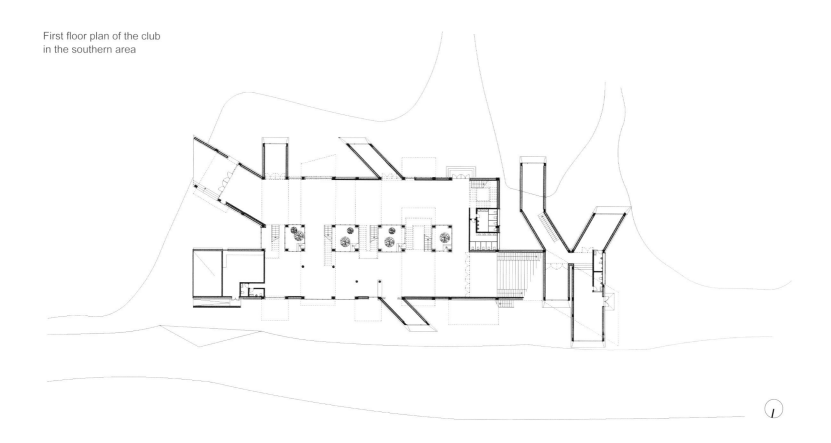

Xixi Learning Community

Wang Yun

Atelier Fronti

Location Hangzhou, China
Gross building area 40,903 ft² (3800 m²)
Site area 643,682 ft² (59,800 m²)
Completion 2010

Site plan

This project was a part of the 12 programs in the third phase of the Arts Village in Xixi Wetland. The site is scattered around and separated by ponds. The client wanted a comprehensive space for writing, interacting, and exhibiting. To meet this requirement for functional concentration and dispersion, the architects adopted a discrete settlement layout.

White

The Chinese character 白 (white) appears frequently in Chinese words and expressions. This expresses the cultural gene of the character 'white.'

Floating

The character 浮 (floating) describes a temporary, moveable, and unstable status. This project is located over floating grass in the wetland, which means its location may change at any time, just like the constant changing characters of time, and its skin.

Disperse

The character 散 (disperse) conveys a sense of individual independence, which is a characterization of this information era. Though the wetland buildings are in a state of dispersion and separation, they actually have an invisible, objective, and structural connection.

A1 schematic plan

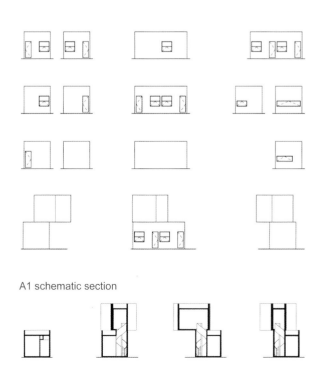

A1 schematic elevatio

A1 schematic section

0   5m

A1 first floor plan

A1 second floor plan

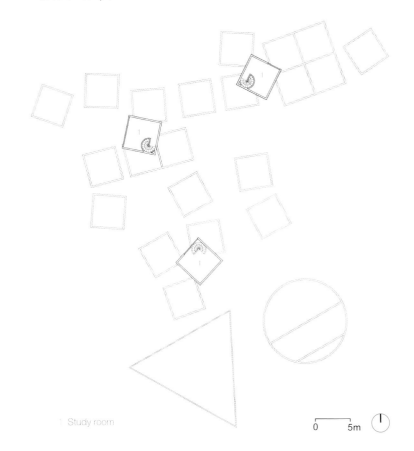

1 Guest room
2 Storage room
3 Pool
4 Activity room

1 Study room

0   5m

Zhangjiajie Museum

Wei Chunyu
Wei Chunyu Studio of Construct

Location Hunan, China
Gross building area 176,980 ft^2 (16,442 m^2)
Site area 152,632 ft^2 (14,180 m^2)
Completion 2014

Site plan

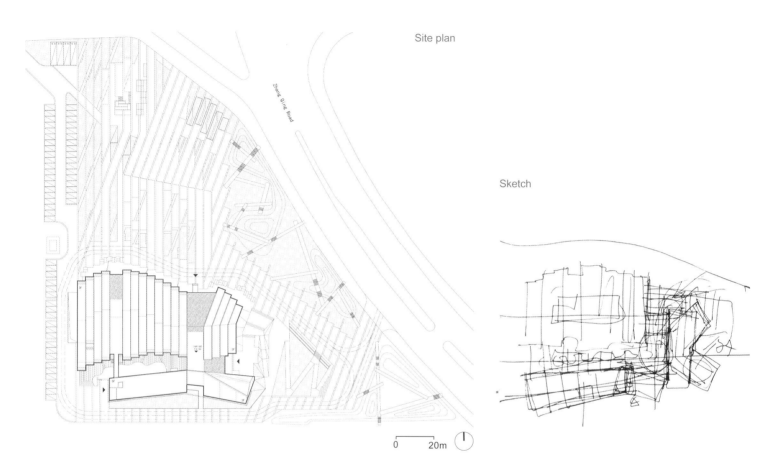

Sketch

0   20m

East of Zhangqing road in the city of Zhangjiajie, facing a wetland river and surrounded by mountains, the project consisted of the Zhangjiajie City Museum, the Urban Planning House, and the Bureau of Cultural Extensive Study, taking mountain-shaped portals as basic units. The buildings roll and wind following the topography, blending into distant mountains and nearby views.

Shape prototypes

The residential building in Zhangjiajie has many unique characters. The most representative one is the stilted houses, which are built on hills. Stilted houses play an important role in the daily life of minority nationalities in the western part of Hunan province, so their construction, functions and styles reflect local cultural traditions. With the passing of time, stilted houses have become a long-standing memory for local residents. Based on this, the architects attempted to seek the form that has a universal meaning and reflects the characteristics of the diversified and complicated types of stilted houses in the form of a prototype. They materialized this prototype by means of geometry and implanted it into the architecture as an abstract gene, so as to awaken people's memories about local dwellings and life in the past.

Fractal landscape

Zhangjiajie has a unique natural characteristic of quartz sandstone landform. The architects attempted to find out the relationship between architectural form and natural features, so as to increase people's sense of identification and belonging with the architecture and the city. Based on the analysis of stilted houses, they broke up and differentiated the prototype and produced several similar units, so as to get a continual architectural form with changes by sequential arrangement and organization of these units.

Landscape texture

The square to the north of the building was expanded into a city square for pubic activities due to the existence of the museum. It is an extension of architectural functions, appearance, and characteristics, as well as a narrative spatial place. The design scheme adjusted the duality of the square and the building through a series of topographic methods, thus integrating the ground with part of the architecture to form a landscaping expression and creating material basis for the narrative place.

Axonometric

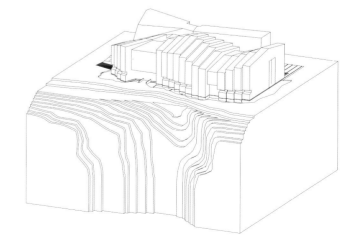

Diagram

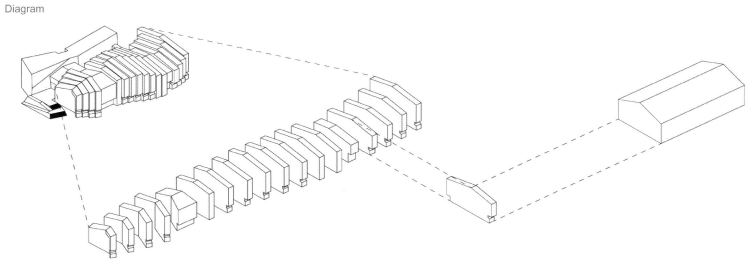

Diagram

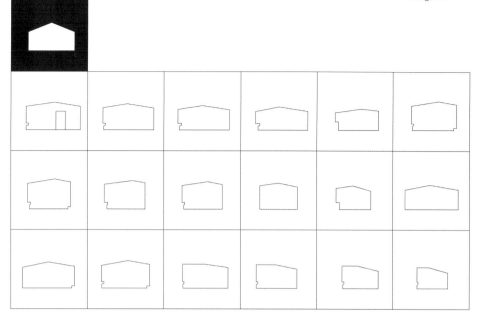

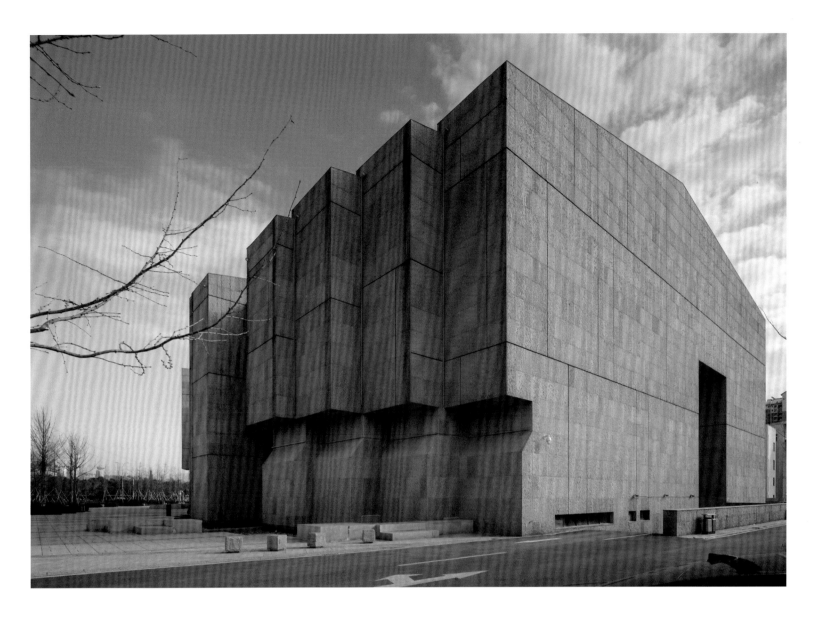

Diagram

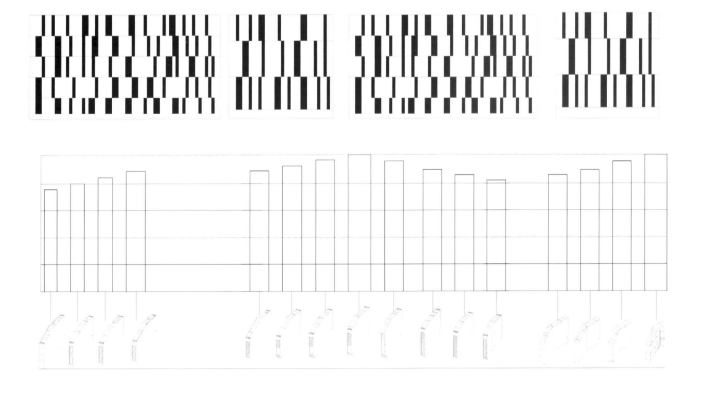

East elevation

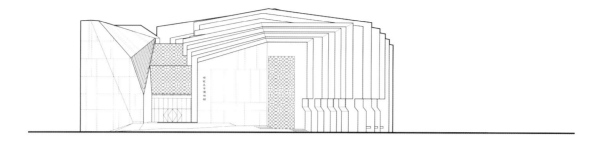

West elevation

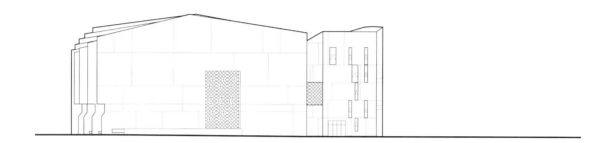

South elevation

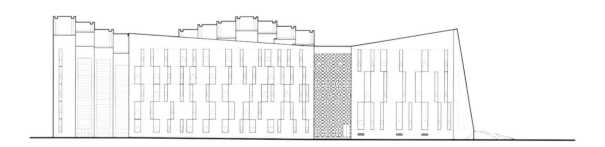

North elevation

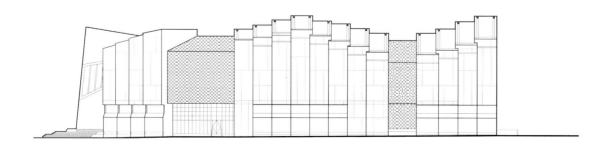

0   10m

Beijing Longshan Church

Zhang Ying, Knud Rossen, Wu Gang, Chen Ling
WSP Architects

Location Beijing, China
Gross building area 41,042 ft² (3813 m²)
Site area 14,854 ft² (1380 m²)
Completion 2006

Site plan

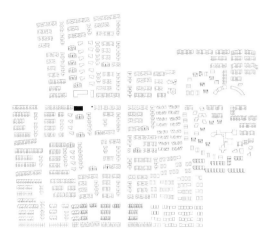

Models

Set in the scenic area of Huairou in the new Longshan village in Beijing, the initial conception came from the ideal mode analysis of the current plot and surrounding structures. Considering most residential buildings nearby are two and three floors only and following the rolling outline of the West Hills, the architects adopted a sloping roof. As the site is narrow, the bell tower, square, and the front and main volume of the church were organized into a sequence, creating a separated but not disconnected relationship of landscaping space and transportation.

Architectural arts

Churches bring a special humanistic culture to the wholesale of the development mode and are in huge quantity in China. The two volumes of the Beijing Longshan Church were connected to form the main body of the church. The attached courtyard at the entrance is a 27.5 x 27.5-square-foot (8.4 x 8.4-square-meter) internal space with 13-foot (4.2-meter) bays. The front courtyard to the main lobby offers another space for purifying one's spirit. The gray pebbles paved in the courtyard and the naked concrete on the walls rightly spread the instilled artistic conception into the thickness and texture of the materials. The main lobby stands side by side with the front courtyard. The main and attached roofs both have a 45-degree slope, yet correspond to contrast spaces: one big and the other small; one sunken and the other protruded; one constrained and the other flaunting. These spaces integrate visual changes into the modest religious space.

Container of light

The light on the surface is an extension and development of modulus. As per the visual line, the elevation divisions and the exterior windows are organized into five, four, three, and two equal partitions from down to up in height. The horizontal division alternatively uses three different module patterns. The exterior windows are 7.9-inch (20-centimeter) wide fillet windows and their height varies with changes of modules. The resulting elevation is an open window system with a changing rhythm. The front lobby highlights the user-friendly space with bright and direct light. In contrast, the light in the main lobby is reasonable, temperate, and mysterious. People in the main lobby are showered in a pure greyish-white, gentle and even light. Standing in it, people can talk to their souls without distracting thoughts.

Temperature of materials

The architectural elevations were built with richly-textured blue-gray basalt, which emits a sense of heaviness and solemnness. The natural color difference of varied mineral substance left on the stone by the changes of earthcrust, together with the big and small bubbles formed in volcanic activities, create beautiful veins. From a distance, Longshan Church looks like a huge gray stone grown from the ground in wild grassland in autumn. Just like one of the doctrines of Christianity, temperance—which means simplicity—is the ultimate sophistication and the design scheme makes everything the simplest: gray stones, warm yellow stones, white painted walls, and hard log pews. Sunlight enters the church through high and low windows and adds warmth to the solemn space, guiding the purification of every soul.

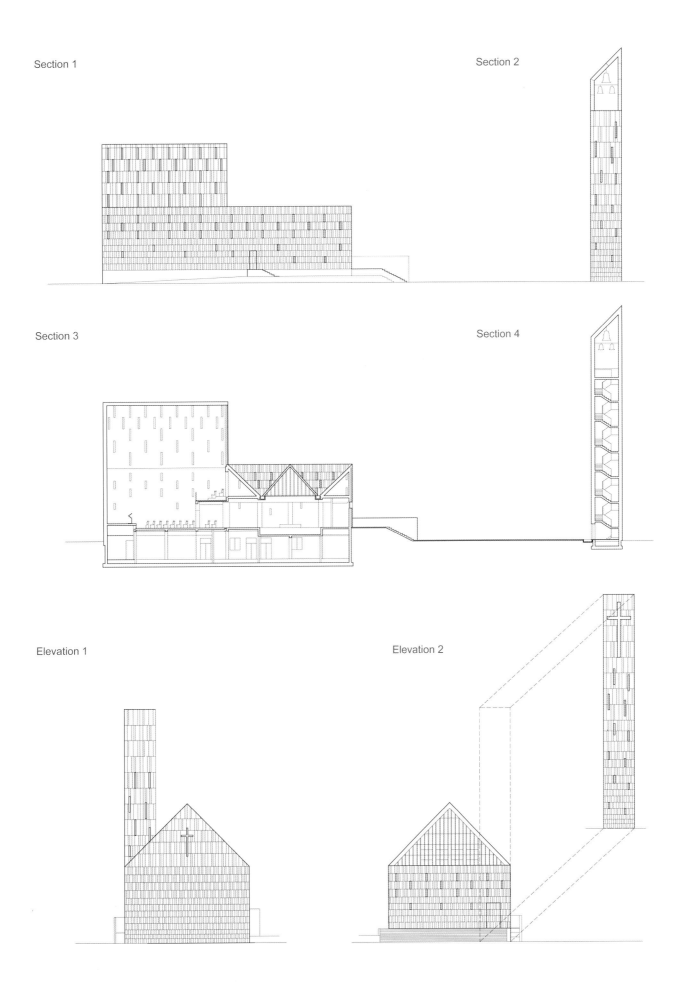

Section 1

Section 2

Section 3

Section 4

Elevation 1

Elevation 2

Roof plan

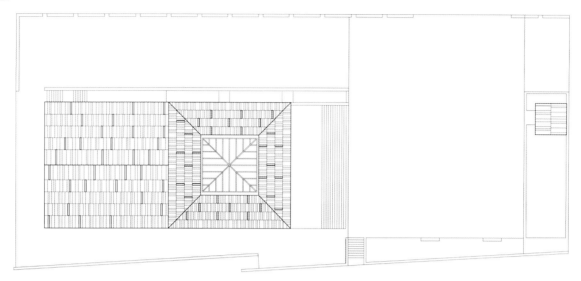

Second floor plan

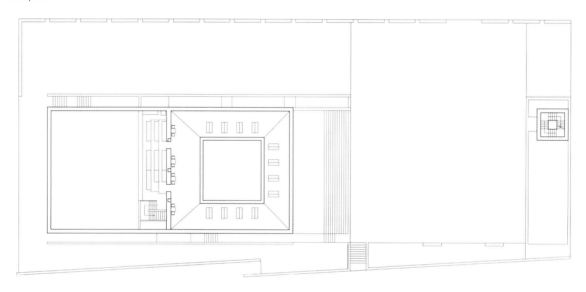

First floor plan

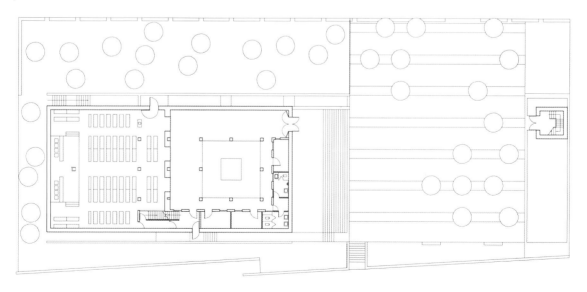

0   5m

Zhejiang Campus Library of Tongji University

Zhang Bin+Zhou Wei
Atelier Z+

Location Jiaxing, China
Gross building area 331,958 ft² (30,840 m²)
Site area 140,092 ft² (13,015 m²)
Completion 2014

Site plan

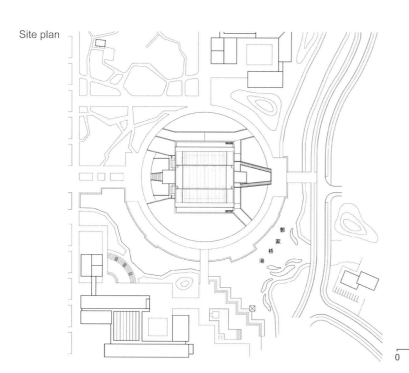

郭
家
桥
港

0   20m

The project is located at a round ground surrounded by a ring road at the middle of the main east–west axis of Zhejiang Campus. To the west is the main entrance to the campus, while to the south and east is a winding river with two bridges connecting the opposite riverbanks. In the campus planning, the central location of the library and its volume meant that it was the only 'monument' in the whole campus and this memorial character helped to support the whole spatial structure of it.

Symbolism

The library was a structural center in the planning of the campus space. The key conception of the project was how to make it the truly most-important special carrier of campus publicity in a fast-built supersize campus space. Here, the corresponding relationship between exterior forms and internal functions proposed by classic modernism was canceled, while the exterior form and internal spaces were separately developed and the campus space was given double definitions: the library is both a symbolic monument for the campus and an internalized urban special gene. From the outside, as a huge symbol with obscured dimensions, the building gives the campus a form order; from the inside, the buildings create increasingly rich and dramatic sensory experiences.

Narration

In contrast to the constrained external form, the open atrium of the library, as a part of the campus public space, is a vertical theater with rich visual experiences and filled with a utopian atmosphere. It creates a special scene with rich mixed senses of urbanity and reveals public activities as a leading character in the space. This dynamic video of public activities underlies the role played by the library as a public space. Different from the symbolic exterior form of publicity, the internal publicity appears as a 'functional' landscape, strengthening the special narrative of looking and being looked at.

Dramatization

The symbolism of exterior forms and the sense of scenario of internal spaces create a miracle contrast that is transformed into a dramatic spatial architecture. The horizontal body movement is replaced by vertically distributed crisscrossing visual lines: at the very center is a utopian urban wonder, which forms two completely different metaphors of publicity in matter and in image together with the exterior 'monolith': with dramatization methods, it creates instant and fragmented sensory experiences with rich perception, and becomes an architectural representation of urban experiences, and the urban gene also turns into another symbolic form. This project shows the common conflicts faced by modern architecture—how to find an architectural opportunity between external super-form and internal spatial scene. The answer given by Atelier Z+ is urban spatial pieces built in a dramatic architectural language.

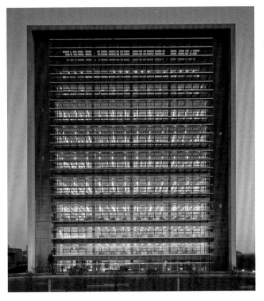

East elevation

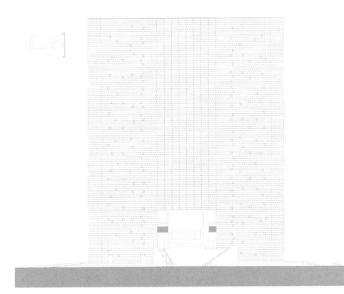

West elevation

Section XIII

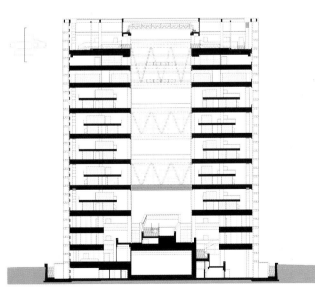

Section VI

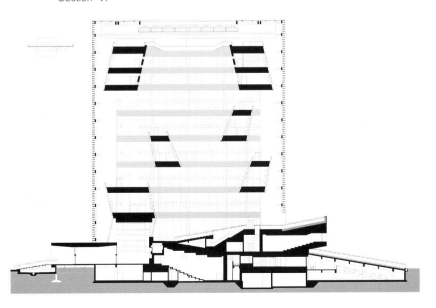

0　　10m

Ninth floor plan

Tenth floor plan

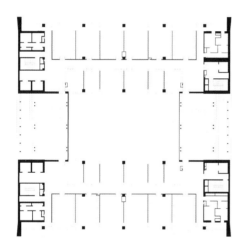

First floor plan

Second floor plan

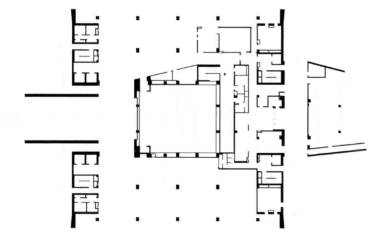

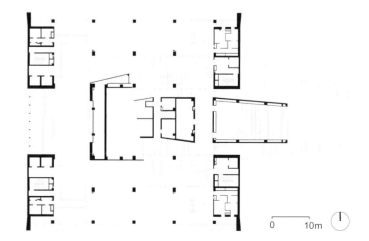

0   10m

Jianamani Visitor Center

Zhang Li
Atelier TeamMinus

Location Yushu, China
Gross building area 12,335 ft²
(1146 m²)
Site area 38,642 ft² (3590 m²)
Completion 2013

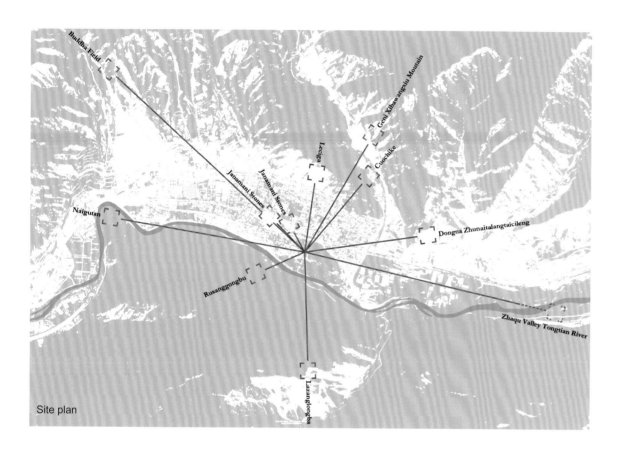

Site plan

The project was one of the major reconstruction structures after the great earthquake in Shuyu in 2010. It directly served the Tibetan Buddhism holy land—Jianamani Stone Scrip City (Shijing city). The Stone Script City suffered severe damage in the earthquake, and the reception service facilities, which were unsound originally, were all destroyed in a day. The new service center mainly serves as a public display for the religious history of Jianamani Stone Script City. It consists of a post office, a bank, a medical station, and public toilets, providing modern services for visitors and local residents.

Direct connection

The project directly responded to Jianamani Stone Pile in Xinzhai, the largest stone pile in the world. It expresses the history and culture of Jianamani from the view of time and space. Eleven viewing platforms face different directions and provide a completely new spatial experience. The design disconnects from any pure symbolic or metaphor forms and realizes cultural continuation in the most simple and direct way.

Cultural continuation

Other than as a modern visitor center, the unique architectural spaces of the project encourage people from different cultures to exchange with each other. It has a selling space co-managed by local Tibetans and foreign investors; an exhibition space for local architectural historians to share history; an idyllic place for the daily turning of prayer wheel and praying of Tibetans—the corridor surrounding the building; the central courtyard providing a close space for community activities; and the viewing platform on top of it for interactions between local residents and visitors. Through obscuring the boundary between the building and the landscape, the structure blends into its surrounding environment.

Local workmanship

The geometrical relationship of the building is modern while its materialism is local. The exterior walls were built with local stones by local artisans. The heating and ventilation systems capitalize on local traditional wisdom. Wooden handrails were spliced with new wood and recycled architectural members from earthquake ruins. Taking advantage of as many local resources and techniques as possible, the building became a convincing case of sustainable construction in high-altitude areas.

Section

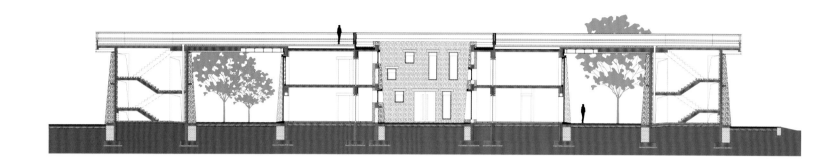

Roof plan

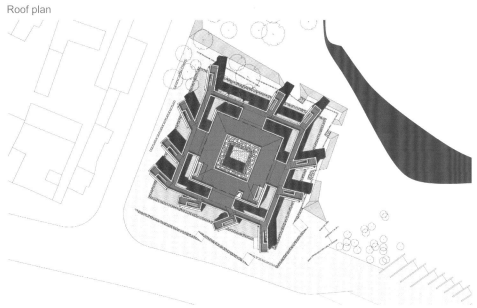

First floor plan

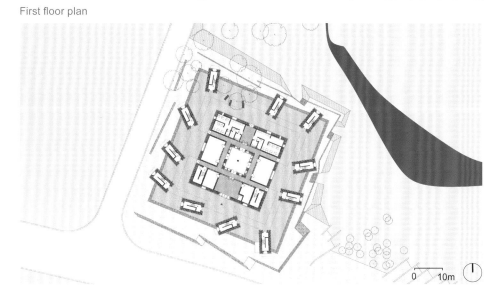

0   10m

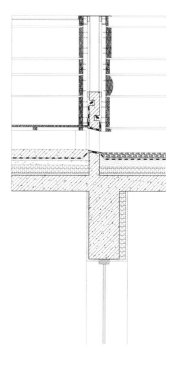

Details 1

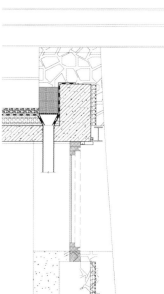

174

Details 2

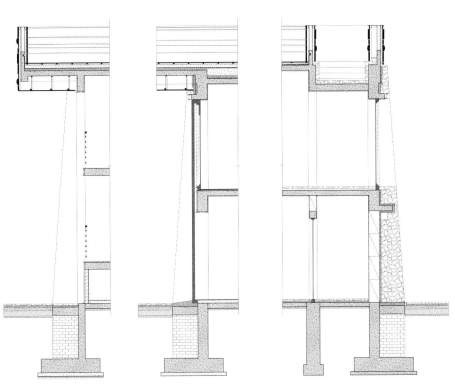

176

Fan Zeng Art Gallery

Zhang Ming+ Zhang Zi
Original Design Studio

Location Nantong, China
Gross building area 75,649 ft²
(7028 m²)
Site area 220,972 ft² (20,529 m²)
Completion 2014

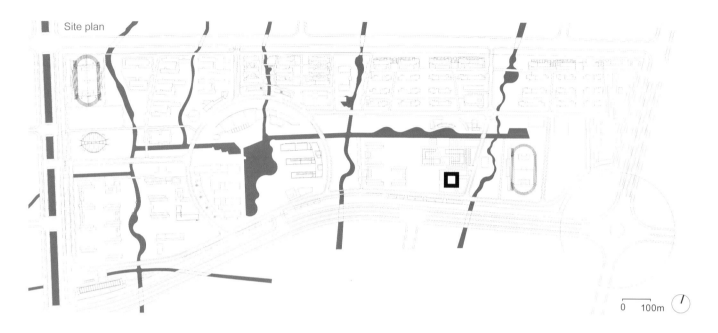

Site plan

0   100m

The project, located at Nantong University, was built for exhibiting, interacting, studying, and displaying a collection of Fan Zeng's calligraphy and painting works and the literary family of Fan in Nantong. The design scheme takes traditional quadrangle courtyards as the prototype and explains it in modern architectural language. Fan Zeng Art Gallery breaks the courtyard away from materialized relationships and shows the integration of touring with visualizing building an artistic conception of 'describing the present while creating an ancient atmosphere.'

Courtyard of Relationships

The Courtyard of Relationships presents three forms of courtyard: the 'Well Courtyard' at the first floor of the building, the Water Courtyard and Stone Courtyard at the second floor, and the Enclosed Courtyards at the third and fourth floor. With these courtyards as the main structures, they build a superposed three-dimensional courtyard. The original idea of a superposed courtyard is to break down the building in the limited site, namely to break the huge mass into three small volumes, to interpret the courtyard at a human-body scale. The architects started from a loose and local relationship instead of the big order of integrating the whole layout with a grid-like control system. The seemingly unrelated three forms of the courtyard are organized by different connections, with a result that was beyond expectation.

Courtyard of Visualization

The Courtyard of Visualization juxtaposes the relationships of parts and builds a sequential order to create possibilities for touring visualization. It offers various viewpoint angles, rather than fixing the viewpoint in a spot, like Chinese classic calligraphy and painting, which usually show intended views at different times and places. Since the design doesn't pursue a perspective relationship at a single viewpoint, it creates a space filled with strong tension. In segments of views, which appear at different times and places, and the relationship between the parts is presented in sequence. Though they are placed in the same place, their relationships disclose layers of progression.

Courtyard of Artistic Conception

The Courtyard of Artistic Conception seeks to create an artistic conception of treating white as black, imposing control between with and without, and revealing fullness in hollowness. It doesn't use a whole framework to include all plots into one clear main line, but creates on its own an order according to the three types of courtyards and extends it into a slightly loose partial relationship. The so-called Hazy Atmosphere refers to sequentially revealing the world and slowly spreading out an atmosphere. The reconstruction and superposition of the courtyard relationships in the art gallery subversively change the courtyards themselves. The courtyards in three simple prototypes have not totally broken from traditional forms, but only present a different appearance after integration. The artistic conception of ancient expression and present meaning stresses that it doesn't rely on forms, but shall focus on spirit.

光音藝術館

Courtyard analysis

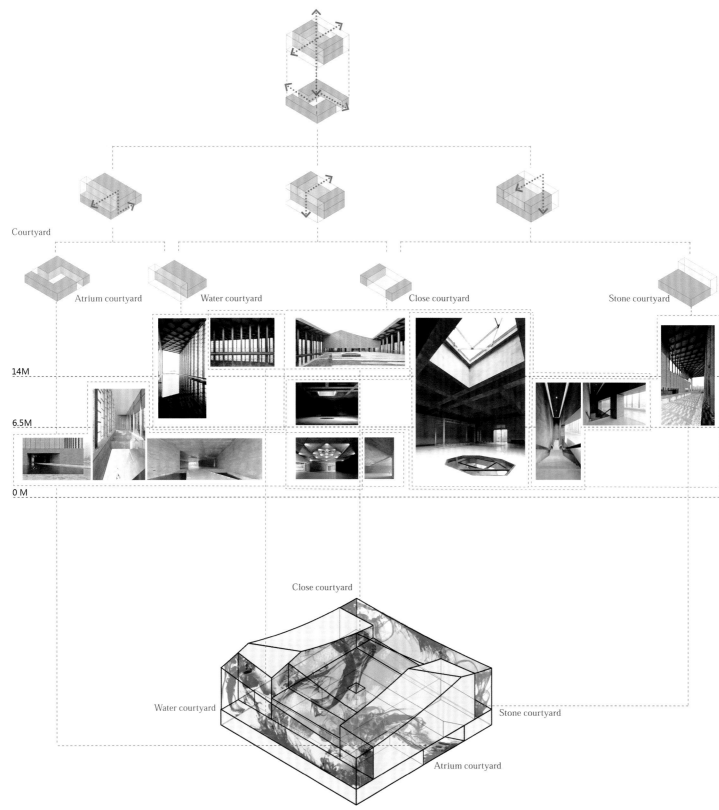

Courtyard

Atrium courtyard   Water courtyard   Close courtyard   Stone courtyard

14M

6.5M

0 M

Close courtyard

Water courtyard

Stone courtyard

Atrium courtyard

Form analysis

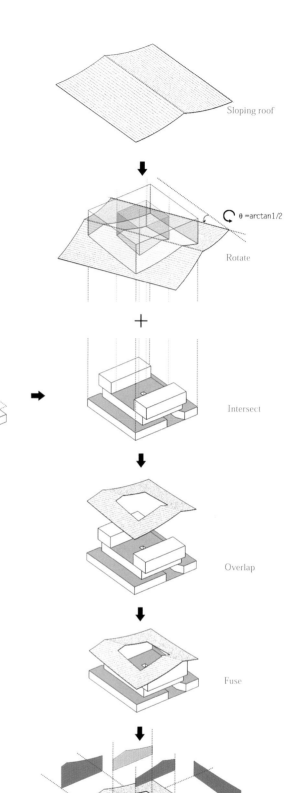

Sloping roof

$\theta = \arctan 1/2$

Rotate

+

Intersect

Overlap

Fuse

Enclose

Generate

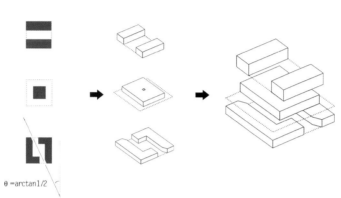

$\theta = \arctan 1/2$

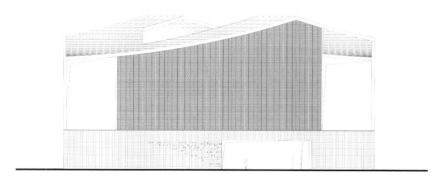

Elevation 1

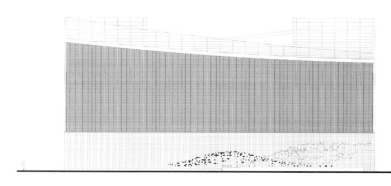

Elevation 2

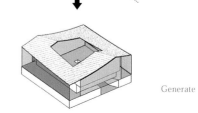

Section 1

Section 2

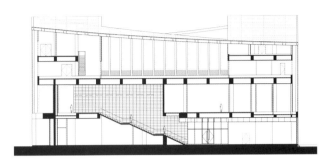

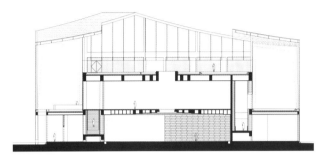

Third floor plan

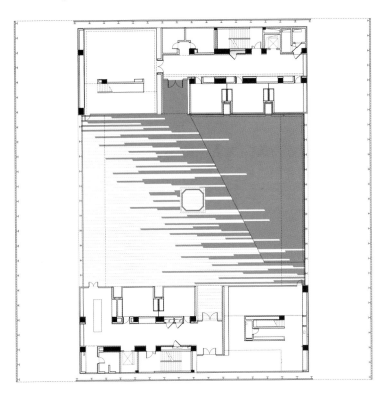

Fourth floor plan

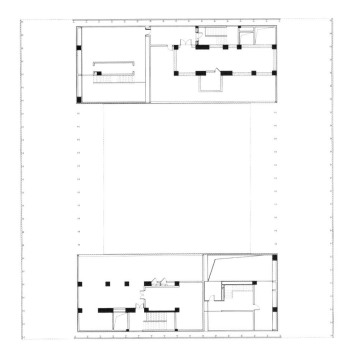

First floor plan

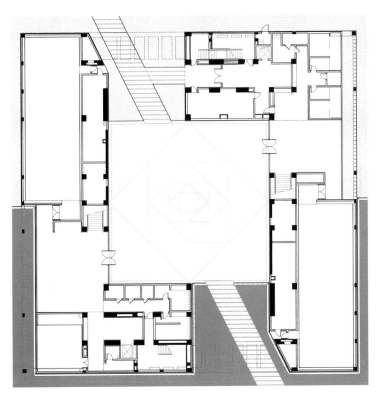

Second floor plan

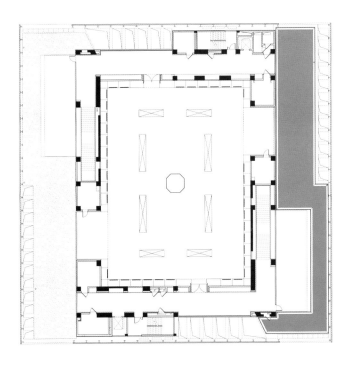

Kenya MCEDO school expansion

Zhu Jingxiang
The Chinese University of Hong Kong(CUHK) + Unitinno

Location Nairobi, Kenya
Gross building area
5167 ft^2 (480 m^2)
Site area 7965 ft^2 (740 m^2)
Completion 2014

Figure-ground relatio

Situated in a slum at the northeast of Nairobi, the capital of Kenya, the design of this project gave full play to the advantages of prefabricated light structure. It not only realized remote project design, but has exerted strict control over onsite construction time to deal with complicated social status.

Light-weight structure

Light-weight structures can not only bring about varied construction forms, but also generate new architectural design, organization, and construction techniques. The emphasis on light-weight buildings has multi-values in social and ecological aspects. For manufacturers, developers, and far-sighted city administrators possessing huge resources, unimaginable hidden resources could be found through light-weight structure construction. Light-weight structures could be built beside, on or even inside heavy-weight architecture.

Due to geological conditions (such as earthquake, bearing capacity of the stratum), construction techniques or policies, light-weight structures have become the main body of the urban built environment. This project was an effective experiment in light-weight structure. Giving consideration to multiple factors—such as site conditions, geological environment, and so on—the architects designed the specific forms of prefabricated components according to local conditions, which could be used to build light-weight structures under proper local environmentally conditions with high efficiency and fast speed, so as to explore the new possibilities of prefabricated architecture.

Foldable structure

The core of the project was a folded structure, which is convenient to transport. It allows for fast construction while not losing architectural beauty. Its development and design involves both structural and mechanic knowledge. The upper and lower floor slabs in standard sizes were connected to four Y-shaped supports at the ends. Each support has three hinge points, one of which has a bolt. When the bolt is removed, the basic structural unit could be flattened and folded. This structural module could be expanded into a complicated housing system. The design of this construction system gave full play to a system through a deep understanding of local conditions and standardized industrial production. It allows people to build a structure within days that is extremely convenient and highly efficient.

Informal settlement

MCEDO School is located in an informal settlement in the northeast of Nairobi. It has very complicated historical elements and current social environment. Therefore, how to build a house in an informal settlement became a key problem in understanding the site. In this project, from the design of the construction technique of the light-weight structure to the general situation of the building, all revealed vividly its non-modernity as a post-colonial rural landscape. The deep understanding of local land, climatic conditions and social status, the new knowledge of construction systems of informal settlements, and the innovations based on them, all create new possibilities for the intervening design.

West elevation

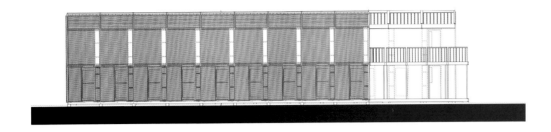

Roof plan

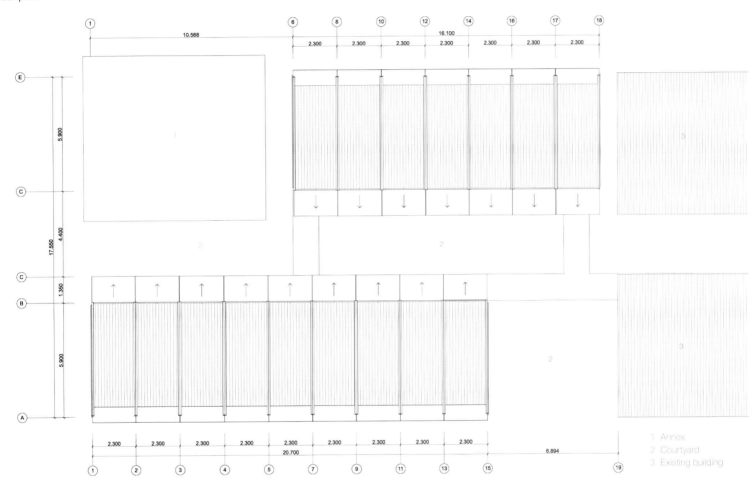

1 Annex
2 Courtyard
3 Existing building

Section

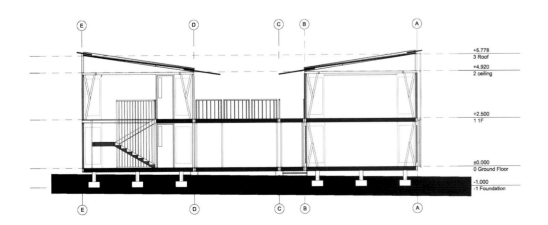

Diagrams

Component transportation

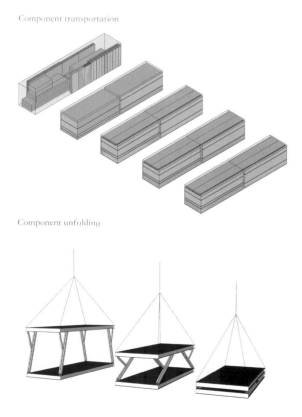

Folding structure

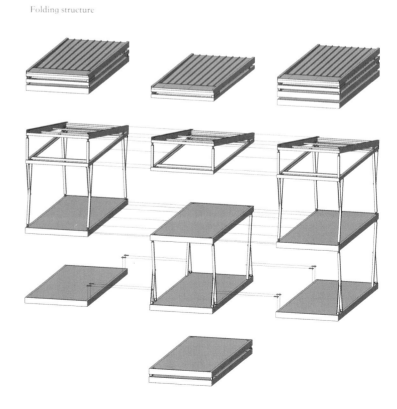

Component unfolding

Second floor plan

1 Classroom
2 Courtyard
3 Corridor

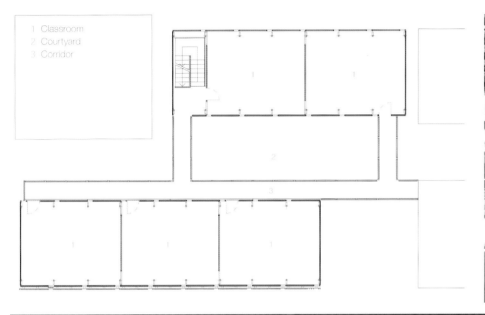

Jingdezhen Imperial Kiln Museum

Zhu Pei
Studio Zhu-Pei

Location Jingdezhen, China
Gross building area 112,989 ft² (10,497 m²)
Site area 9420 ft² (9753 m²)
Completion 2018

Site plan

0   50m

Sketch

The project is located at the center of the historical block in Jingdezhen, adjoining the sites of imperial kilns of Ming and Qing dynasties and with lots of big and small historical kiln sites scattered around. Inspired by these old kiln sites, the architects designed many brick arches of different sizes and volumes in the layout. These arches appear close and separated, and like many trees, create a relaxing, occasional, handmade, and natural atmosphere. Walking among these brick arches and courtyards, can aroused in people a familiar and strange spatial experience.

Ceramic kilns

The conception of the spatial form of this project started from the influences of local living style and climatic conditions imposed on local architectural form. Jingdezhen was born because of kilns and became well-known for them. Kilns are cells of the city, an incentive for the living style and origin of culture. Kilns are not only factories for producing ceramics, but also familiar living places to local people. In winter, the producing kilns become important public spaces for the Jingdezhen people. Many schools gather around them to fend off the coldness. In summer, the standing kilns turn into playgrounds for young people. The spatial prototype and materials of ceramic kilns are the starting point of the Imperial Kiln Museum, while the local people's living experiences are the contents it wants to catch. The architectural form of the museum is not only a reconstruction of local spatial relationships, but also a creation of modern reading and new experience founded on the basis.

Porcelain clay

Through the capture of local geographic conditions and the concentrated presentation of them, the unique regional culture could be expressed and underlined in a natural way. In this project, the uniqueness of earth gives birth to the ceramic culture of Jingdezhen. Some earth could be used for making porcelain, some for making bricks and some for rammed-earth. Soil layers, like growth rings of trees, clearly record the changes of times in Jingdezhen. The Museum of Imperial Kilns in Jingzhende blends into the architectural relics of Ming and Qing dynasties. The soil layer cuts vertically from the interior of the building and becomes a part of the walls, grounding the museum deeply into this special earth.

Handicraft art

Handicraft is the essence of Jingdezhen culture. People make porcelain with their hands and, thus, build a special, close relationship with porcelain. People's feelings and emotions are distinctly recorded in the production of porcelain. At the same time, kilns are also built by people. Without scaffolding, the shape of kilns is different from that of arches in Rome times. They are not exactly geometric, all depending on the fingers of people, relaxing and random, just like the porcelain of Jingdezhen—simple, pure, light, and thin. The shape design of the museum is based on local artisans' handicraft. The shape and size of each arch is slightly different. The internal relationship of porcelain and kiln as well as the relationships between people, kiln, and porcelain become the most remarkable appeal of the museum. The construction of kilns also follows similar logic. It gives space to the artisan for creating freely, which finally produces a unique, handmade effect.

Section 1

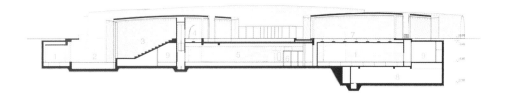

1 Exhibition
2 Courtyard
3 Lecture hall
4 Elevator hall
5 Underground lobby

6 Rest room
7 Cafe/book shop/souvenir
8 Storage room
9 Mechanical room

Section 2

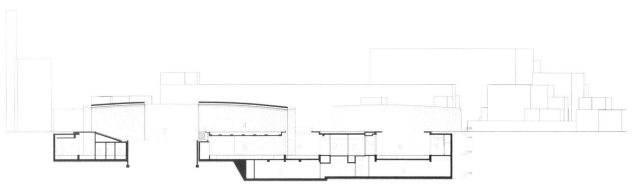

1 Temporal exhibition
2 Rest room
3 Relics of Ming Dynasty
4 Exhibition (outdoor)
5 Exhibition
6 Courtyard
7 Mechanical room
8 Storage
9 Relic repair room

First floor plan

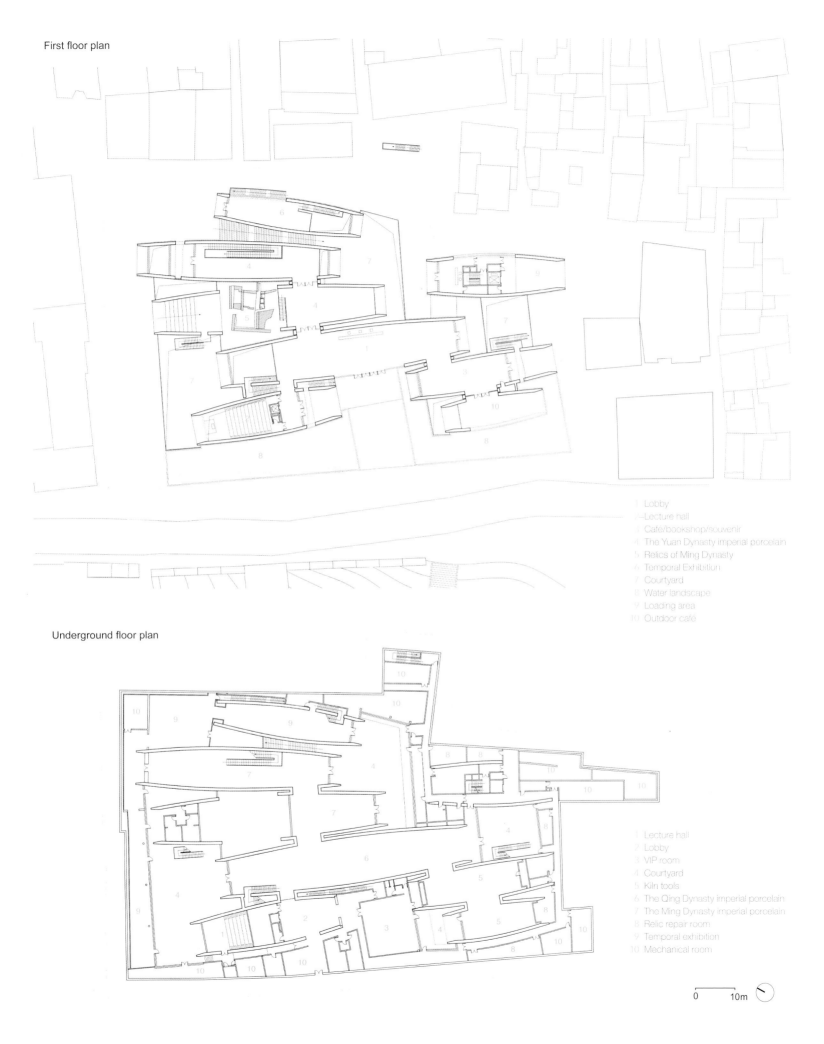

1 Lobby
2 Lecture hall
3 Café/bookshop/souvenir
4 The Yuan Dynasty imperial porcelain
5 Relics of Ming Dynasty
6 Temporal Exhibition
7 Courtyard
8 Water landscape
9 Loading area
10 Outdoor café

Underground floor plan

1 Lecture hall
2 Lobby
3 VIP room
4 Courtyard
5 Kiln tools
6 The Qing Dynasty imperial porcelain
7 The Ming Dynasty imperial porcelain
8 Relic repair room
9 Temporal exhibition
10 Mechanical room

0   10m

197

Huaxin Center—Shanghai Google developers' group starup incubator

Zhu Xiaofeng
Scenic Architecture Office

Location Shanghai, China
Gross building area 7859 ft² (730 m²)
Site area 59,202 ft² (5500 m²)
Completion 2013

Site plan

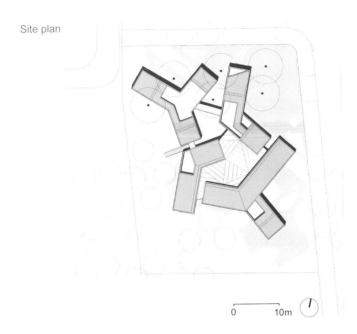

0   10m

Sketch

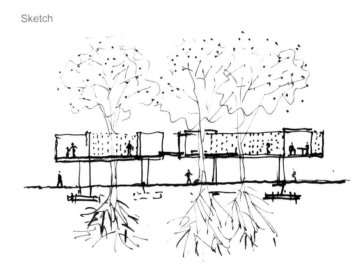

Huaxin office complex is situated at west Guilin Road, Xuhui district, Shanghai, with a greenbelt to the south of its entrance. The building starts from an open greenbelt, which faces an urban artery and has six large camphor trees. First, the main body of the building was elevated to the second floor to maximize the open green space; second, the six trees were kept to establish a close interactive the relationship with the buildings. The structure and texture of the buildings interweave with the limbs and leaves of these big trees, creating many pure exterior and interior spaces.

Settlement

Nowadays, the world tends to present a loose and dynamic settlement pattern based on the gathering of diversified individuals. New settlement buildings may become one of the building types that reflect this trend. Compared with mechanic and centralized spaces, contemporary settlements need to provide more internal flexibility and external identity and create exchanges between different settlements and among individuals, nature, and society. The new settlement, not necessarily like a traditional settlement, which consists of a group of independent buildings, may be a whole composed of many interconnected spaces. The units in a settlement may not be in a purposely simplified form, but an intricate individual with particular requirements and detailed roles.

Shanghai Google Developers Group Startup Incubator (Huaxin Center) was one of a series of the architectural experiments on new settlements. This micro-settlement is located between city roads and an open office community. Four interconnected structural units were organized in a small woods, establishing a balanced positive relationship between users, nature, and city.

Perception

Perception is a bridge between people and architecture. People can understand their relationship with a built environment only through perception. In this building, perception was the key to driving the design process. The architects elevated the buildings to make them cross the tree trunks freely. They provided privacy in the second floor while opening the pubic space on the ground. The organization of courtyards and paths allows people to feel the layers and changes of space. The interweaving of the structure and camphor trees creates close communication between people and nature. The interaction of multi-perceptions forms the whole experience of the building.

Tectonic presence

Architecture is not only a matter of material elements in constructing buildings, but also about arousing one's perception through its expression. Whether logical or intuitive, abstract or figurative, direct or implicit, the expression of architecture can always reflect the attitude of architects toward it, or how they use it to meet functional, experiential and psychological requirements. The two floors of the structure are presented in different architectural forms, one concealed and the other revealed. The forms thus trigger people's different perceptions of special boundaries and are subtly infused with people's feelings, acts, and thoughts in the space. Therefore, the architectural expression helps people step into the spiritual field of architecture.

Section

1 Exhibition
2 Meeting room
3 Signing office
4 Courtyard
5 Water courtyard
6 Pool

Roof plan

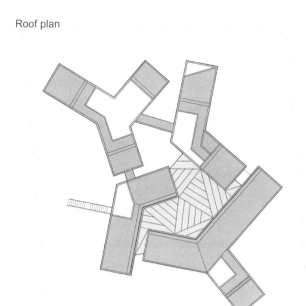

Second floor plan

1 Exhibition
2 Meeting room
3 Signing office
4 Office
5 Accounting room
6 Archives room
7 Changing room
8 Cleaning room
9 Reception
10 Courtyard
11 Pool

First floor plan

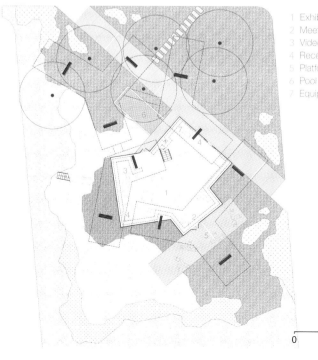

1 Exhibition
2 Meeting room
3 Video room
4 Reception
5 Platform
6 Pool
7 Equipment

0   5m

Residential ▶

The ownership of land by central government in China coupled with the real-estate development of housing has established restrictive conditions under which Chinese architects are unable to directly meet the demands and needs of their clients. Development projects have pushed the public preference in a market-tested direction, favoring mass-developed units over custom-tailored design schemes that often entail higher construction costs. Under these circumstances, residential projects rarely deliver breakthroughs or experimental approaches in design, despite the titanic scale of China's housing market.

The residential projects selected here represent the continued effort that Chinese architects have put into testing different typologies as well as providing affordable housing for low-income residents in urban or rural areas. These projects reflect an increasing social agenda and highlight the work of Chinese architects that resist the mass production of market-driven housing and its appeal to the Chinese public.

Stepped Courtyards

Li Hu + Huang Wenjing
Open Architecture

Location Fuzhou, China
Gross building area 411,214 ft²
(38,203 m²)
Site area 479,747 ft² (44,570 m²)
Completion 2014

Site plan

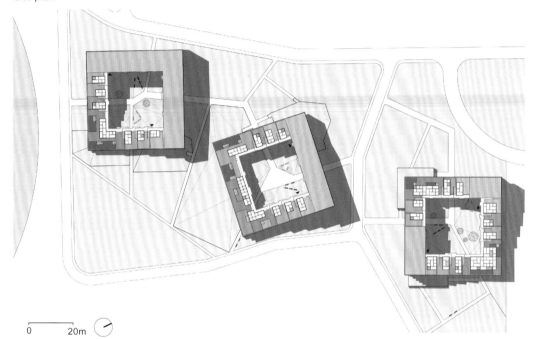

0   20m

The project, located at Fuzhou city, is a dormitory building for NetDragon Websoft's new headquarters. The site is virgin land near the seashore in an area without many surrounding conditions or clear boundaries. The designer wanted to create a strong sense of community through creating an internal and relatively independent 'collective commune.' Three courtyard-like buildings, which resemble Hakka people's earth buildings, were arranged on the site to form a new NetDragon commune.

Creation

As social animals, humans firstly create the conception of group living and work. They originally lived nomadic lives as huntsmen, or settled down as farmers. Later, due to the increase of population and urbanization, a denser architectural formed: urban collective housing, which is a pile-up of early building types emerged at the right moment. In modern times, the Soviet Union has created the unit compound—a living mode that combines collective life and work. Unit compounds become the model of modern collective housing and were introduced to China in early socialism times. From 1960s and 1970s, the unit compound became not only a basic place for living and working, but also a symbol of individual collectivism.

Reinvention

Today, though living and working are gradually separated in large cities, unit compounds are revived as headquarter parks of private companies. Most of them are built in the remote outskirts of cities

with higher quality living and working environments. The new headquarters base of NetDragon in Changle Fuzhou is one of them. NetDragon's new dormitory building is a rather obscure composite architectural type that originates from the re-creation of a series of architectural prototypes, such as European street-block housing, earth buildings of local residents in Fujian, and complex buildings in modern cities. These architectural circles were reintegrated and reshaped in Stepped Courtyards. The result is a composite architectural complex that features comfortable living environments, convenient working spaces, open views, and rich leisure and entertainment activities.

Creative intervention

Undoubtedly, architectural environment has a deep influence on collective living. The spatial forms of architecture even intervene in people's basic living modes. In this project, the air corridors at the six floors connect 12 sky courtyards that are unique in form, dimension and materials, and even functions. Rich social spaces bring people together and establish maximum exchanges between people and nature. The spaces can be used according to people's requirements, and with the development of living and new demands of the occupiers, they also change. When people move up and down in the building or enter into and exit from the courtyards, the potential power of buildings is constantly exerting positive influences upon their daily life.

Section

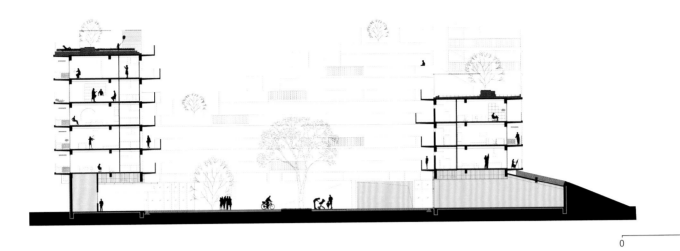

0   10m

Concept diagram

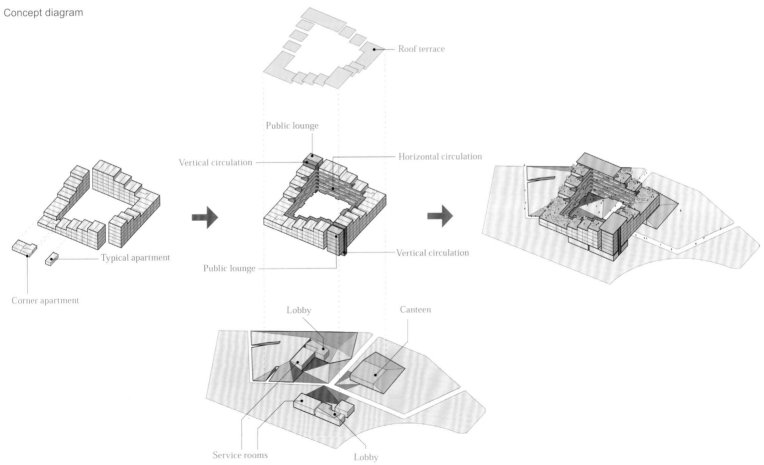

Roof terrace

Public lounge

Vertical circulation

Horizontal circulation

Typical apartment

Vertical circulation

Public lounge

Corner apartment

Lobby

Canteen

Service rooms

Lobby

First floor plan of Building 3

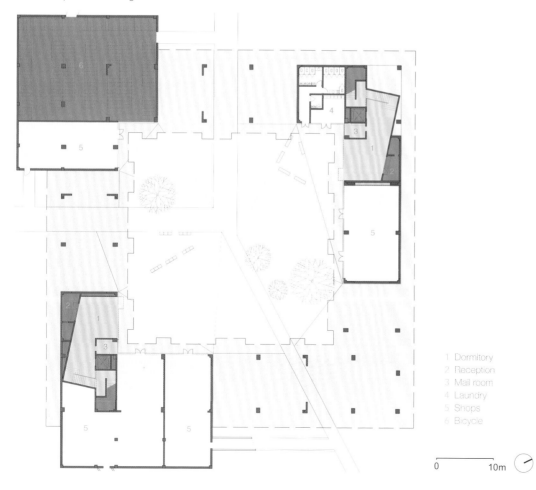

1 Dormitory
2 Reception
3 Mail room
4 Laundry
5 Shops
6 Bicycle

0   10m

West Village·Basis Yard

Liu Jiakun
Jiakun Architects

Location Chengdu, China
Gross building area 33.5 acres
(135,522 square meters)
Site area 450,609 ft² (41,863 m²)
Completion 2015

Master plan

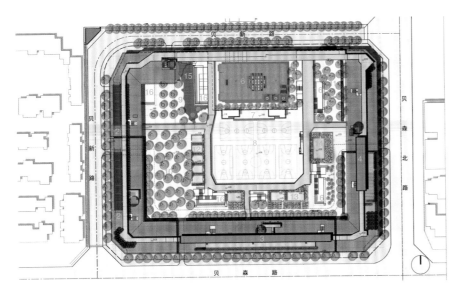

1 Runway
2 Bamboo shelf
3 Gallery
4 Gallery bridge
5 Little theatre
6 Multi-function hall
7 Stage
8 Sports field
9 Bambusa chungii
10 Bambusa emeiensis
11 Bambusa multiplex
12 Cabins in bamboos
13 Big houses in bamboos
14 Bamboo plaza
15 Pool
16 Atrium

Located in Chengdu, the project intended to integrate all social resources to create a local living space cluster including sports and entertainment, culture and art, fashion and creation in one. It needed to meet diversified actual requirements and become an urban pacer that continually triggers the vigor of the community. Holding the architectural idea of 'use modern skills and restore historical memories,' the architects adopted the spatial prototype of unit collective compound with the idealistic color of collectivism in planned economic times and endeavored to transform it into the modern architecture mode and design language of Basis Yard.

Commonness

West Village purposely softened its urban image and architectural language to return to the basics. It adopted a framework design with functional facilities. The design allows secular life rich with personalities to freely move in the space, while all these living activities are sorted by the huge dimension of the compound and finally form an 'everyday life.' This brings together these daily life contents that seem to grow in corners only and forms a combination of secular scenes, manifesting the strong expression power of group creation.

Genius loci and leisure culture

West village is built along the edge of the street block and occupies all spaces of the whole block. It is a supersized enclosed courtyard, like a park, offering as many sport and recreational spaces as possible and accommodate a maximal street population in the limited space. It turns into a 'green basin' that is high on the edges and low in the center, corresponding to the primitive landscape of Sichuan Basin.

The 'green basin' holds all kinds of public life. Courtyards with bamboo groves nestle layer upon layer and are open to the public, allowing people to walk among the bamboo trees and successfully represent the regional living environment. It wakes up local people's collective memories and carries on the traditional leisure life mode under beloved bamboo groves of the Chengdu people.

Simultaneously, an elevated leisure track circles the compound and climbs up to the roof and then makes another circle there. It provides runners and bikers with new, free, exciting activities and injects extraordinary experiences into the traditional living space that they get accustomed to.

Vernacular craftsmanship

The reply to actual construction conditions, whether it is folk design wisdom or civilian architectural language, or an improvement on traditional countryside building prototypes, can all become a strong starting point in architectural expression and architectural aesthetics basis relied on by designers. The West Village includes many special applications and expressions of basic materials and techniques; for example, it uses local handmade bamboo pallets as template. This act gives plain concrete unique textures and helps it build an abstract relationship with local natural elements; the manufacturing of broken bricks reveals the inner aggregates of reclaimed bricks; blocks with big holes are used for roof planting, ventilation in the machine room, and penetrated boundary walls; blocks with small holes are used for vertical greening; porous blocks are used for fixing exhibits on the exhibition walls; and gangue bricks as a common filler are used for plain exterior walls. All these measures are environment-friendly and cost-effective, while endowing West Village with highly localized material characters.

Sketch

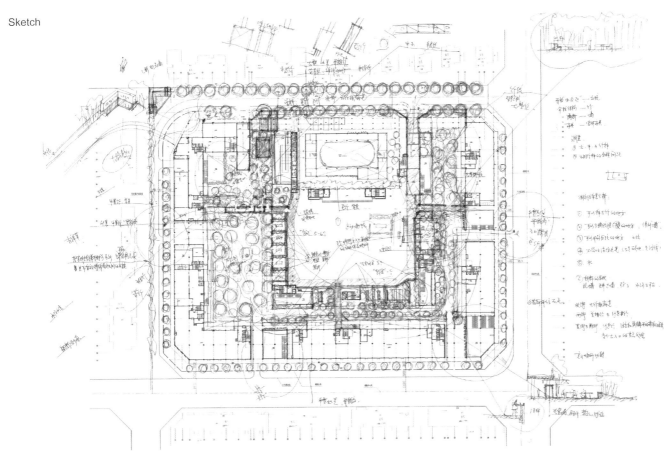

Ventilation diagrams

Section

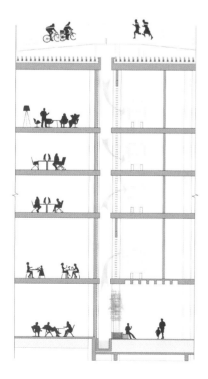

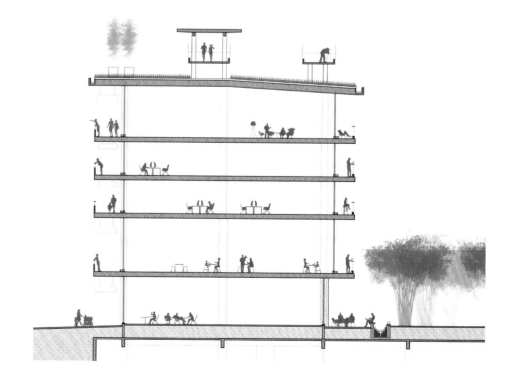

Inner-courtyard diagrams

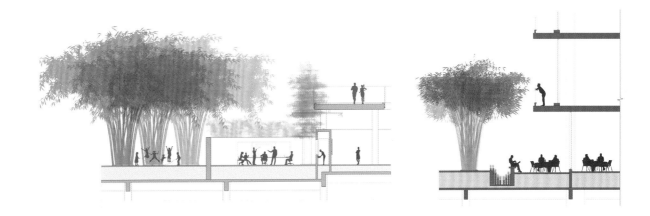

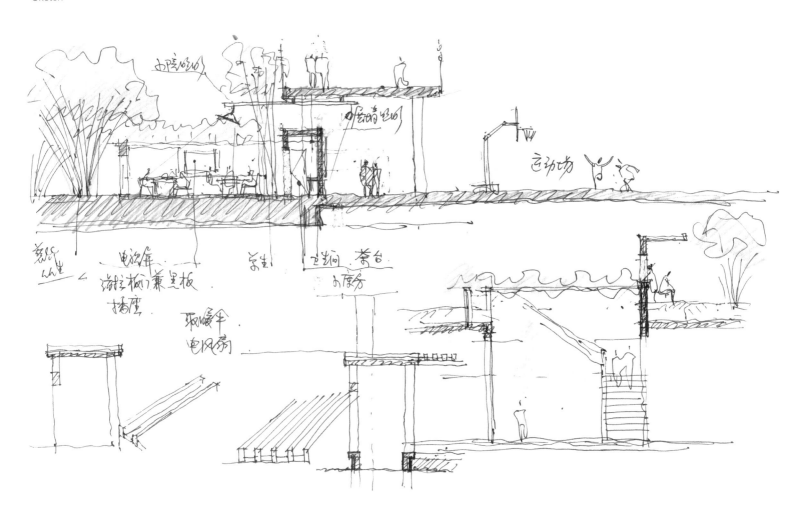

Section

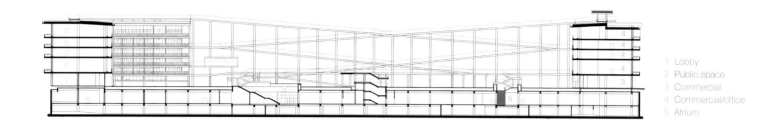

1 Lobby
2 Public space
3 Commercial
4 Commercial/office
5 Atrium

Sports activity analysis

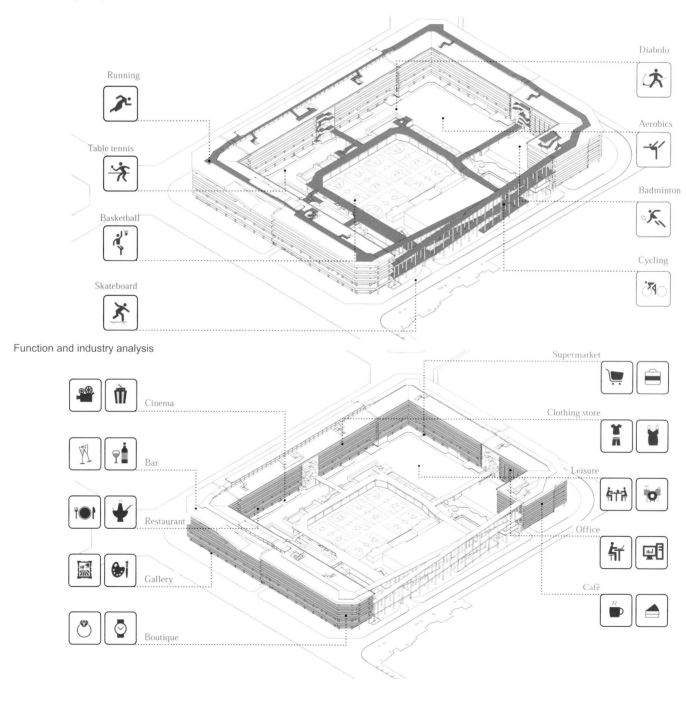

Running

Table tennis

Basketball

Skateboard

Diabolo

Aerobics

Badminton

Cycling

Function and industry analysis

Cinema

Bar

Restaurant

Gallery

Boutique

Supermarket

Clothing store

Leisure

Office

Café

Tulou Collective Housing

Liu Xiaodu, Meng Yan
URBANUS

Location Nanhai, Guangdong, China
Gross building area 147,584 ft²
(13,711 m²)
Site area 87,629 ft² (9141 m²)
Completion 2008

Site plan

0 12m

Unit types

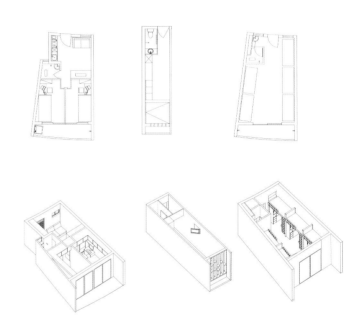

Based on the study of traditional Hakka people's earth buildings, the architect adopted a highly recognizable form and provided high-quality economic houses for low and middle-income people in the fast urbanization process.

Hakka earth buildings

Migrating southward from central China, the Hakkas built earth houses by clans—Tulou, which are unique in China and around the world. Designed for defensive purposes, the buildings are built with only one entrance, a courtyard, and a circle of walls where up to four-story houses consisting of standard units are constructed. Its architecture design strongly resembles collective lifestyles of the modern era. Inspired by the earth buildings, the Tulou Collective Housing has applied the Chinese traditional living culture of the Hakka Tulou to the design of contemporary social housing.

Social housing

The social housing includes low-rent housing and government-subsidized housing in China. The Tulou Collective Housing is a

pioneer, pilot project of low-rent houses with the participation of civil society. The unique architectural design of earth buildings is used for the disposal of idle lands in urban areas. It is also a new way of providing high-standard affordable houses to people on low incomes. With the emergence of the Tulou Collective Housing, the living conditions of low-income urban dwellers will attract more attention.

Migrant workers

With China's rapid economic development, the gap between the rich and the poor keeps growing. The poor living conditions of low-income migrant workers in Chinese cities have long been an issue that remains to be resolved, partly because it fails to attract adequate public attention. The Tulou Collective Housing will allow migrant workers to enjoy small but relatively high-quality housing at affordable prices while having essential things every apartment needs. The Tulou Collective Housing shows that low-budget social housing is not necessarily the synonym for low quality. Low-income city dwellers also have the right to a high standard of living.

Section

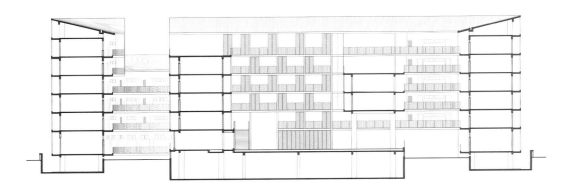

0   6m

Axonometric

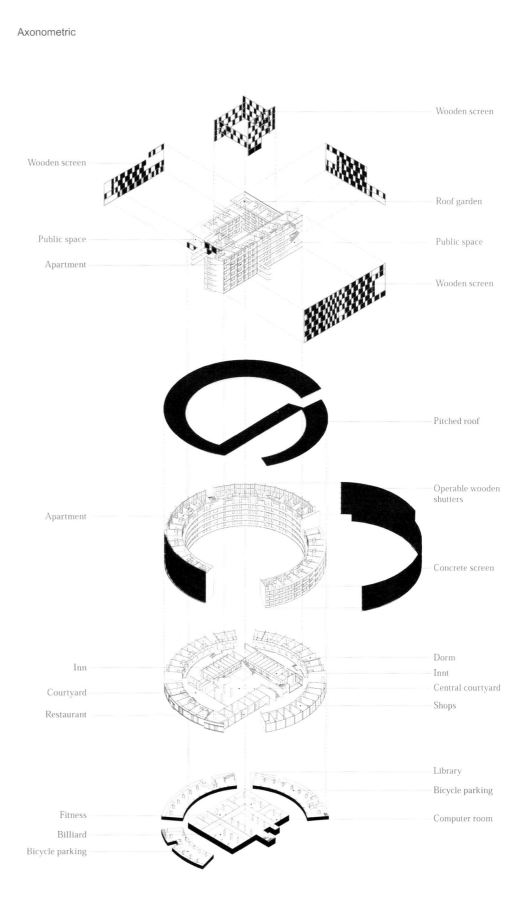

Wooden screen

Wooden screen

Roof garden

Public space

Public space

Apartment

Wooden screen

Pitched roof

Apartment

Operable wooden
shutters

Concrete screen

Inn

Dorm

Innt

Courtyard

Central courtyard

Restaurant

Shops

Library

Bicycle parking

Fitness

Computer room

Billiard

Bicycle parking

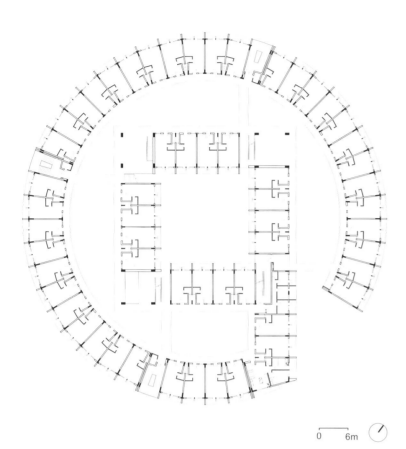

0 — 6m

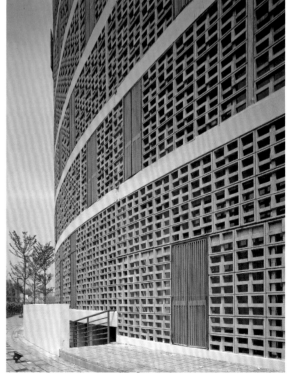

Father's House

Ma Qingyun
MADA s.p.a.m

Location Xi'an, China
Gross building area 3789 ft² (352 m²)
Site area 2153 ft² (200 m²)
Completion 2013

Elevations

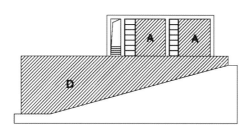

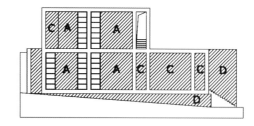

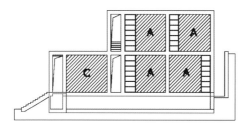

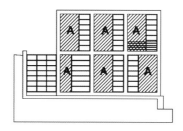

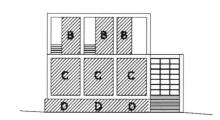

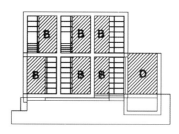

Located at Yushan Town, Lantian County, in the southeast of Xi'an, the project is a residence designed by the architect for his father. By using local wood and stones, the design glows with a regional artistic sense of beauty.

Geography

The site, with the roughness of northwest China, is at the junction of Qinling Mountains, Ba River, and White Deer Plain. The building is sited at a gentle slope, which is saturated with the atmosphere of Yutian County. It faces Wangchuan, an old villa of the great poet Wang Wei, and is filled with the glory of outstanding people. The structure, together with the front court, forms a basic spatial pattern, while its exterior walls are oriented to endless mountain scenery.

Framework

The architect determined the column grid of the building and courtyard walls through an axis grid. He establishes the fundamental generation rule by constructing a framework and filling-up. He sets up a consistent concrete framework in a three-dimensional space and then filled it with substance. Most exterior walls were filled with pebbles from local rivers; the surfaces of the interior walls and ceiling were tiled with bamboo plates, while the floor is paved with pebbles to create a rough surface. As such, the materials are consistent with the space.

Axes

Beginning from the courtyard, a strict axis grid was built lengthwise in the whole structure. It controls the spatial proportion from the front door, through the front courtyard and corridor, and to the back walls. Horizontally, it forms four even open spaces, contrasting with the vertical rhythm. This axis grid reflects the rationalism of the architect and shows an uncompromising intervention in the site.

First floor section

Second floor section

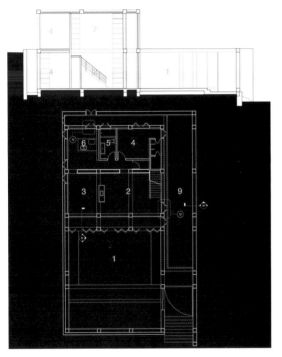

First floor plan

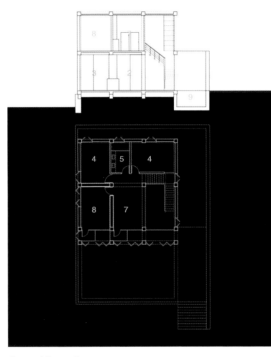

Second floor plan

1 Courtyard
2 Living room
3 Dining room
4 Guest room
5 Bathroom
6 Kitchen
7 Study room
8 Master room
9 Swimming pool

0   3m

The Concave House

Tao Lei
TAOA

Location Benxi, China
Gross building area 32,291ft² (3000 m²)
Site area 53,819 ft² (5000 m²)
Completion 2009

Site plan

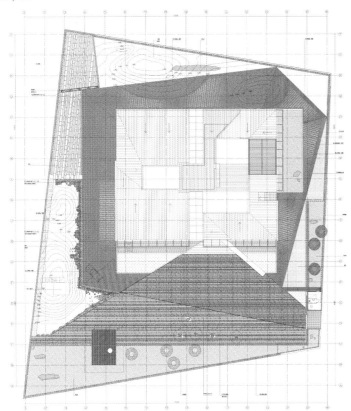

Volume analysis

Designed for the artist Feng Dazhong, the project combines a residence, workshop, and art gallery together in this Benxi, Liaoning location. Though sited in the major urban area, it also enjoys a natural mountainous landscape in the front. The brief required the construction of a quiet space for creation and living and to give visitors a cultural sense of peace and depth.

The AO (凹) shape

In this project, the building was designed to be a 凹 (concave) shaped 'brick box.' The concave space in the roof converges in the center and forms a whole together with three internal courtyards. The large spatial tension draws the whole sky into its architectural interior. There is a wooden roof in the center that is accessible to people. Due to the shielding function of the concave roof against the surrounding city, there is a strong sense of place on the wooden roof. Here, one can only see faraway mountains, the sky, and the moon, and feel the cycle of seasons and the existence of the soul.

Inner courtyards

In this square 'brick box,' the insertion of the Study Courtyard, Bamboo Courtyard, and Mountain Courtyard makes the internal space rich and poetic. These inner courtyards transform the building into an independent world with solemn heaviness outside and flexibility inside. The inserted inner courtyards light the whole space like lanterns, while natural light creates a boundless dramatic atmosphere. Under the premise of following the traditional Chinese sense of space, culture, and current values, the architects attempted to create an oriental internal space by changing some rules.

The brick skin

Due to the regional coldness in Northeastern China, the architects made 2.4-inch (600-millimeter) THK large bricks with warm color and good heat insulation. They believed that the exterior protection system of the architecture should present an expression opposite to the properties of the heavy and rough materials. Therefore, the bricks were built in a stretched net-fabric structure, which forms a gradual change from opacity to transparency, endowing the building with new texture and tension. The new form built through a combination of bricks creates a sense of transparency with Chinese traditional lattice windows. Light enters the interior through the gaps of the bricks and obscures the limit between the interior and the exterior.

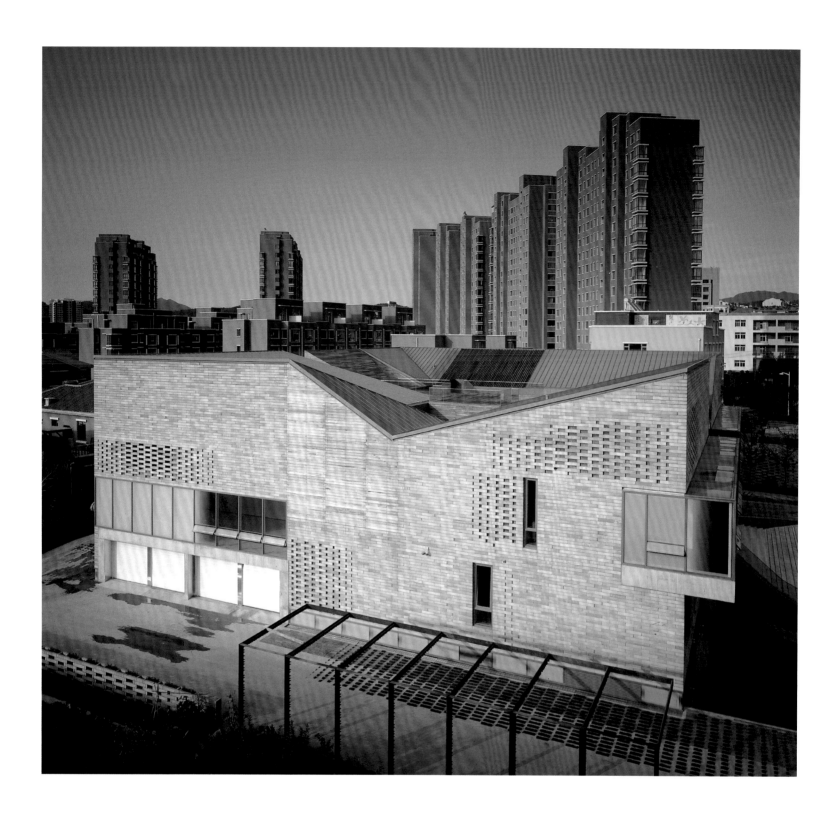

South elevation

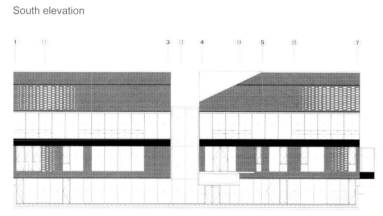

East elevation

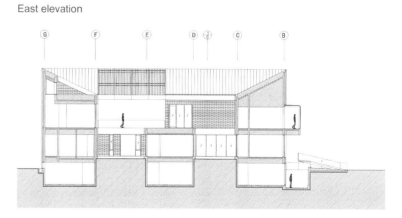

1   Atelier 1
2   Bedroom
3   Study room
4   Painting storage
5   Book storage
6   Paper storage
7   Gallery
8   Atelier 2
9   Family room
10 Master's room
11 Central hall
12 Washroom
13 Liberary
14 Bamboo house
15 Mountain house
16 Terrace
17 Living room
18 Monitor room
19 Entertainment
20 Dining hall
21 Kitchen
22 Family dining room
23 Main entry
24 Sub-entrance
25 Hallway
26 Car park
27 Pool house
28 Ramp
29 Storage
30 Activity room

First floor plan

Underground floor plan

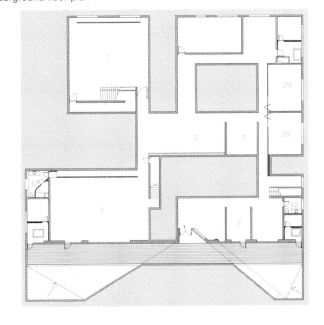

Wang House

Wang Hao
Run Atelier

Location Ningbo, China
Gross building area 2368 ft² (220 m²)
Site area 2799 ft² (260 m²)
Completion 2012

Site plan

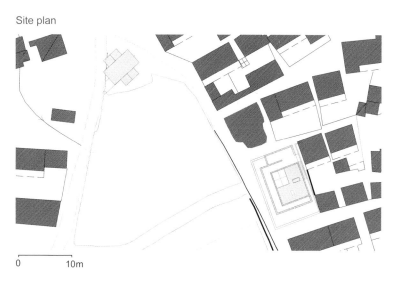

West elevation

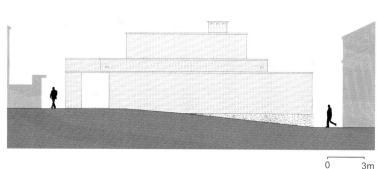

0   10m

0   3m

The project is located at a seaside village in Chunxiao, Ningbo, where the architect Wang Hao spent his childhood. The traditional horizontal and flat rural structure was completely preserved, simple and plain. The house site, handed down for generations, is about 2691 square feet (250 square meters). The new house was expanded from two farmhouses. It was intended to be a space for working and vacationing as well as the residence for his mother.

Internality

In contrast to thousands of foreign-style houses currently in the Chinese countryside, the design of the house attempted to present the simplicity of life itself from a perspective of peace and plainness. All architectural materials and furniture are made from a kind of local material, red bricks, to express the primitive vitality of the material and strongly indicate the internality of the house. The concrete structure further liberates the space with light and beam-columns to create flowing structural spaces between walls and floor slabs. The comparison of the structures of internal and external spaces precisely matches the aesthetics of antithesis in Chinese traditional houses.

Free structure

The design aspired to create an enclosed and simple countryside residence with a modest traditional building material. Three hollow cross walls, arranged concentrically, guide space gradually to a second-story patio, which is the center space for daily life, and finally go back to the traditional 'inward' spatial experience. Three cross walls arranged from low to high create a traditional enclosed architectural appearance and sketch the horizontal tension of the

house in extremely simple outlines. As a response to the large-scale enclosure on the exterior, the new internal structure is organized in a free style, which inserts floor slabs, beams, and columns between walls as independent elements and organizes them with traditional overlap joints for free transmission of gravity power.

With flexible columns, functional spaces could be divided and adjusted. A sense of layers and division is reinforced by beams at different heights and with different sections. These together create a structural flowing space. The traditional textural materials (bricks) exist as fillers and were constantly inserted into the original walls and segments (the old house before renovation) and sometimes with old bricks joining in. Bricks can reduce the simplicity of the walls and increase the dominance of the free framework as the main body. Even the floor slabs in general buildings are replaced with prefabricated plates, forming a textured surface.

Primitive materials

The aesthetics and the simplicity of primitive materials are protected and fully presented. The pigments of the naked red bricks deposit with the pass of time, and strike a stable visual balance with plain concrete and terrazzo floor. Some traditional rural furniture, such as handmade bamboo chairs, brick-built sofas that copy countryside heated brick beds, straw rain cape, and a kitchen rebuilt from a brick hearth, create an atmosphere of a farmhouse. The contrast of the exterior wall surface and the internal free linear structure comes from the most common aesthetic knowledge, namely internalization, of Chinese traditional dwellings.

Section 1

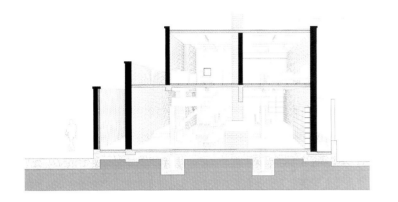

Section 2

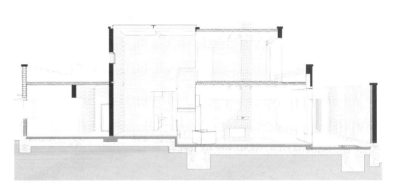

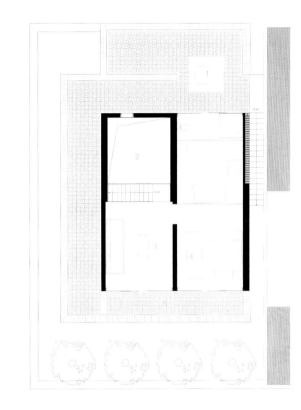

Second floor plan

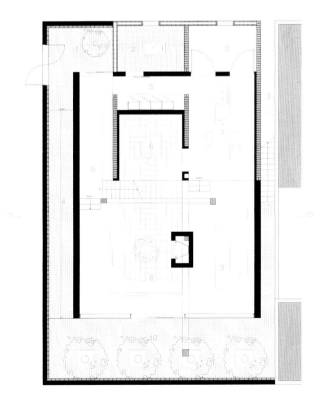

1 Terrace
2 Light well
3 Living room
4 Bedroom
5 Balcony

1 Backyard
2 Toilet
3 Storage
4 Lane
5 Gallery
6 Light well
7 Kitchen
8 Saloon
9 Atlier
10 Yard

0   3m

Post-disaster reconstruction of Yangliu Village

Hsieh Ying-Chun
Hsieh Ying-Chun Architects+ Third Architectural Office

Location Abazhou, China
Gross building area 126,185 ft² (11,723 m²)
Site area 295,351 ft² (27,439 m²)
Completion 2009

Site plan

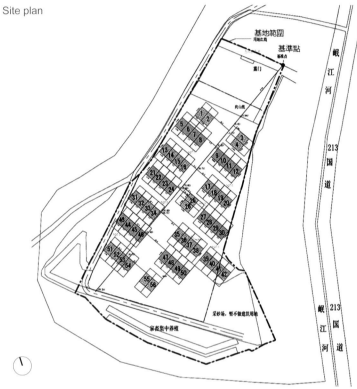

Bird's view

This was a post-disaster reconstruction project, located at Yangliu Village of Mao County in Sichuan. Yangliu village, originally a village of the Qiang ethnic minority, was relocated from the top of the hill to the bottom. There are 56 reconstructed households in the form of four townhouses, thus saving a lot of room for building many roads and public spaces. The design adopted a light-steel system to construct the major body. It not only followed the living customs of the Qiang ethnic minority, but was also cost-effective.

Quality versus quantity

The architectural practice of Hsieh Ying-Chun reflects his thoughts about human dwellings. His design, based on a strengthened light-steel structure and centered on the use of bolts, corresponds to socialized quantity (or, say, construction ability of the mass itself) with technical quality (namely oneness and accuracy), and then promotes industrial transformation of design organizations and production modes. The key is that the more open and accurate the design organization is, the more successful the terminal integration becomes, and the higher the realization degree of factory mass production and field assembly achieved.

The production of space

The architectural practice of Hsieh Ying-Chun could be understood as a space production plan from the perspective of 'social architecture,' in that the design organization should keep its openness and accuracy; attention should be paid to environmental sustainability and locality; the construction techniques should be simplified; and the cost should be lowered. The dwelling problem of disadvantaged groups should be allowed to be confronted with a corrective attitude that follows the direction of industrial development while decomposing the power produced in this process by transferring it to more general, non-professional classes to give full play of the construction ability of the mass.

Regional criticism

In the architectural practice of Hsieh Ying-Chun, the 'critical regionalism' has been transformed into 'regional criticism.' In the view of the former, the 'regionalism' facing the architects refers to the re-affirmation to historical cultural symbols or local material techniques. Here, a post-modern rhetoric is used to cure the harm caused by modern generalization; while for the later, it refers to giving up the initiative and monopoly with which the architects respond to 'regionality' and delegates the power to 'people' or 'commoners' coexisting with 'regionality,' and finally becomes 'regional criticism' plan of a newer social production mode.

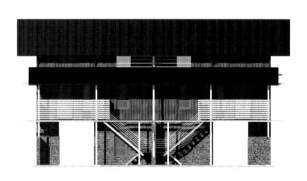

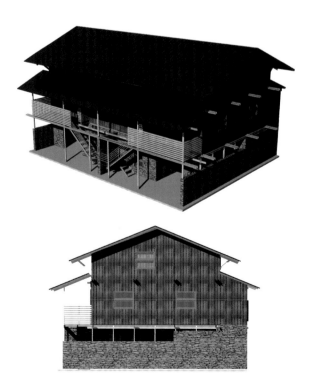

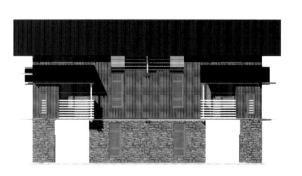

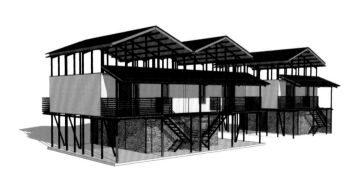

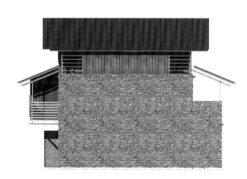

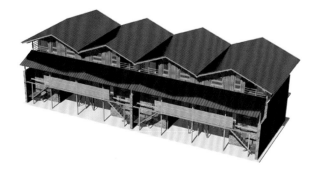

First floor plan   Second floor plan   Third floor plan

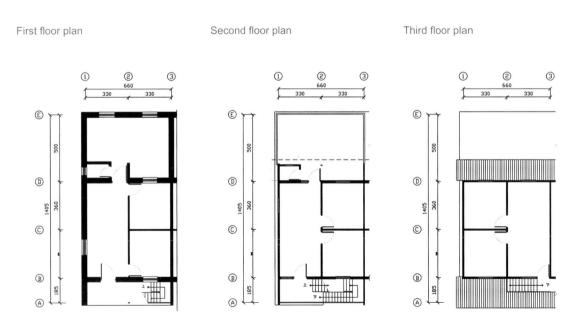

Regeneration ▶

Over the past three decades, cities in China have developed at a remarkable rate, unparalleled in the West. In many instances, urban high-rises proliferated at a rapid pace, dismantling the historic streets and blocks that once weaved together with these ancient cities. However, with the outward sprawl of Chinese cities reaching its threshold, the inward growth has regenerated more and more built-up areas in the urban fabric. Innovative design solutions are emerging in the city centers, including in Beijing and in Shanghai where urban regeneration is in full swing.

Rather than erasing the existing urban fabric, buildings constructed out of traditional as well as modern industrial materials are rehabilitated and often combined with newer additions. The conscious decision to maintain aspects of the city's heritage is an expression of a new design strategy, reflecting the Chinese public's nostalgia for the past. Yet, in order to counter an architectural language that is overtly historicized without self-reflexivity, a critical attitude that scrutinizes the relevance of the historical past on the contemporary moment needs to be further developed.

Wei Yuan Garden

Ge Ming
School of Architecture, Southeast University

Location Nanjing, China
Gross building area 21,549 ft² (2002 m²)
Site area 23,276 ft² (2162 m²)
Completion 2015

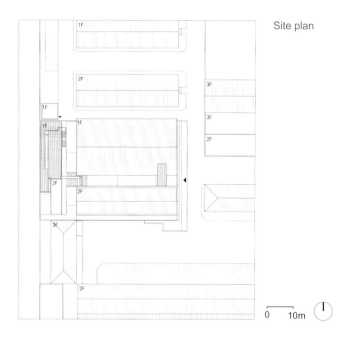

Site plan

0   10m

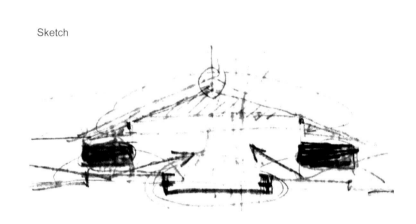

Sketch

The project involved the renovation of a factory in Nanjing to rehabilitate a group of unrelated old factory houses into a calligraphy museum through expansion and addition.

Six Principles to Garden

As a contemporary design method, 'Six Approaches to Garden' was proposed, which consists of Changing of Living Mode, Type-Form, Myriad Living Things, Structure/Material/Po-Fa, Generating, and Real/False.

Void

The double-pitch rooves of the old factory were extended, making space for exhibiting paintings and calligraphies, and the space within the original factory became 'a void in the house.' The first floor of southern house was integrated, and 'a void between the houses' became special. 'The void in the house' was partly descended to a lower level, and 'the void between the houses' was dug for another 'void', making the inside-outside undistinguished and the 'voids' endless. Construction itself became weaker in the site, and the spaces arose, which brought a sense of distance.

Viewing

A special viewing at varied body gestures and sight levels was suggested in the spaces, derived from the specific viewing in the Song Dynasty. The overlap of elevations was deliberated to make the greenery infiltrate into the spaces, to lower focus of the spaces, and to indicate various 'divisions' and 'distances.' Spaces became vivid because of the viewing.

Structure

The main girders in the White Hall were wrapped, and the beams in the Black Hall were used for suspending panels in order to make the structure and the spaces work together. The longitude beams of the White Hall were weighed discreetly in a subtle position between 'what is above for eyes' and 'what is related to the body,' reacting with the cabinets, producing ambiguity and pushing the space further. Two pillars in the Ancillary Hall were reduced, featuring two special upstand beams, to create a sense of mutual relation, separation and promotion among the voids, spaces, porches, and greeneries.

Stones

Stones were to be the resort of spaces, so they were to form a 'tendency' in the plan, meandering forward from the outside to the inside, making the spaces up-and-down, extended-and-compact, as well as accurate and meaningful. Moreover, the stones were varied in the height levels, tilts, weights and tones, changing the focuses and directions of spaces, highlighting their characteristics on the void, changing constantly and reveal their characters.

Section A-A

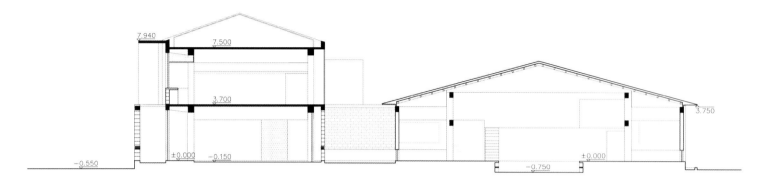

Section B-B

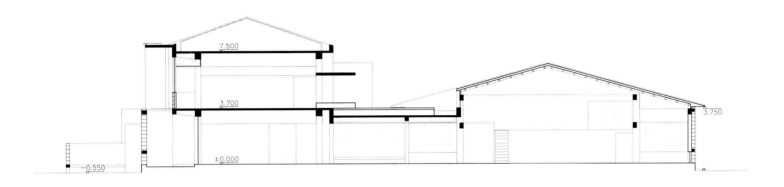

7.500

3.700

3.750

±0.000

−0.550

First floor plan

Second floor plan

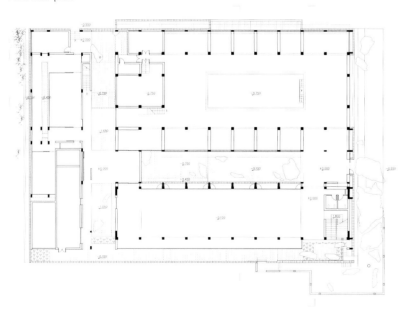

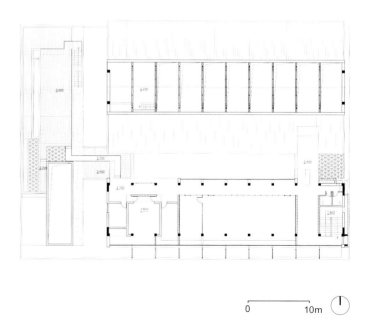

0   10m

Tea House in Hutong

Han Wenqiang
ARCHSTUDIO

Location Beijing, China
Gross building area 4844 ft^2 (450 m^2)
Completion 2015

Site plan   Models

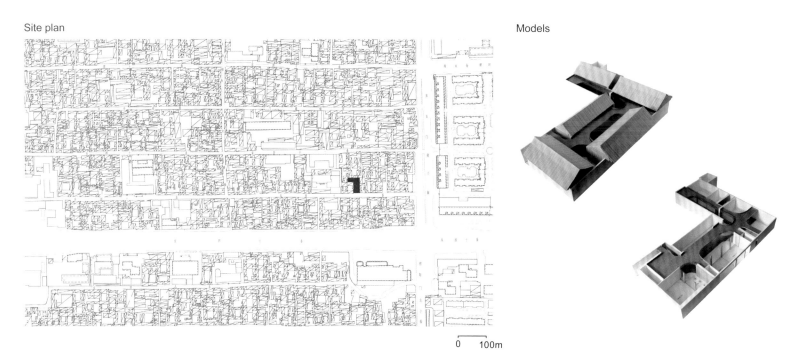

0   100m

The project, located in a Hutong block in the old town area in Beijing, is an L-shaped little courtyard with an area of about 4844 square feet (450 square meters). The courtyard includes five old houses and several temporary structures of colored steel plates. Originally a corporation club, the yard fell into disuse for quite a long time due to improper operation. The yard was renovated into a tea house for people to read and drink, also serving meals for the odd customer.

Overlap

Old buildings are seen as a result of overlapping historical traces while the renovation brings about a new overlapping status. Therefore, the architects divide the design into two parts. First, to organize and protect the quality historical information in the old building through partial restoration and renovation, and intentionally keep the traces of house left in different ages. Second, the winding corridor under the eaves of the old building connects the originally-disparate old structures and contains some necessary infrastructure (air-conditioner, floor heating system, thermal insulation, and so on) of contemporary living to meet spatial demands of the occupiers. The light and transparent corridor space contrasts strongly with the heavy and closed old structures, thus creating an interesting sense of spatial experience produced by the overlapping of the old and the new.

Inside and outside

Traditional quadrangle courtyards usually have a clear inside-outside relationship, which would be obscured by renovation. This could be seen from:

- The infiltration of space. The winding corridor, like forked branches, extends from the exterior to the interior of the old building. It forms three little curved courtyards and brings outdoor landscape into indoor spaces. The courtyard structure with rich layers creates a sense of endlessness and spreading in this narrow space.

- Transparency of materials. The curved glass curtain resembles a floating curved screen. It projects the bamboo grove landscape and old structural form onto the tea house, creating changing images and reflections along with the movement of people.

Activation

How to inject new energy into an old structural space was a general problem produced in the reconstruction of the old town in Beijing. This reconstruction project sought to transform the old residence into a public commercial space. The architect tried to strike a balance between the historic value of the old structure and the functional value of new commercial activities. In dealing with their relationship, the architect developed an actual environment with rich experiences. The experiential and flexible space was gradually transformed into an operation mode of culture plus business. Besides offering tea and meals, Chinese culture courses, art shows, and business activities are regularly held there. The vitality of historical architecture was preserved through 'being used' by people, while the way of 'being used' constantly change the historical architecture itself.

Sections

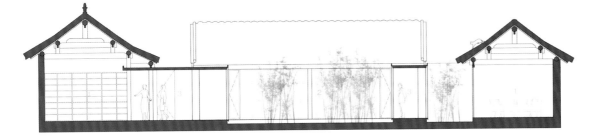

1 Restaurant
2 Courtyard
3 Corridor
4 Book bar
5 Kitchen

0   5m

Diagrams

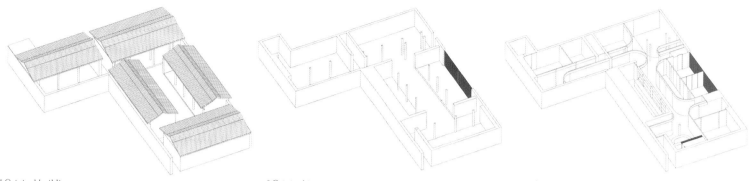

1 Original building

2 Original interior space

3 Inserted wall

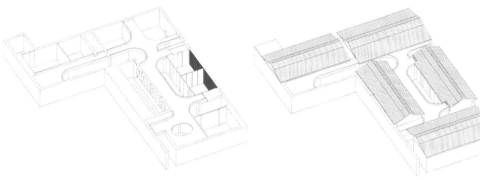

4 New ceiling

5 Renovated building at the juxtaposition of old and new

First floor plan

1 Main entry
2 Front desk
3 Courtyard
4 Restaurant
5 Tea room
6 Book bar
7 Kitchen
8 Office
9 Washing room
10 Storage

0   3m

Courtyard House Plugin

He Zhe, Shen Haien, Zang Feng
People's Architecture Office Co., Ltd

Location Beijing, China
Gross building area 150 to 500 ft² (4.6 to 46.5 m²)
Site area 150 to 3000 ft² (13.9 to 278.7 m²)
Completion 2015.9

Function plan of Sanjing Neighborhood

Office
Library
Classroom
Washing room
Rentals
Moved house
Homestay
Washing room
Kitchen

Diagram

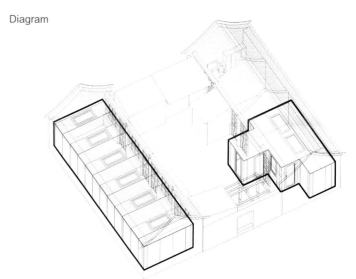

This project involved a prefabricated construction system applied in old quadrangle courtyards, whereby the prefabricated module plugins were installed in the old courtyards and residents were provided with an energy-efficient living environment to meets modern living quality standards.

Regeneration without demolition

Courtyard House Plugin is a new mode of minimal intervention in reconstructing old houses without the need to remove them. In China, many old town areas were demolished without second thoughts, and people were forced to leave their homes, severing the close community relationships for short-term benefits. By contrast, Courtyard House Plugin provides a healthier development mode with long-term social benefits: residents can create private, disparate, high-efficient, and energy-saving infrastructure without the need for dismantling the houses or relying on large civilian infrastructure, which means that they can directly improve their living quality.

Compared to reconstructions with huge investment from the minority, micro-investment from a large quantity of individual residents plays a much more enduring and efficient role in the development of traditional urban areas. The Courtyard House Plugins purchased by the Beijing government and individuals have already been widely applied. Each plugin could be a base point that influences its surrounding, and to combine all of these scattered base points is nonetheless a good way to deal with the decline of communities.

Architecture as a product

Courtyard House Plugin is an architectural product. It is also a systematic solution that could be replicated and updated. It can provide a living standard with higher quality in a wider community.

The plugin developed by architects could be constructed into a structure with insulation, pipes, doors and windows, and exterior and interior finishes. The boards are light, easy to manage, cheap to transport, and can be fixed with a hexagon wrench. Even several inexperienced people can assemble a complete plugin in one day. The finished house plugin has good insulating and airtight properties and is relatively cheap. The Courtyard House Plugin is equipped with diversified plug-in accessories, such as inter-layers, accordion houses, upturning houses that connect the interior with the yard, sliding walls, and large pushing walls. All of these features create many possibilities.

Ordinary people as clients

Courtyard House Plugin is affordable to ordinary people. As a systematic product, it uses standard boards. It is realistically priced, convenient for transportation, and easy to build. Therefore, it can be mass-produced, purchased, used, and assembled by ordinary people. The industrialized prefabrication mode can reduce cost while improving the quality of the product. It can provide many options. The architects also developed a system for purchasing products and allow people to freely choose the dimension, function, surface material, color, equipment, and others elements on their own.

Ordinary people need only invest a minimal amount to highly improve their living quality of life. This new market was developed by Courtyard House Plugin under Chinese land system.

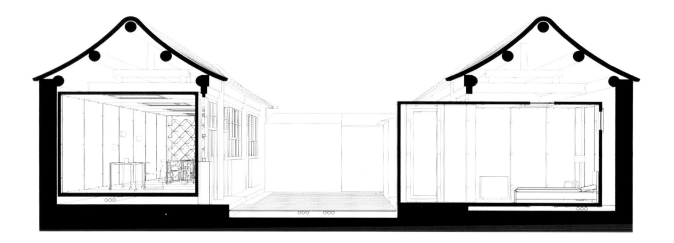

Before

After

Floating Entrance—Fufa Glass Factory renovation

Doreen Heng Liu
NODE Architecture & Urbanism

Location Shenzhen, China
Gross building area Existing 6781 ft²
(630 m²)
Site area 60,277 ft² (5600 m²)
Completion 2013

Site plan

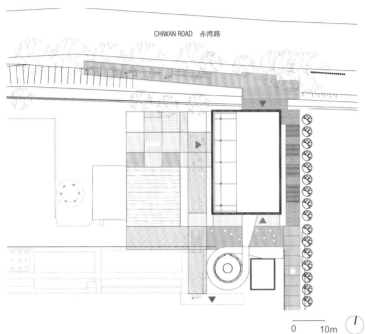

0   10m

Sketch

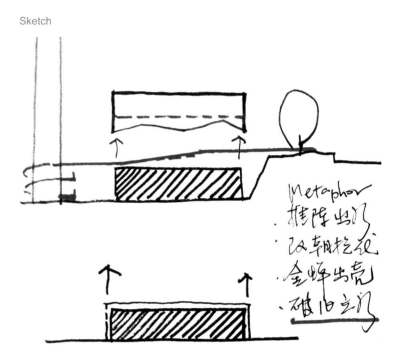

The project took place just before the 2013 Bi-City Biennale of Urbanism/Architecture to renovate the entrance of the Fufa Glass Factory, which is a warehouse that was originally going to be removed. The addition separates the new volume from the old warehouse by a new structural system, thus creating contrast and comparison.

Urbanism conservation

The progress of urban renewal is not only about the creation of new structures, but also about the renovation of old buildings and conservation of urban traces so as to preserve cultural and historical contents for the city. Old buildings without any feature but with time values, though not dismantled, can also be extended and acquire new functions, create unique spatial features, and add richer public contents for this age. The project was a bold and effective experiment of keeping original urban textures in expanding and renovating an old architectural structure. The new structure was stacked directly onto the original one. In this strong contrast, the quality of the old and the new are both underpinned, and the time properties of urban construction are also shown.

The 6th façade

The new parts of the project are separated from the original structure and float over them. In this design, a new public space grows, without being noticed, from the gap between the new and the old.

Here, the entrance area is right in between the semi-reflection folding ceiling and the old architectural roof of the 6th façade. It defines the factory area and is naturally connected with the unique chimney structure. The slant entrance platform directs the population to the spiral ramp circling downward towards the chimney, then leads to the factory ground and provides an experience space in the transition field. The waving lighting in the night creates an obscure and mysterious contrast distorted by the mirror surface between the old and the new spaces of the 6th façade, creating an ambiguous and attractive space between structures with varied qualities.

Contrast of the new and the old

In the renovation of the main entrance, the old warehouse, which was originally going to be removed, was kept with the aim of organically combining it with the new entrance. As such, the new volume is supported on the new light steel structure erected from the old traditional frame concrete structure. The new and the old structures are similar in volume and form interesting contrasts in times and technology. From the outside, the structural volume and the old building are similar in appearance but different in essence. A double layer of metal curtain and glass covers the façades of the new structure and creates a sense of lightness and mystery. It also contrasts with the enclosed façades of the old building in color and material. The design also successfully reflects the attitude of the city towards the new and the old.

South elevation

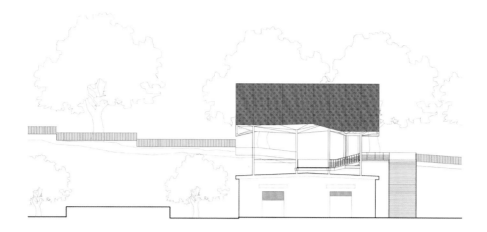

East elevation

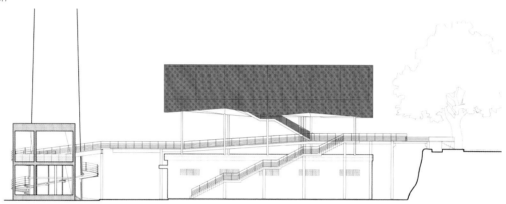

Section D-D

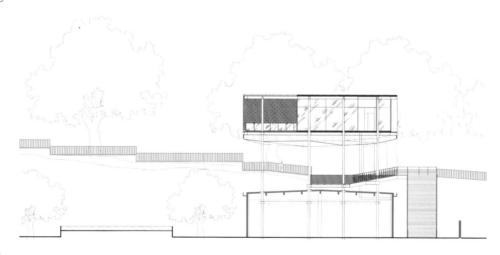

Section A-A

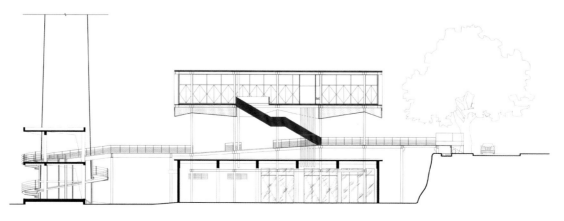

Axonometric diagrams

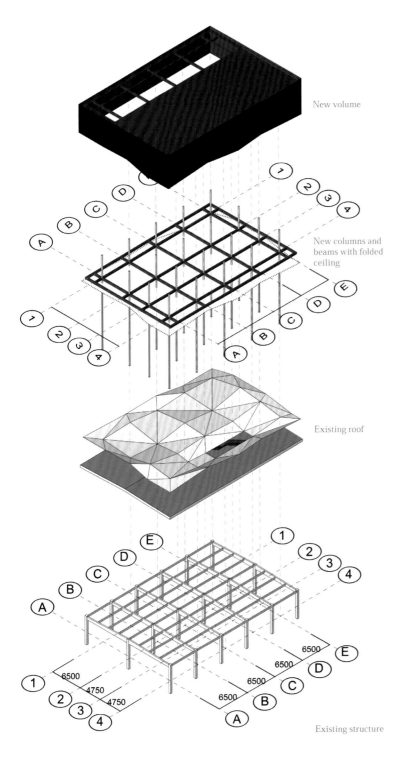

New volume

New columns and
beams with folded
ceiling

Existing roof

Existing structure

Diagram of folded ceiling

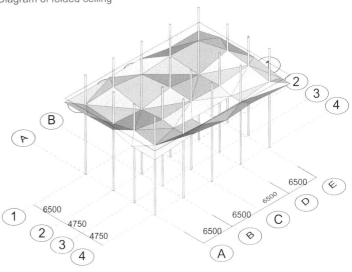

Serial number of folded
ceiling plates

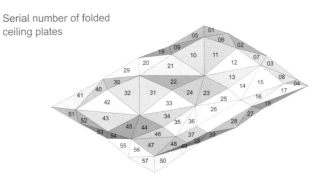

Size of folded ceiling

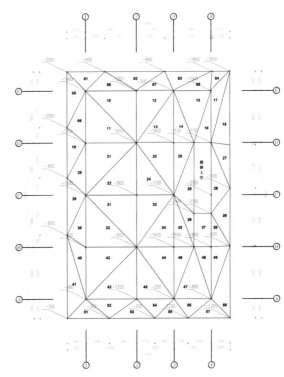

Third floor plan

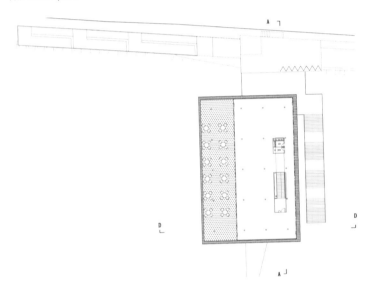

Roof plan

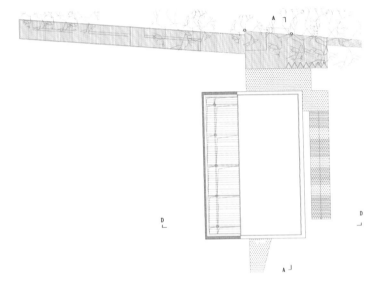

First floor plan

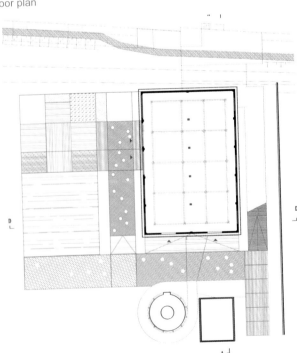

Second floor plan

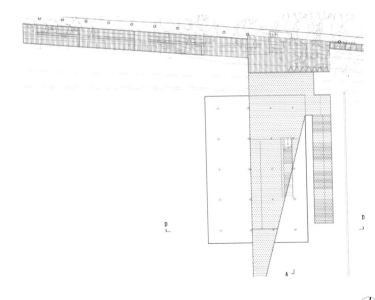

The Waterhouse at South Bund

Guo Xi'en+Hu Rushan
Neri&Hu Design and Research Office

Location Shanghai, China
Gross building area 30,139 ft^2
(2800 m^2)
Site area 8611 ft^2 (800 m^2)
Completion 2010

East elevation

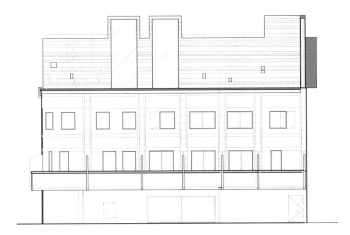

East section

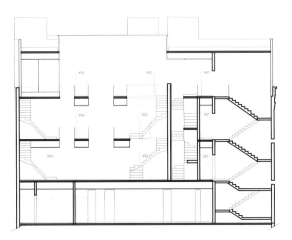

Located at the new developing zone in the old pier at South Bund in Shanghai, the project involved the creation of a four-floor boutique hotel with 19 guest rooms. It is close to Huangpu River, looking towards the skyline of the Pudong district glowing with lights across the river.

Old and new

The building, originally Japanese barracks, came to life under Neri&Hu Design. The decayed skin was peeling and the building was on the edge of ruin, so the hard skeleton had to be carefully renovated before the new façade was created. The new weather-proof steel structure added to the building not only corresponds to the industrial background characteristic of the region but also transforms the roof platform into a socializing space with pleasing views. Inside, various small and accurate cuts reveal the traces of the walls with its turbulent past, awakening people's memories of the building's history. Both internally and externally, the details are balanced between the new and the old to create a new whole.

Public and private

To describe the relationship between the new and old, the boundaries between the public and private were intentionally obscured. The architects attempted to break through limits on images, substance, and atmosphere in private space. As an iconic restaurant of the hotel—the first platform of the Bund crosses the street through the whole building and extends to the inner courtyard, which is an infiltration of public space into a private area. There is a cut in the roof of the restaurant that allows upper-floor guests to experience the scene as they dine. With carefully planned cuts, smartly arranged mirrors, and an unexpected circuit, there are endless possibilities for people-gazing.

Travelers and tourists

While casual tourists are often easily satisfied, experienced travelers place higher value on the spatial sense. As such, the water shed concept raised the question of how to create a home-like atmosphere in such an unusual environment, which was solved in the design, allowing even daily-living customs like bathing to become a unique experience. The layouts of the guest rooms are comfortable and distinctive, with unexpected surprises for guests. The original marks and scars of the building reflect the more sophisticated mindset of experienced travelers; all thirst and joy, hesitance and pursuit, are woven into unique textured materials and enrich the meaning of the place and existence itself.

East section

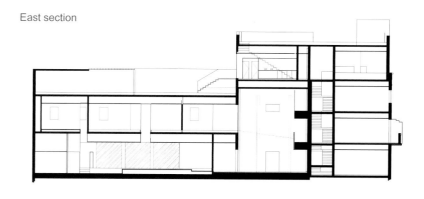

Third floor plan

1 Lift lobby
2 Bridge
3 Corridor
4 Back of house
5 Fire exit stair
6 Void
7 Bedroom
8 Bathroom
9 Terrace
10 Existing stairs

Fourth floor plan

1 Lift lobby
2 Bridge
3 Corridor
4 Back of house
5 Fire exit stair
6 Void
7 Bedroom
8 Bathroom
9 Roof garden
10 Existing stair
11 Mechanical room
12 Stairs to roof bar

First floor plan

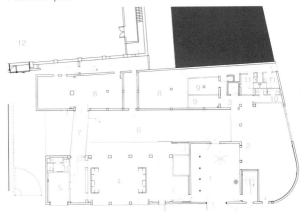

1 Lobby
2 Lounge
3 Lift lobby
4 Restaurant
5 Private dining room
6 Courtyard
7 Corridor
8 Kitchen
9 MEP room
10 Washing room
11 Changing room
12 Warehouse

Second floor plan

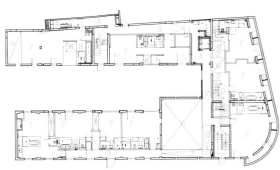

1 Lift lobby
2 Bridge
3 Corridor
4 Back of house
5 Fire exit stair
6 Void
7 Bedroom
8 Bathroom
9 Terrace
10 Existing stairs

0   5m

Roof plan

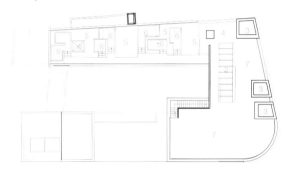

1 Stairs to roof bar
2 Skylight
3 Periscope
4 Bar
5 Sunken garden
6 Seating pocket
7 Seating area
8 Void to guest room

1178 Waima Road warehouse renovation

Shui Yanfei, Ma Yuanrong, Su Yi-Chi
Naturalbuild

Location Shanghai, China
Gross building area 10,333 ft²
(960 m²)
Site area 10,333 ft² (960 m²)
Completion 2014

Location map

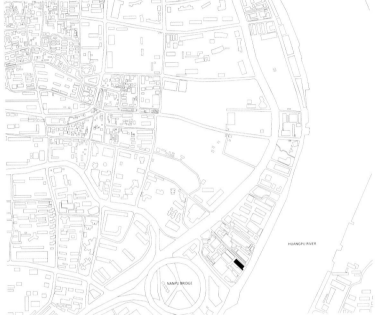

Plan

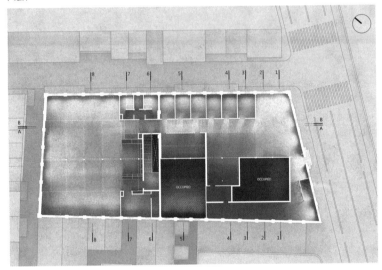

The project involved the renovation of the Naturalbuild office in an old warehouse of nearly 10,764 square feet (1000 square meters) at South Bund in Shanghai, which Naturalbuild designed themselves.

Weathering

Generally, a newly completed building is at its prime, after which time it gradually weathers. Yet, if it is recognized that this is the formal beginning of an architectural life cycle, the weathering can be predicted and the continuation of architectural process can be considered sooner in order the accept the process, and not resist the unavoidable time traces. The renovation plan of the warehouse sought to positively represent the traces left by years of natural weathering rather than eliminate them, so as to enable people to feel the influences exerted upon the surface of materials by the air, water, and time.

Specificity

The working mode of Naturalbuild stressed a study of reasonable deduction and materialization. It sought to explore the natural characters of design and construction and get away from all artificial and pretentious elements. During the renovation of the warehouse, all measures taken by the architects indicated preciseness, abstinence, and a sense free of metaphors. Naturalbuild felt that some forms, sounds, colors, and even the appearance itself weren't representative of their objectives.

Due to the building quality and architectural insight, the delicate ideas of the project were mostly used on conceal systems such as the electricity supply, heating and ventilation, and wiring and piping. Ducted air-conditioning was concealed in the symmetric overhanging ceiling; the air-conditioning condenser pipes were hidden in the attached inverted triangle under the roof truss; under the elevated floor, the bathroom water pipes were concealed. The dumbbell-like layout forms a path and produces a Venturi effect that introduces the river breeze to the backfield workplace. Different forms of ceilings were integrated with the electromagnetism system to meet energy requirements of an open and closed space and produce changes in light and shadow around the clock and seasons.

Serenity

Based on the design principles of Naturalbuilt and because of limited cost, the project sought to strengthen the original elements in the new spatial scene with the least amount of intervention. The way of juxtaposing the old and new highlights the old in the space and expresses a sense of serenity and simplicity brought about by the old, with even a hint of plain aesthetics. Therefore, the finishing materials were reduced to a minimum. The large areas of white walls are used as exhibition space for the museum, contrasted against the mottled roof and floor.

Sections

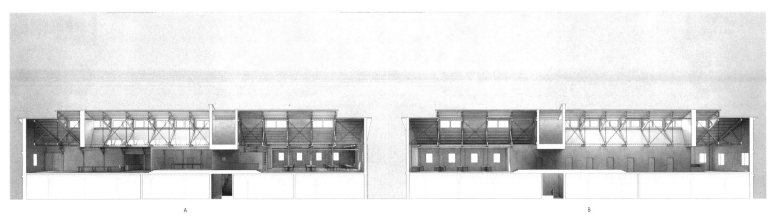

A

B

Sections

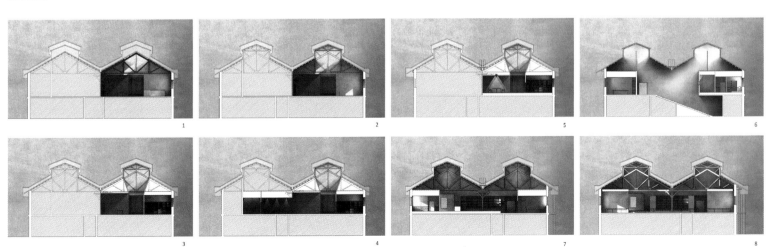

1   2   5   6

3   4   7   8

Section through meeting room and office

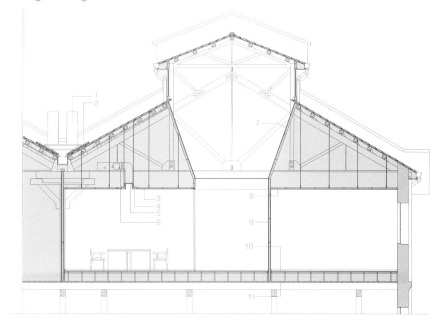

1 HVAC
2 Steel and wood plinth roof
3 Painted gyp board ceiling
4 Painted plywood light covets / translucent lens
5 Stainless-steel diffuser
6 FCU on steel frame welded on original roof truss tension member
7 Painted gyp board wall / rockwool insulation layer
8 Painted gyp board ceiling
9 Painted gyp board wall with rockwool insulation layer
10 Raised composite wood floor
11 Original wood deck floor

Section through working space and loft

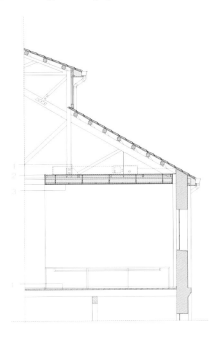

Wood deck reinforced steel frame welded on original roof truss tension member
Painted stainless-steel trim
Painted gyp board ceiling
Wax finishing or original wood floor

The Five-Dragons Temple environmental face-lifting

Wang Hui
URBANUS

Location Ruicheng, China
Gross building area 2874 ft² (267 m²)
Site area 32,840 ft² (5838 m²)
Completion 2016

Site plan

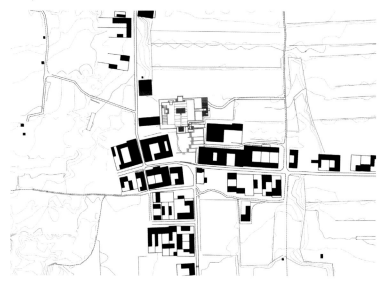

Sketch

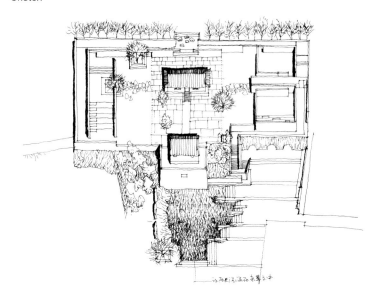

This project involved the overall environment improvement of Five-Dragon Temple (or Temple of King Guangren) in Ruicheng, Shanxi. The temple, built in 831 in the Tang Dynasty, is the earliest existing Taoist architecture and the key historical site under state protection. Yet, its historical position was out of place with its environment. The Five-Dragon Spring was under the earth ridge in front of the temple, but had dried up due to fall of the water level in recent years. As such, it had lost its spiritual position in the villagers' mind, along with the disappearance of rain-praying rituals in the Five-Dragon Temple and the decline of the center of the village neighborhood.

Protection of cultural relics

The 'Long Plan,' initiated by Vanke and some other organizations, was a domestic public welfare campaign invested by the legacy of the Vanke Pavilion of 2015 Milan Expo. Part of the funds were raised by crowd-funding along with Vanke's donation for the Project of the Five Dragons Temple Environmental Improvement. The 'Long Plan' soon received a positive social response, in addition to Shanxi Province's cultural relics authorities and the local government of Ruicheng city show of acceptance and support. This initiative would then go on to become the precedent where the government and private funds cooperated for cultural relics preservation, as well as the promotion of cultural protection through the platforms of internet and the international Expo.

Activation of cultural relics

For architects, the design in the field of cultural relics' protection might be conservative. They opposed radicals but would not give up the exploration of new paths in the existing environment, and produced new ideas on how to activate the cultural relics in present context. After the environmental improvement, people would start to read the place through various perspectives instead of the common bland way of viewing cultural relics. The visitors would then be surrounded by visual experiences offered by the Five Dragons Temple, allowing for a deeper understanding and meditation of the history over time. The series of spaces surrounding the center temple was designed as the outdoor museums of Chinese ancient history and a country school. The exploration of innovations in this context helped the cultural relics flourish and be more valuable and all the more charming.

Daily life

The design of the environment renewal for the Five Dragon Temple was centered around two themes. The foremost was to create layers of overlapping spaces around the main building in order to tell the history of the temple and ancient Chinese architecture in a narrative way. Through this theme, people would learn about the knowledge of traditional Chinese architecture thus better understand the importance for the preservation of heritage. And at the same time, people would gain a pleasantly unique experience in this ancient cultural relics environment. The latter theme was to restore the temple into an area of public gathering in the village, as well as alleviating the environment to encourage contemporary lifestyles harmoniously with the realms of ancient architecture. The rural spiritual values would then have an opportunity to be remolded in the design, which in turn integrates itself into the daily rural life.

Detail section

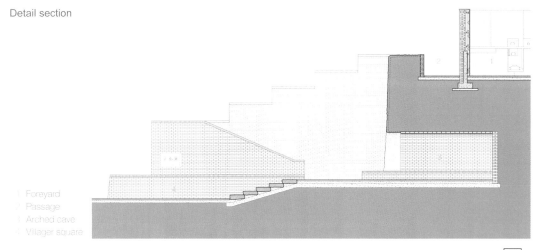

Foreyard
Passage
Arched cave
Villager square

0   1m

Section 1

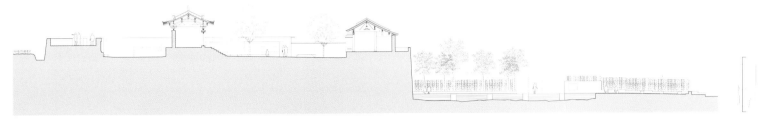

Section 2

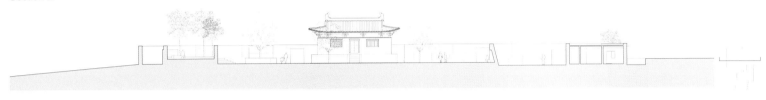

Section 3

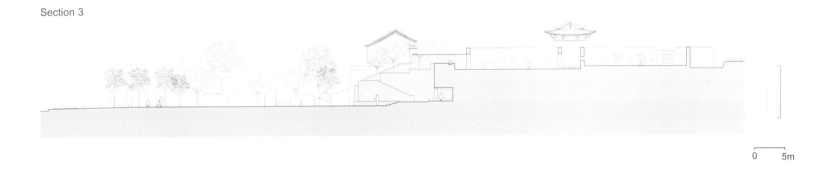

0   5m

Axonometric

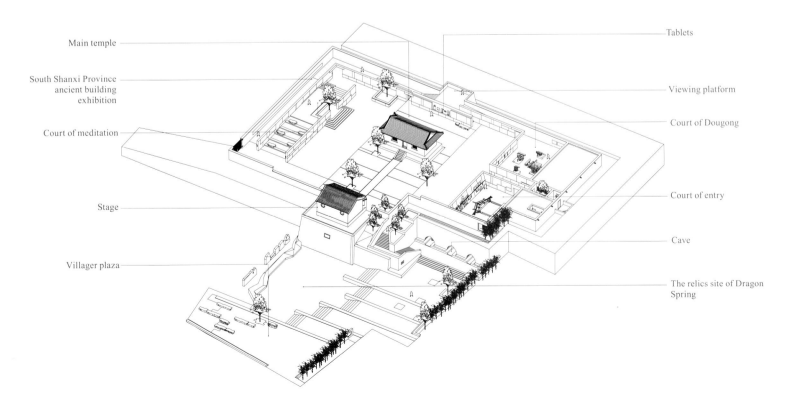

Main temple

South Shanxi Province
ancient building
exhibition

Court of meditation

Stage

Villager plaza

Tablets

Viewing platform

Court of Dougong

Court of entry

Cave

The relics site of Dragon
Spring

Plan

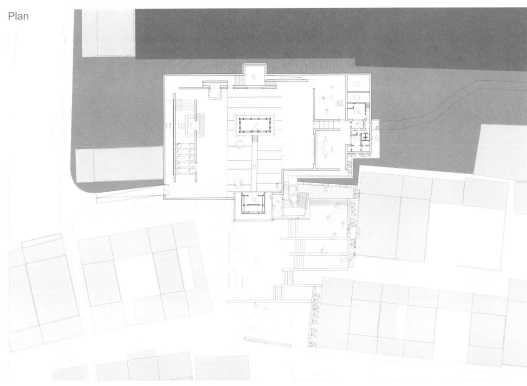

1 Villager plaza
2 The relics site of Dragon Spring
3 Cave
4 Court of entry
5 Court of Dougong
6 Viewing platform
7 Main temple
8 Main temple plaza
9 Stage
10 Court of meditation
11 South Shanxi Province ancient building exhibition
12 Fire pool
13 Water pump room
14 Generator room
15 Ticket office/control room
16 Toilet

0   10m

Water Tower Pavilion

Wang Shuo
META-Project

Location Shenyang, China
Gross building area 323 ft² (30 m²)
Site area 2153 ft² (200 m²)
Completion 2012

Embedded installation exploded diagram

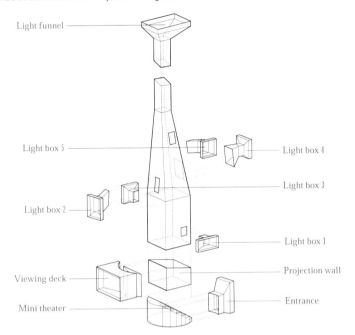

Sectional axonometric drawings

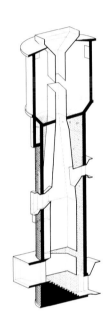
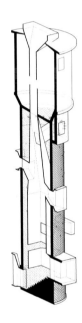

The project aim was to renovate a water tower in an old factory in Tiexi, Shenyang. The reconstruction sought to implant a new reality in a sophisticated and clever way into an old industrial site, showing architectural wisdom in a small space.

Collective fragment memory

The water tower is located in an old factory in Tiexi, Shenyang. It was originally the No.1102 Factory of CPLA, a military factory found in 1959 in the Great Leap Forward period. Shenyang is one of the major heavy industrial cities in China. Here, the water towers that are seen everywhere seem to have become unique landmarks that reflect the history of that period. Luckily, after great changes to surrounding urban spaces in recent years, the water tower had survived intact. As a collective fragment memory of original industrial history, the architects aimed to rebuild the water tower into a new space with a certain public function for the future.

Spatial–temporal continuum

Spatially, it is located right at the boundary area between the industrial texture left by Tiexi and the emerging resident community. The aim was to get rid of its heavy industrial history, yet the transformation and quick development of Shenyang again pushes it to the convergence point of the new and old. Based on this, the architects developed a renovation idea about how to put the water tower in a continual time-space. The façade of the renovated water tower transformed an art feature in the urban landscape, while its interior provides a new public activity center for the newly built surrounding communities.

Reality embedding

The reconstruction was carried out with due respect to history and current constraints. Consideration was given to how to embed the new reality into the historical context, integrating them to produce a new vitality. While the architects endeavored to not touch the intact water tower and only do the necessary structural reinforcement, in the newly-added part is a complicated and delicate device embedded into the inside of the water tower. The main body in between consists of two inverted funnels. The smaller one was placed on the top of the tower, while the bigger one was connected inside the tower with several lighting boxes that look like camera lens. These environmental lights were directed into the lighting box inside the water tower through indirect reflection and 'grow' from every possible opening.

At the bottom of the tower, seating steps were built with recycled red bricks at the connection of the entrance and elevated viewing platform to create a little theater for people, and providing a small place for activities and rally screening for the surrounding public. Looking up at the water tower, the light enters the tunnel in the center of the tower through the light tunnel in the roof and all the window openings display different forms and colors, changing constantly around the clock.

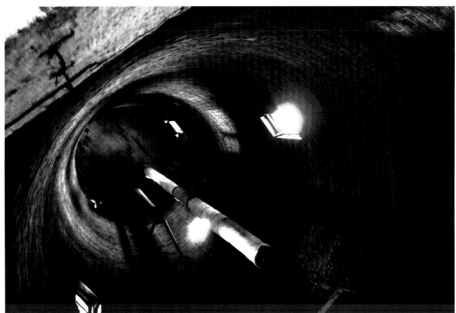

Axonometric

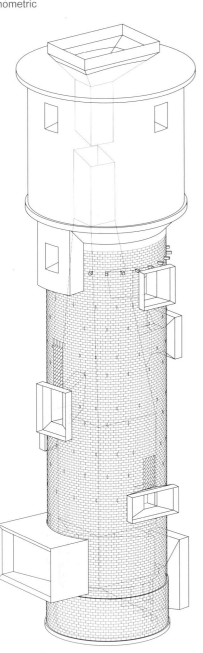

Diagram

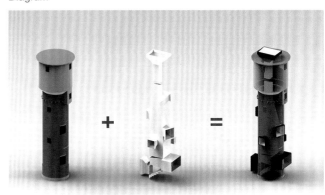

H=+25.000

H=+15.200

H=+13.000

H=+9.000

H=+6.500

H=+2.000

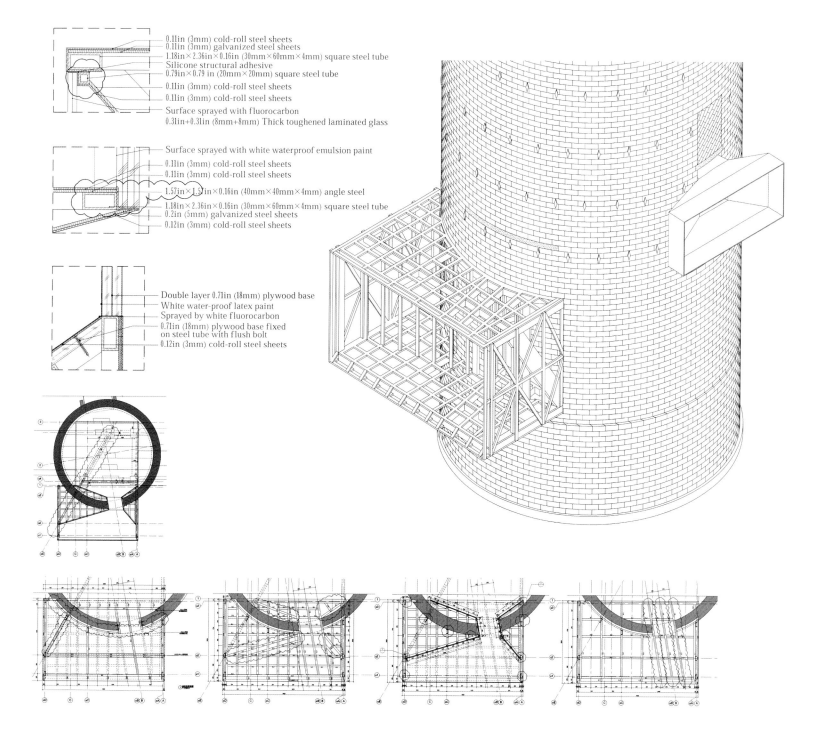

0.11in (3mm) cold-roll steel sheets
0.11in (3mm) galvanized steel sheets
1.18in×2.36in×0.16in (30mm×60mm×4mm) square steel tube
Silicone structural adhesive
0.79in×0.79 in (20mm×20mm) square steel tube
0.11in (3mm) cold-roll steel sheets
0.11in (3mm) cold-roll steel sheets
Surface sprayed with fluorocarbon
0.31in+0.31in (8mm+8mm) Thick toughened laminated glass

Surface sprayed with white waterproof emulsion paint
0.11in (3mm) cold-roll steel sheets
0.11in (3mm) cold-roll steel sheets
1.57in×1.57in×0.16in (40mm×40mm×4mm) angle steel
1.18in×2.36in×0.16in (30mm×60mm×4mm) square steel tube
0.2in (5mm) galvanized steel sheets
0.12in (3mm) cold-roll steel sheets

Double layer 0.71in (18mm) plywood base
White water-proof latex paint
Sprayed by white fluorocarbon
0.71in (18mm) plywood base fixed
on steel tube with flush bolt
0.12in (3mm) cold-roll steel sheets

Sections

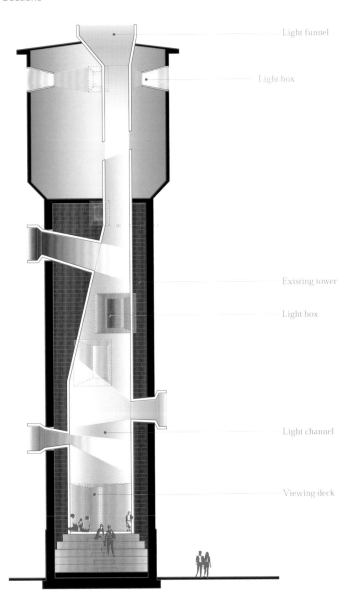

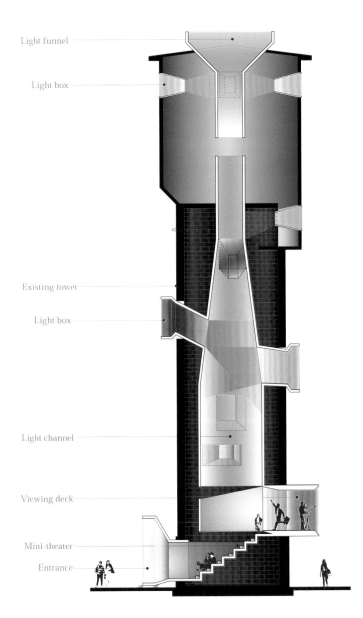

Light funnel

Light box

Existing tower

Light box

Light channel

Viewing deck

Light funnel

Light box

Existing tower

Light box

Light channel

Viewing deck

Mini-theater

Entrance

Looking down

Looking up

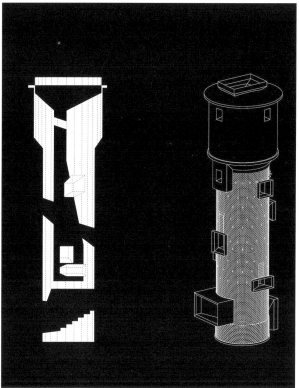

Shanghai Painting & Sculpture Institute Art Museum

Wang Yan
GOA Architects

Location Shanghai, China
Gross building area 32,292 ft² (3000 m²)
Site area 645,83 ft² (6000 m²)
Completion 2010

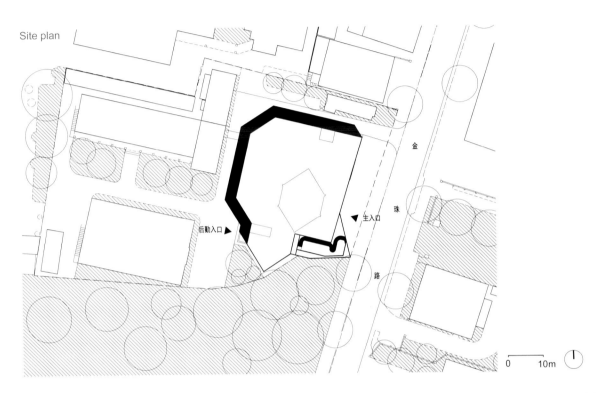

Site plan

后勤入口　主入口　金珠路

0　10m

In consideration of the loss of area due to set-back for building a new art museum in Changning, Shanghai, the architects choose to restore the original building and renovate the irregular road interface. Like a hard stone cut into a geometric polygon, the building lies at the side of Jinzhu road. Being steady and angular, its simple and massive volume liberates passers-by from the feeling of decorative architectural façade of the neighboring building.

Locality

The designers believed that architecture shouldn't be divorced from its location. By responding to specific problems on the site, architecture can grow from the ground and actively shape a unique spirit of the site. Shanghai Painting & Sculpture Institute Art Museum was rebuilt from a property management building. Keeping the original space, new architecture filled vacant corners and infused a good spatial relationship between the architectural volume and the street. In the design, the original enclosed bounding wall was replaced with an entrance square open to the public. The inclined stainless-steel net wall directly inserted into the art museum creates a distinct entrance image, which was a unique result from the connection of the original exterior boundary wall with interior columns.

Material

Proper use and expression of new materials, including new uses of traditional materials, made interesting subjects in the contemporary architectural design. In 2007, architects tried to use prefabricated concrete to build a curtain wall system in Shanghai Painting & Sculpture Institute Art Museum, which was the first instance in China. The minor color differences produced in the coagulation of hanging boards created a natural and large-scaled mottled effect in the whole wall. Thus, the wall looks like a structure built by huge natural square stones, waiting to be carved into by an artist creating an artwork.

Perception

Perception not only refers to physical perception of space, but also means psychological perception under a specific social and cultural environment. The 6.6-foot (2-meter) high massive prefabricated concrete hanging boards of the museum are close to the height of people. The entrance, which was formed by inserting an inclined wall into the architectural volume, creates a strong sense of guiding and spatial pressure. The construction method of the beveled handrails for the indoor staircase makes the whole hanging square cover practically as light as a piece of paper. The creation of bodily perception could be transformed into psychological perception of the modern art space.

Section A-A

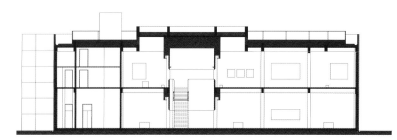

Section B-B

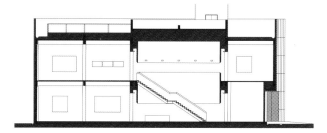

West elevation

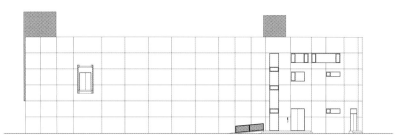

Section C-C

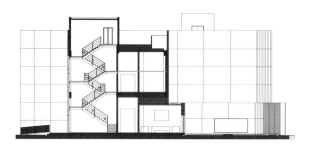

Details

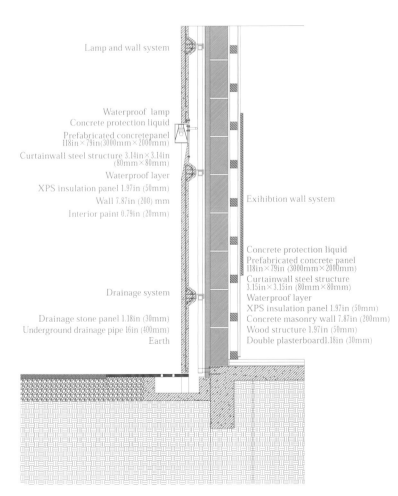

Lamp and wall system

Waterproof lamp
Concrete protection liquid
Prefabricated concretepanel
118in×79in(3000mm×2000mm)
Curtainwall steel structure 3.1in×3.14in
(80mm×80mm)
Waterproof layer
XPS insulation panel 1.97in (50mm)
Wall 7.87in (200) mm
Interior paint 0.79in (20mm)

Exihibtion wall system

Concrete protection liquid
Prefabricated concrete panel
118in×79in (3000mm×2000mm)
Curtainwall steel structure
3.15in×3.15in (80mm×80mm)
Waterproof layer
XPS insulation panel 1.97in (50mm)
Concrete masonry wall 7.87in (200mm)
Wood structure 1.97in (50mm)
Double plasterboard1.18in (30mm)

Drainage system

Drainage stone panel 1.18in (30mm)
Underground drainage pipe 16in (400mm)
Earth

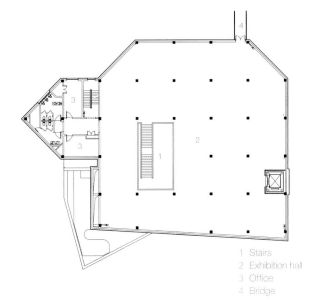

Intermediate floor plan

1 Stairs
2 Exhibition hall
3 Office
4 Bridge

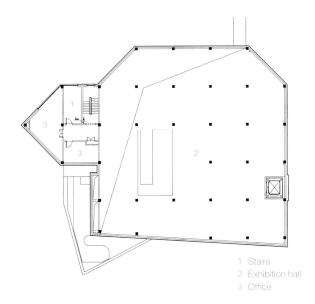

Second floor plan

1 Stairs
2 Exhibition hall
3 Office

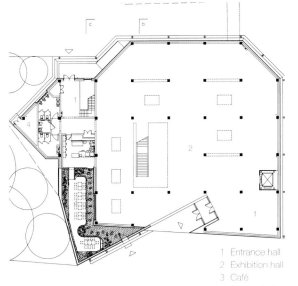

First floor plan

1 Entrance hall
2 Exhibition hall
3 Cafe
4 Mechanical room

313

TJAD new office building

Zeng Qun
Tongji Architectural Design (Group)
Co., Ltd.

Location Shanghai, China
Gross building area 694,509 ft²
(64,522 m²)
Site area 750, 245 ft² (69,700 m²)
Completion 2011

Site plan

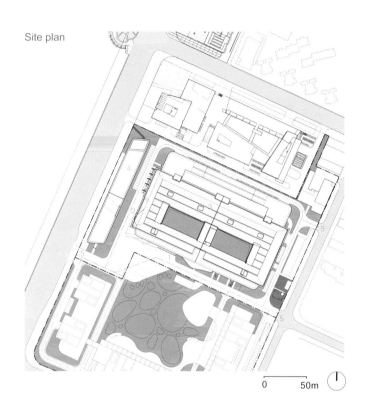

0   50m

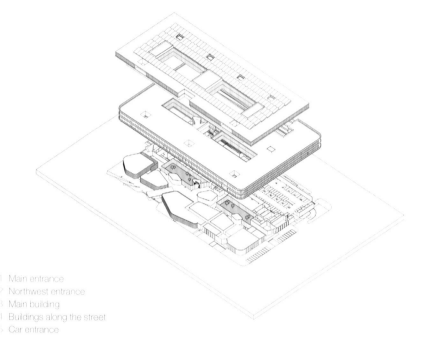

1 Main entrance
2 Northwest entrance
3 Main building
4 Buildings along the street
5 Car entrance

For the TJAD new office building at Yangpu, Shanghai, the project was rebuilt from the parking garage of Shanghai Bus No.1 over a two-year period. The original garage was the largest vertical bus garage in Shanghai. The renovation strove to protect the original main parking space and structure while also adding a steel structure to the top of the building to expand functional spaces. The outcome is a total area of over 645,835 square feet (60,000 square meters).

Space regeneration

Along with the rapid urbanization of China, urban spaces have undergone quick development, which resulted in further space regeneration. To meet new urban requirements, many buildings needed to adapt to the new age through spatial renovation. From the viewpoint of space regeneration, it upgraded an industrial space into an office building for a large architectural design group.

Place transformation

Built in 1999, the parking garage of Shanghai Bus No. 1 had completed its initial mission only 10 years after construction and was urgently awaiting regeneration. The garage was a typical building that stressed the principle of 'forms serve functions.' As a transportation building without any surplus members, its space expressed a pure sense of place. The garage was a three-floor

frame structure of 16.4 to 19.6 feet (5 to 6 meters) high with 24.6 feet (7.5 meters) horizontal column spacing and 49.2 feet (15 meters) vertical column spacing. It had a very strong structural rhythm and a simple, or even, dull space. Therefore, the challenge in this project was to strip off and dismantle the original field used by machines and rebuild it into a space for people today.

Symbiosis of old and new

As initially the design of the garage only considered the basic functional requirements of parking buses, it naturally became a building with purely transportation functions. It was totally supported by columns with fixed dimensions and a repeated rhythm. With respect to the original space, the architects attempted to create a unique spatial environment in which the new and old coexist. Therefore, the design started from extending the legible structure and spatial form of the original architecture. It follows three principles: authenticity, which refers to strengthen the sense of identity of the old building; historic significance, which defines the boundary between the old and the new structures; and wholeness, which means to realize the coexistence of the new and the old building areas. The juxtaposition of the old and the new in this project was presented mostly in the status of wholeness, while the application of many new techniques and the experiment of partial skin were both remarkable.

South elevation

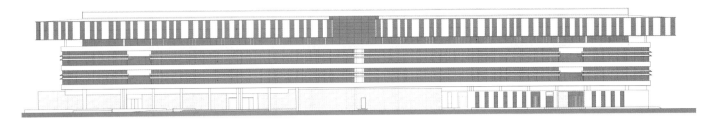

North elevation

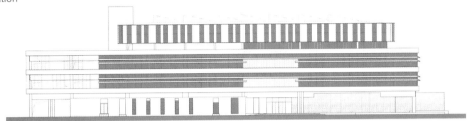

Section A-A

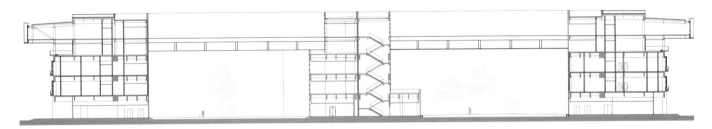

Section B-B

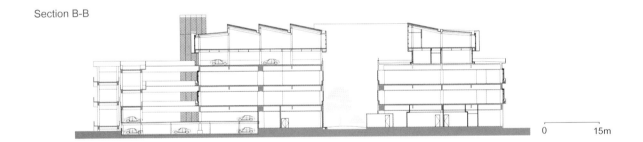

0   15m

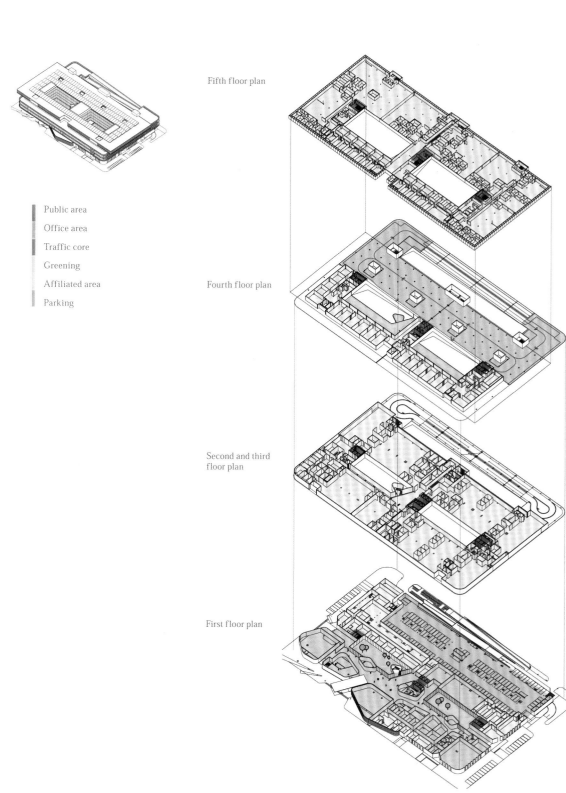

Public area
Office area
Traffic core
Greening
Affiliated area
Parking

Fifth floor plan

Fourth floor plan

Second and third
floor plan

First floor plan

Axonometric drawing

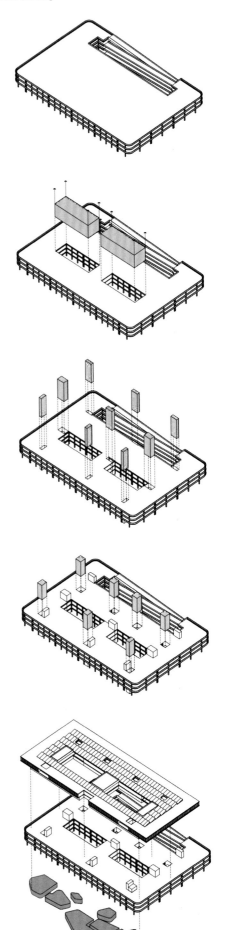

Third floor plan

Second floor plan

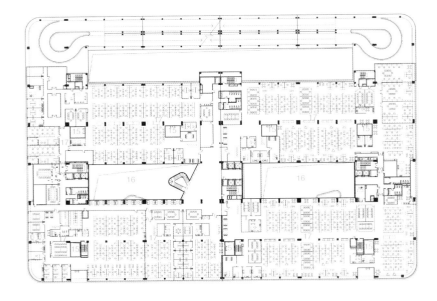

First floor plan

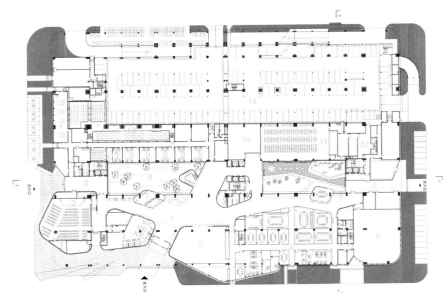

Fifth floor plan

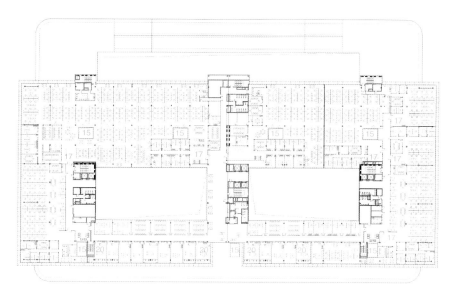

Fourth floor plan

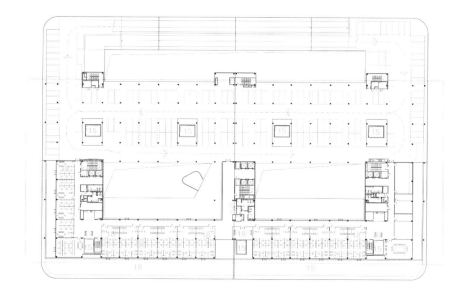

1   Entrance hall
2   Sub-entrance hall
3   Lecture hall
4   Café
5   Exhibition hall
6   Meeting
7   Reception
8   Inner courtyard
9   Offices
10 Activity room

11 Cafeteria
12 Pantry
13 Picture archive
14 Garage
15 Light well
16 Above the inner courtyard
17 Offices
18 Studio
19 Rooftop terrace
20 Director's office

0   15m

Micro Hutong

Zhang Ke
ZAO/standardarchitecture

Location Beijing, China
Gross building area 355 ft² (33 m²)
Site area 355 ft² (33 m²)
Completion 2016

Site plan

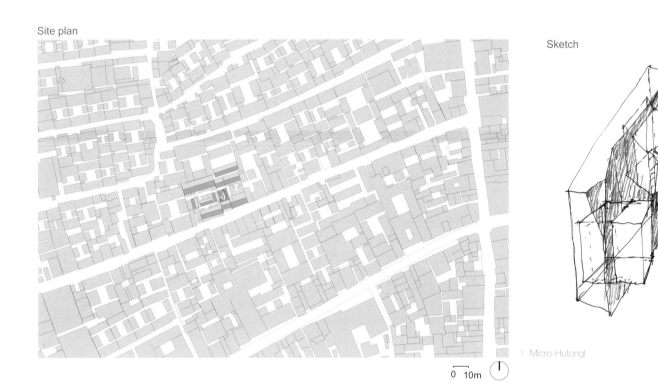

0 10m

1 Micro-Hutongl

Sketch

Located in the Dazhalan area in Beijing, the project was an experimental construction of standard architecture in Yangmeizhuxie street. It strove to explore the possibilities of building super-miniature social housing for multi-users in the limited space of traditional Hutong.

Micro-urbanism

Micro Hutong is a traditional Hutong courtyard within 15 minutes' walk from Tiananmen Square. Being a functional dwelling building, it was a residential experiment developed into a 377-square-foot (35-square-meter) area with an extremely limited space in a traditional Beijing Hutong. The project expressed a possibility of micro-urbanization: just like reshaping the whole body through improvement of cells, this project treated the Hutong courtyard as a newer basis unit in a city. It initiated changes from a micro-dimension and then affected the whole macro-environment in reality. The project endeavored to explore a new mode to protect and renew Hutong by the provision of many living spaces with different sizes in Hutong.

Inwardness

Similar to the form of traditional Beijing quadrangle courtyard dwellings, Micro Hutong architecture is also in the form of inward independent living units—five overhanging rooms are staggered in the direction of the little courtyard and use the spatial organizational form of traditional enclosed living courtyards. Differing from general reconstruction projects of Hutong courtyards, Micro Hutong is not an independent dwelling that is completely isolated from the local Hutong community, but an inward architectural form. It is integrated into the antechamber directly connected with the street.

The preserved slope-roofed structure is the 'urban antechamber' and also a transition space from the private house to the outdoor street. This space could be share-used by occupiers and Hutong neighbors, thus transforming the courtyard into a possible place for community activities. While improving the spatial quality, micro Hutong extends the dimensional sense of traditional Hutong courtyards in spatial form. It also strengthens the social characteristics of the space and increases exchanges between neighbors.

Ink concrete

The main body of the Micro Hutong building was site-casted in place with ink concrete. Ink and concrete were mixed at a certain ratio so that the material achieved a special tone. As the major exterior architectural material, ink concrete and gray bricks integrated Micro Hutong properly into its surrounding traditional environment. Meanwhile, the warm-color laminate boards of the windows imply the modern keynote of the contemporary interior. The ink concrete was an experimental attempt at a new material by the designers and can be seen in other more recent projects developed by Standard Architecture, such as Micro Tenement Yard and Co-living Yard.

Section A-A

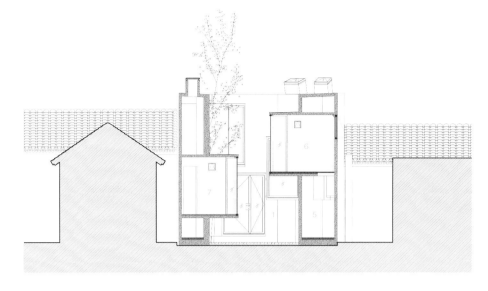

Section B-B

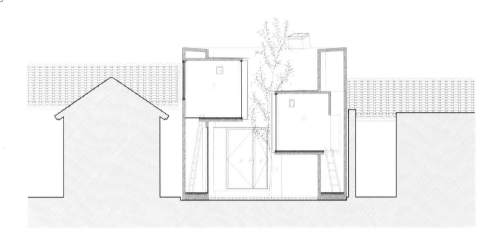

Section C-C

1 Courtyard
2 Exhibition room
3 Dining room
4 Kitchen
5 Corridor
6 Bedroom
7 Study room

0   1m

First floor plan

Second floor plan

Roof plan

0 1m

Details

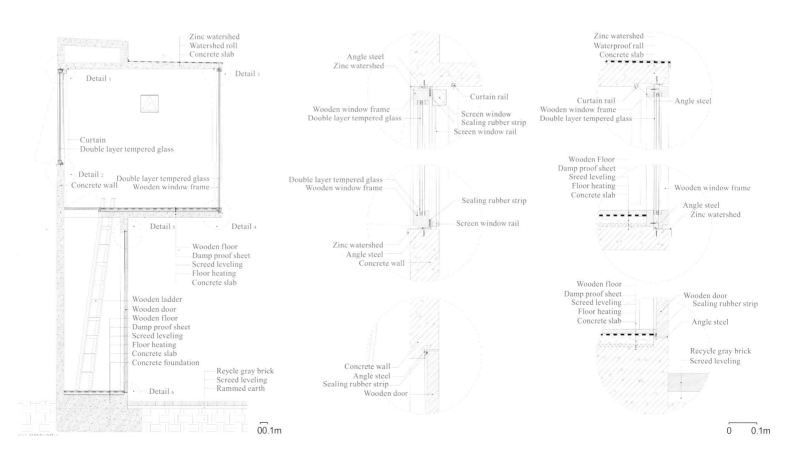

Zinc watershed
Watershed roll
Concrete slab

Detail 1
Detail 3

Curtain
Double layer tempered glass

Detail 2
Concrete wall

Double layer tempered glass
Wooden window frame

Detail 5
Detail 4

Wooden floor
Damp proof sheet
Screed leveling
Floor heating
Concrete slab

Wooden ladder
Wooden door
Wooden floor
Damp proof sheet
Screed leveling
Floor heating
Concrete slab
Concrete foundation

Recycle gray brick
Screed leveling
Rammed earth

Detail 6

00.1m

Angle steel
Zinc watershed

Curtain rail

Wooden window frame
Double layer tempered glass

Screen window
Sealing rubber strip
Screen window rail

Double layer tempered glass
Wooden window frame

Sealing rubber strip

Screen window rail

Zinc watershed
Angle steel
Concrete wall

Concrete wall
Angle steel
Sealing rubber strip
Wooden door

Zinc watershed
Waterproof rall
Concrete slab

Curtain rail
Wooden window frame
Double layer tempered glass

Angle steel

Wooden Floor
Damp proof sheet
Sreed leveling
Floor heating
Concrete slab

Wooden window frame

Angle steel
Zinc watershed

Wooden floor
Damp proof sheet
Screed leveling
Floor heating
Concrete slab

Wooden door
Sealing rubber strip

Angle steel

Recycle gray brick
Screed leveling

0   0.1m

Façade renovation for No.8 building at Lane 890 Hengshan road

Zhuang Shen, Ren Hao, Tang Yu, Zhu Jie
Atelier Archmixing

Location Shanghai, China
Gross building area 4628 ft^2 (430 m^2)
Site area 2476 ft^2 (230 m^2)
Completion June 2014

Conceptual diagram for façade renovation

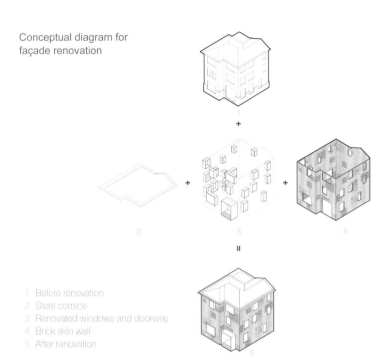

1 Before renovation
2 Steel cornice
3 Renovated windows and doorway
4 Brick skin wall
5 After renovation

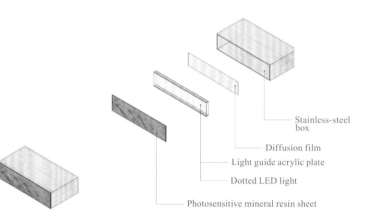

Stainless-steel box
Diffusion film
Light guide acrylic plate
Dotted LED light
Photosensitive mineral resin sheet

This façade renovation project is a small part of a big urban regeneration program, Hengshanfang, which tends to transform a historical residential district with Lilong houses built in 1934 and villas built in 1948 into a boutique commercial area.

Façade renovation

The site is in Xujiahui, one of the busiest commercial centers in Shanghai, where constant change plays a crucial role in guaranteeing economic and urban vitality. Thus, for Atelier Archmixing, the biggest challenge was how to achieve iconic difference as well as commercial dynamics without sacrificing the coherence of a historical preservation area.

Everyday changing

In order to balance the integration and distinction between the old villa and surroundings, the architect decided to cover the three-story structure with a changeable skin, which keeps elegantly quiet during the day while sending out charming allure during the night. Instead of using a conventional curtain wall or floodlighting, they applied illuminated brick, an originally designed and customized product to achieve this dramatic effect. The historical building, now a boutique shop, is covered with an envelope combining two different materials, traditional gray bricks mixing with this unique illuminated bricks, both share same size and similar color. Therefore, during the daytime, with a pure brick texture, it would easily integrate into its surrounding. When night falls, the wall suddenly becomes shinning, just like lighting up a lantern with rich pattern, successfully distinguishing

itself, at the same time attracting and amusing the pedestrians. What makes the building stand out among this downtown commercial area is the dramatic fact that this is an everyday transformation of the building itself instead of neon light effect. Moreover, this sophisticated design of difference, changing from daytime quietness to nighttime brilliance, also conveys a sense of Shanghai character, no matter in a mode of withdrawn seriousness or open enchantment, it would always keep restrained elegance.

Luminous brick wall

The illuminated brick is a complicated product composed with five different segments. A stainless-steel box in the size of a normal brick serves as the main structure, inserted with a lighting facility made of three different layers, among which, a new material called Photosensitive Mineral Resin Sheet plays a key role in creating delicate texture. These bricks were laid alternatively with gray bricks in mortar, just like building a traditional brick wall. Four elevations constitute a continuous skin to achieve unity and simplicity. The illuminated façade is composed of overlapping rectangular lighting patterns of varied size and intensity, intersecting with window frames. Since the LED bricks are of the same size as those gray ones, they can form rectangular lighting areas of different texture. While rectangular is also the shape of windows and doors, it is applied as the basic form. To exaggerate this covering effect and create different brightness, a small size of extremely denser lighting blocks are hidden in those large areas.

Wall section

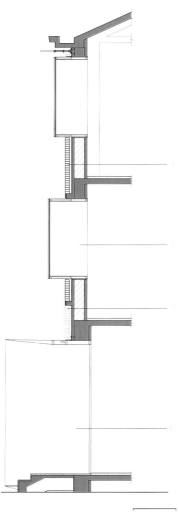

0　　　1m

1 3.96in (98mm) illuminated bricks
2 Copper plate
3 3.96in (98mm) gray bricks
4 Stainless-steel plate

Rural ▶

Architects practicing design and construction in rural areas of China are increasingly conscious of their social responsibility and the corresponding need to develop sustainable modes of construction. Up until a decade ago, architects were concentrating on cities as the base for architectural practice, ignoring the countryside due to its unfavorable socioeconomic conditions. Over the last decade, Chinese city dwellers, seeking an idyllic lifestyle removed from urban congestion and industrial pollution, have begun to relocate to the rural areas.

Following this trend, a growing number of independent architects are implementing their designs in rural settings, participating in the transformation of agrarian societies. Much like artists, designers, and social workers who are determined to directly engage in rural communities, some architects choose to move out of cities and relocate to rural areas. This geographical transition has encouraged architects to develop more sensitive design methods that respect local lifestyles as well as their building typology, materials, and craftsmanship.

Taiyang Organic Farming Commune

Chen Haoru,
Citiarc

Location Hangzhou, China
Gross building area 2756 ft² (256 m²)
Site area 21,528 ft² (2000 m²)
Completion 2014

Section

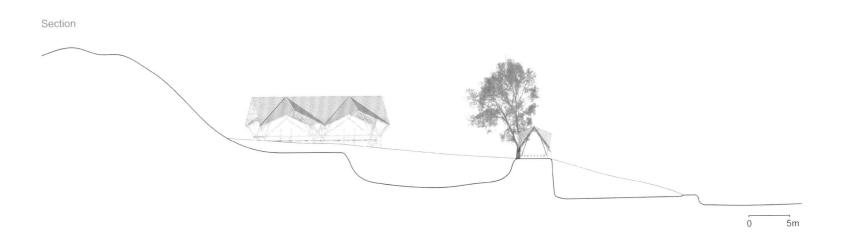

0   5m

Located at Linan, Hangzhou, the project is nestled in Zhuyi Cove, a 1.86-mile (3-kilometer) mountain valley. The structure was built with local construction materials such as Mao bamboo, pebbles, and couch-grass and completed by local artisans within a week.

Natural construction

The area was short of industrial materials and rich in natural materials. Factory products can only reach this mountainous area after a long distance of transportation, but local natural materials are abundant here. In the streams spreading all over the valley is a substantial layer of pebbles. These pebbles, formed in the ancient times, are transported to the cities as paving materials in landscaping projects and are seen everywhere in the rural area.

The Mao bamboo groves behind the mountain houses are also commonplace. The type and quality of bamboo vary a lot with the difference of earth. Mao bamboo is quite unique in the county. Collected in winter, they have a thick outer skin, which can protect them against insects. Many farmers in the area are also bamboo artisans. They make bamboo-wares between busy farming seasons, which is also a historical tradition. The architects had particular interest in the bamboo trees, so they begin to study the bamboo structures. The artisans who build the bamboo house are also partners of architects. This architectural experiment, thus, became an opportunity for reviving the craftsmanship of bamboo architecture.

Foundation in-situ

Groundbreaking is a big event in Chinese rural custom. It is extremely important to select a proper date and location as the changes of earth and Feng Shui are taboos. The site of this project is in a small grove of bamboo of Farmer Luo's Famil, which is in a farmland near the mountain. It is clear and distinct frrom the path entering the valley. The new thatched cottages make use of original ground and gutters without breaking the ground. Without any foundation, they

have more than 10 stone stools as ground supports for the bamboo structure. Similar traditional structures put wooden columns directly on the stone stools embedded in the rammed-earth. The non-rigid connection in the roof structure absorbs the instability produced in the subsidence of the ground.

When visiting ancient architectures, the architects found that Chinese wooden structures gain stability up to down; therefore, they could bear the instability from the ground. In an uncultivated farmland, the whole huge bamboo structure forms an individual stable architecture, just like a large bird perched on a low wall built with pebbles from the creek. The stone stools, like claws of birds, keep a firm hold on the earth. The slope roofs covered by couch-grass stand high, like wide and powerful wings of birds, ready to take flight.

New rural agricultural community

A group of city dwellers with different backgrounds cherished common ideals and a return to the rural area to cooperate with farmers. They intentionally go to foreign countries to learn about new agricultural technology and management modes. They also establish new standards of agricultural production and marketing channels of agricultural products. The farmers grow original crops according to new standards and sell them to the farms after harvest.

The social experiment solved the problem of selling farm products and selecting plant species, but the key strategy was that the farmers could keep the land use right and continue farming in the farmland handed down for generations. This rural experiment is in its inception and laboring farmers have joined in the collaboration, which is so different from that of the past. Architecture plays a subtle and important role in this process. As a modern structure with natural characters or a natural structure with modern characteristics, a new architectural form will emerge under the demand of rural production.

Pavilion elevation

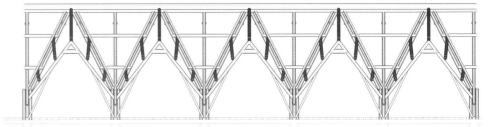

Exploded diagram of the chicken farm

Section of the chicken farm

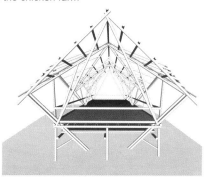

Detail of the chicken farm

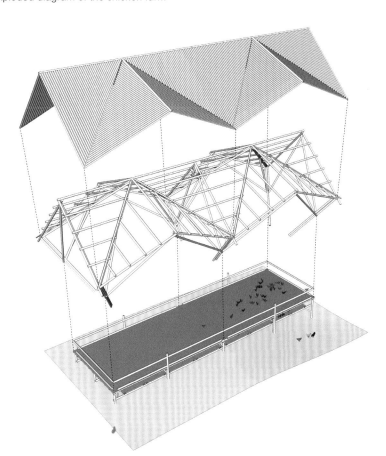

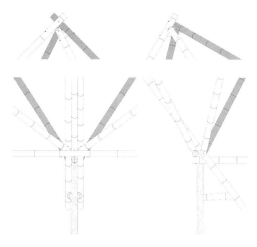

0 10m

Exploded view of the pig barn

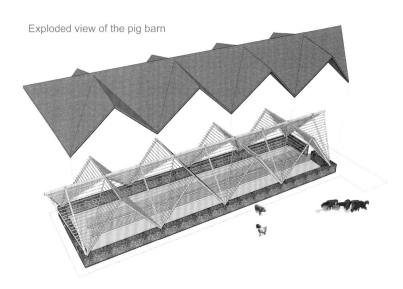

Top view of the pig barn

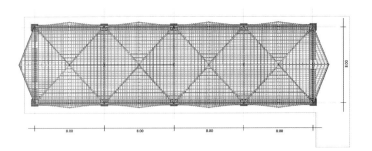

Section of the pig barn

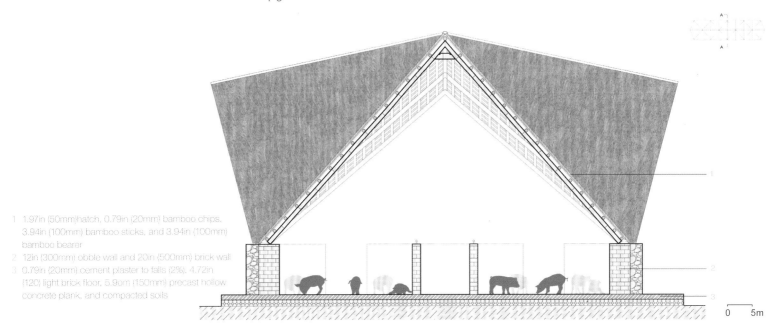

1 1.97in (50mm) hatch, 0.79in (20mm) bamboo chips,
   3.94in (100mm) bamboo sticks, and 3.94in (100mm)
   bamboo bearer
2 12in (300mm) cobble wall and 20in (500mm) brick wall
3 0.79in (20mm) cement plaster to falls (2%), 4.72in
   (120) light brick floor, 5.9om (150mm) precast hollow
   concrete plank, and compacted soils

0   5m

Papa's Hostel

He Wei
3andwich Design+He Wei Studio

Location Lishui, China
Gross building area 2906 ft² (270 m²)
Site area 1615 ft² (150 m²)
Completion 2015

Site plan

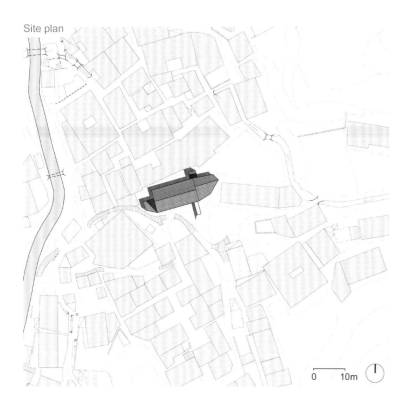

0   10m

Sketch

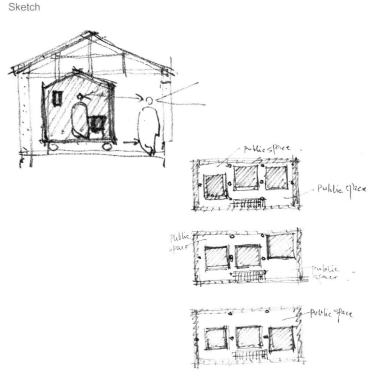

The project—located at Pingtian village, Siping township, Songyang county, Zhejiang province—involved the building of a hostel from an existing civilian house. Surrounded by mountains with beautiful views, the layout and building appearance of the traditional Pingtian village had been kept relatively intact. The existing buildings are mostly rammed-earth and tiled-roof structures.

Contrast

In a renovation project, the relationship between the new and old is a problem architects must solve properly. In this design, as the old building was sited in a traditional village, it became more sensitive to introduced new elements. For the newly built parts, the architects did not adopt the measure of 'restoring the old as the old.' Rather, they intentionally highlight the contrast between the new and old, so as to build dialogues between the new material—sunlight panels and the old rammed-earth texture. Lightness versus heaviness, thinness versus thickness, transparency versus closure. Through these dialogues in the architectural vocabulary, the old structure was given a new meaning to smoothly enter the modern context.

Variability

The architects shaped a variable and flexible space through a 'Houses within a House' design on the second floor. The three sets of

'Houses within a House' could be relocated in the space according to user requirements. When necessary, they could also be easily dismantled and moved to another location and then re-assembled. Therefore, the architectural interior space can be easily rebuilt or restored. The easy shift between white and colored light further stresses this variability: the users, by the control system, can freely change the atmosphere by shifting light and taking advantage of the semi-transparent sunlight panels.

Ambiguity

A hostel is an interesting architecture type. It is a structure between private and public. Though a dwelling space, it is not absolutely private: people don't know each other, but they are willing to live under the same roof. In this design, the architects tried to challenge the boundary between the private and the public by reshaping the house-bed relationship and redefining the interior interface-partition wall. Light rays and visual lines in the space are obstructed, softened, and released by a semi-transparent interface, building an obscure and overlapping spatial relation. From young the middle-aged, the people who live there all experience such complicated perceptions as nervousness, desire, and ambiguity, and this complicated feeling is just the quality the hostel wanted to express.

Section

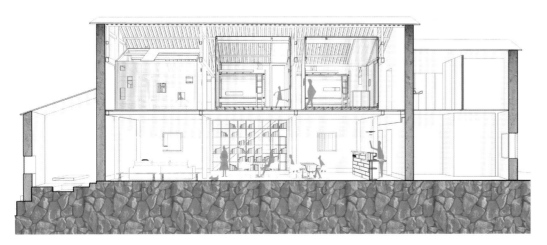

Axonometric

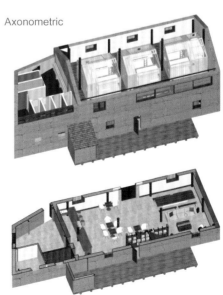

First floor plan

Second floor plan

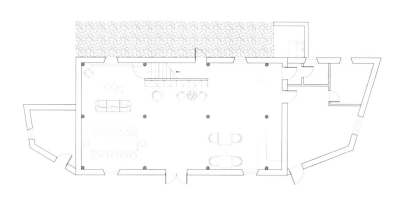

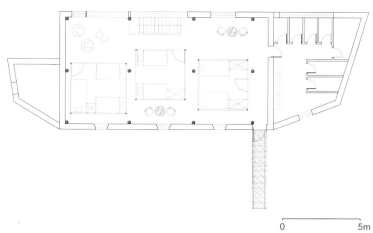

0   5m

Treehouse Qiyunshan

Kong Rui, Fan Beilei
genarchitects

Location Shanghai, China
Gross building area 353 ft² (32.8 m²)
Site area 10,312 ft² (958 m²)
Completion 2016

Site plan

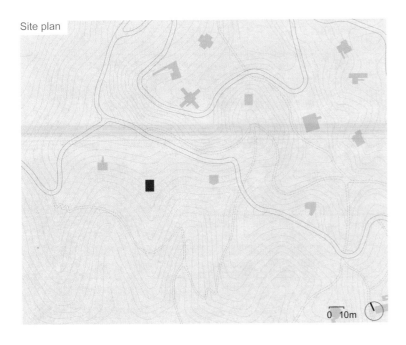

0 10m

Elevation

0   1m

The project is located in Qiyunshan Town, Anhui Province, one-hour drive from the renowned Mount Huangshan. In this small village with about 2000 local residents, tourism is not highly developed. There is only one newly-built hotel with a small number of tourists. Most of them sojourn here since the village is close to Mount Huangshan, which is their real destination. Mount Qiyun, 1.2 miles (two kilometers) away, is one of the sacred Taoist Mountains and also a famous scenic spot for its Danxia landform. Around the village, gentle mountains are densely covered with pine trees and there are no mosquitoes, even in summer. As a part of a distributed hotel, the project stands in the pine groves. The client hoped that the hotel rooms were independent from each other and only connected by meandering roads. Hotel rooms of the first phase were delegated to different architects. They shared three goals: for couples, families, and friend gatherings. This project outlines the couples' accommodation.

Nest

In the design, the architects imagined the couples' space as a nest among the trees, like a bag, with an opening towards the scenery. Its front is lifted a bit, rendering a sense of safeness. People need to pass through a dim entrance and climb into this space. It is so small that people can easily touch the ceiling. Couples can be embraced by this cozy container, like birds in the nest. There is no furniture other than a mattress.

Dualist form

The architects proposed many ideas at the initial stage around the theme of 'between objects and the house.' The camp stools, with crossed wooden legs as supports and canvas and hemp rope

tops, can be folded for easy carrying. The duality form comes from different requirements of the self-use part and supporting part. One can find similar inspiration from the Monument of Witches of Zumthor in Norway: a series of wooden supports pulled up a long tent; the slightly sloping roof shelters people from rain while the metal stays protect it against the tides. Other things in daily life, such as umbrellas, sailboats, suspension bridges, and kites, are integrated in such a way. The supports at the lower part of the dualist form are the load bearing part, while the form at the upper part is to meet the requirements of people, but the two parts are not simply juxtaposed but adapt to each other to offer flexibility.

Objects

The client of the project wasn't aspiring to a one-off unique building, but rather a prototype that could be freely placed in the mountains; one that could be duplicated and adapted to different topography with minor changes. Therefore, rather than a building, the architects viewed the structure as a subject, a piece of furniture, a deformed tent, or a bird nest. The architects regarded the design as a process of combining different objects. The bedroom is a soft and simple space. All the M&E and sanitary equipment is packed in a wooden box, like baggage, and both of them are supported by a self-standing structure.

Plan

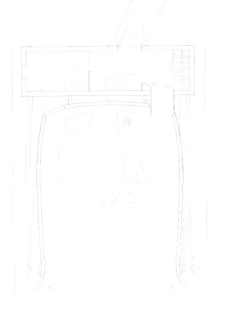

0   1m

Section

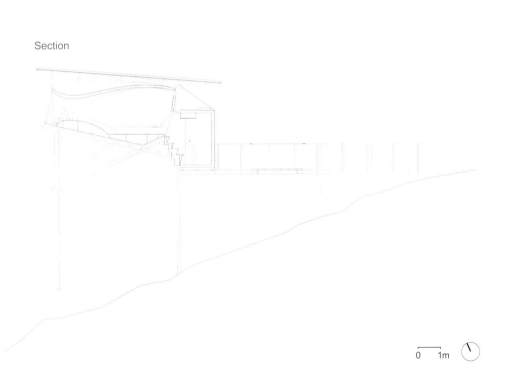

0   1m

Wattle School

Li Xiaodong
Li Xiaodong Atelier

Location Beijing, China
Gross building area 1884 ft² (175 m²)
Completion 2011

Site plan

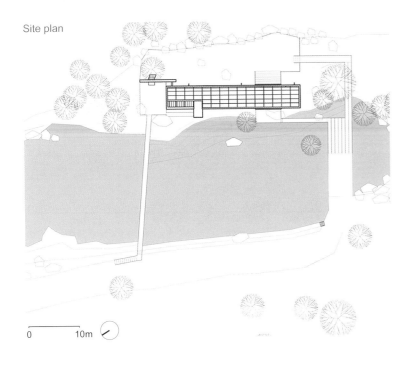

0   10m

Sketch

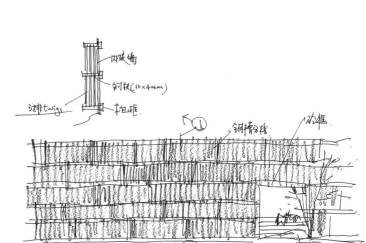

Located in Huairou town on the outskirts of Beijing city, the school was designed to provide a space for free readings and resource for tourists and villagers, while also being a simple hut and elegant garden for interaction between visitors and villagers.

Material

The main structure of Wattle School is welded square steel, while the fence uses tempered glass. The finished elevations were densely covered by 45,000 untreated wood sticks. Wood sticks are one of most abundant natural materials in the local area and also a fuel for heating and cooking for the local people. The use of this local material was environment-friendly while also allowing easy maintenance after long use. The steel and glass basic structure of the architectural elevations is ice-cold but looks more pleasing due to the well-arranged wood sticks. The color of wood sticks changes with the seasons and surrounding mountains. These long and thin sticks are arranged vertically and create gaps due to the varying sizes. The natural light is filtered and evenly illuminates the interior, ensuring lighting while shading the interior.

Space

The interior of the school is simple and direct. The main space consists of wide steps and bookshelves. The steps, with books under them, become a part of the bookshelf. There is a sunken discussion space with relative independence at each of the two ends. This huge area is actually a 98.4-foot (30-meter) long space without any partition or any furniture, thus giving people a more complete sense of space. The only screen is in the concrete door opening of the foyer. Entering the library, readers can take any book they like and find a place for quiet reading.

Sociality

Jiaojiehe village, surrounded with steep mountains, is located in a valley grown with chestnut, walnut, and pear trees. As the site is near Beijing, the young in the village leave the rural area to the city and make a living there. The elderly are left behind and often suffer from loneliness and poverty; as such, the situation in the little mountain village is not good. Fortunately, Hong Kong Lu Qianshou Trust fund donated ¥10 million to support rural projects, which is why the architects decide to build a public library. The original intention was to serve local villagers and make up for the lack of schools and libraries in the village. Now the library has broadened its influence. Some Beijing people drive two hours on weekends to visit it and the local people also benefit from this increased tourism by selling food and drinks.

West elevation

East elevation

South elevation

North elevation

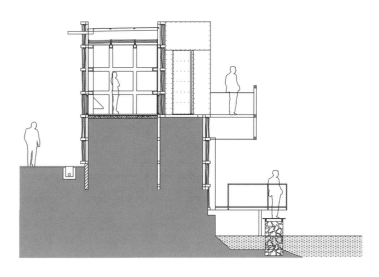

Section 1

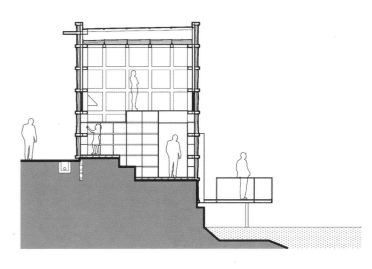

Section 2

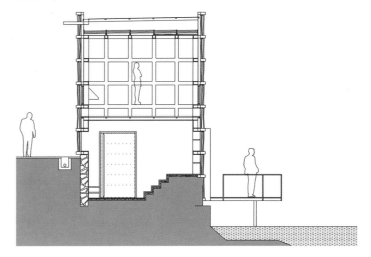

Section 3

Toilet door section Toilet door elevation Toilet door plan Exterior wall

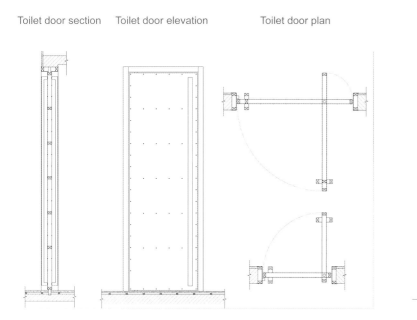
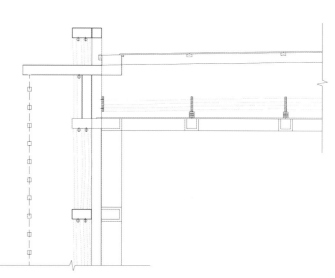

Roof plan

Second floor plan

1 Discussing
2 Reading

First floor plan

1 Reading
2 Storage
3 Rest room
4 Toilet

0   5m

XY Yunlu Resort Restaurant building

Liu Yuyang
Atelier Liu Yuyang Architects

Location Guilin, China
Gross building area 1830 ft² (170 m²)
Site area 39,826 ft² (3700 m²)
Completion 2014

Site plan

0   20m

Sketch

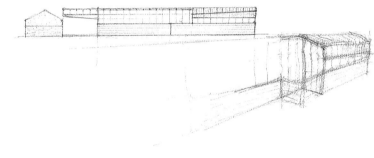

The project, located at Xingping Township Guangxi province, was rebuilt from several dilapidated farmhouses in a natural village and is concealed in the waters and mountains of Lijiang. The architecture gives respect to and takes a serious attitude toward the local culture and surrounding village, creating a natural coexistence of the hotel and its surrounding environment, and harmonious coexistence with the local people.

Time

The architects believed that time confers vitality and flexibility to architecture. With changes due to time and climate, instant flickering of light and shadow, the influences of wind and water, the meaning of architecture goes beyond visual images and forms expression. When it comes into the architectural entity, it becomes a dialogue between a series of spaces, materials, and atmosphere. The new part uses a more low-key architectural language. Its variable section steel structure and axial glass door and window system, together with rubble stones, carbonized wooden grills, and clay roof tiles, form a contrast with old rammed-earth architecture.

Place

The sense of place of a building originates from the specific elements of its location, which give it architectural and cultural meaning. The architecture with sense of place corresponds to the original context of

the place and defines a completely new spirit of place. In the design, the architects organized and rebuilt the narrow and disordered farmhouses and site, and reduced surplus separation between the hotel and surrounding farmhouses. Meanwhile, as the visiting guests are from cities, the coordination between unique experience of the place and living quality turns into the most remarkable feature in the design.

Use

The design covered site planning, construction of a new dining room, renovation of the dwellings, and the landscaping design. The architects rebuilt the five original dwellings into 27 guestrooms through the organization of the villages. The dining room is at the entrance of the hotel and oriented toward the central courtyard. The function and practicability of architectural spaces, on the one hand, reflects the inner demands and desires of people and, on the other, determines the value of the structure. The variable and invariable uses are not only real reasons for the existence of the architecture, but also fundamental conditions of the architectural beauty. The practicability is not defined by existing division of functions, but a result of actual actions in specific time and place.

Section of the restaurant

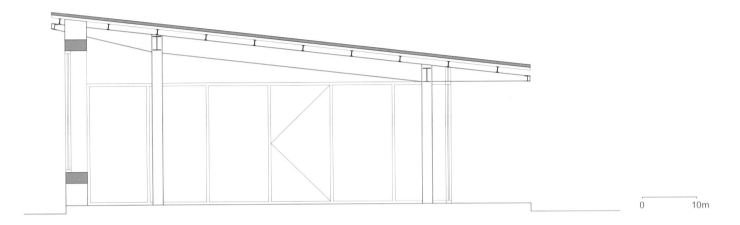

Restaurant plan

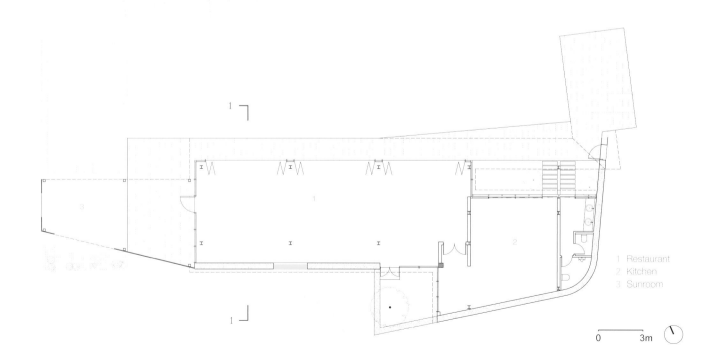

1 Restaurant
2 Kitchen
3 Sunroom

0   3m

Wencun Village

Wang Shu
Amateur Architecture Studio

Location Hangzhou, China
Completion 2016

Sketch

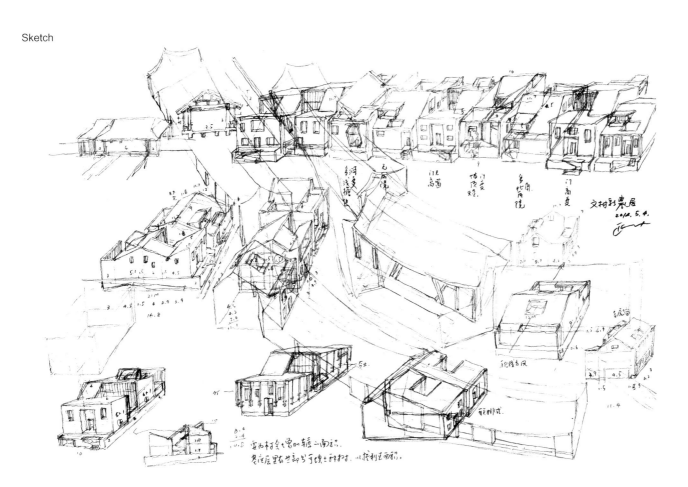

Located in Hangzhou, Zhejiang, the project involved the overall construction in Wencun Village, Dongqiao Township. Other than repairing and renovating the original old buildings and village spaces, over 10 rural houses were built to form a contrast with the original structures. The design, with consideration given to the actual needs of villagers, also embodied strong personal influences from the architect. The practice in Wencun is a trial on traditional practice. While respecting nature, the architecture explored how to make rural housing meet the needs of both modern and traditional living styles.

Inspiration

The legacy left by ancestors can often be preserved more completely by facing threats at any time. Wencun is a common village in the large country areas in Fuyang Zhejiang. The design team was invited to reconstruct the residence for the villagers. Inspiration for the design came from the traditions, natural waters, and mountains, as well as the ethical orders of the village. The villagers live beside waters, rising with the sun and going to bed when it gets dark. The design changed the physical form of the village while maintaining the traditional country life and atmosphere.

A house with a courtyard

The design of Wencun focused on the house and courtyard, spacial elements of such importance in settling down to secure and peaceful living. The design adapted to the local conditions and integrated the house with courtyard by juxtaposing, linking, interlocking, and dislocating. The compact and delicate courtyard allows the occupiers to get close to and abandon themselves to nature. The layout that follows a traditional living mode is quite pleasing and satisfying. The occupiers live in small spaces between the sky and the earth, and return to the true natural and peaceful country life.

Earth and tiles

Earth and tiles were not only used in a new way, but also kept their traditional meanings. The rammed-earth walls reintroduced natural fragrance into the rooms, while avoiding the coldness of concrete. Together with gray tiles and low eaves, they help retain the charm of a water village. The earth and tiles reappear in the villagers' life in a fresh way. Their familiar color and form are merged with the unique contemporary treatment.

Sketch

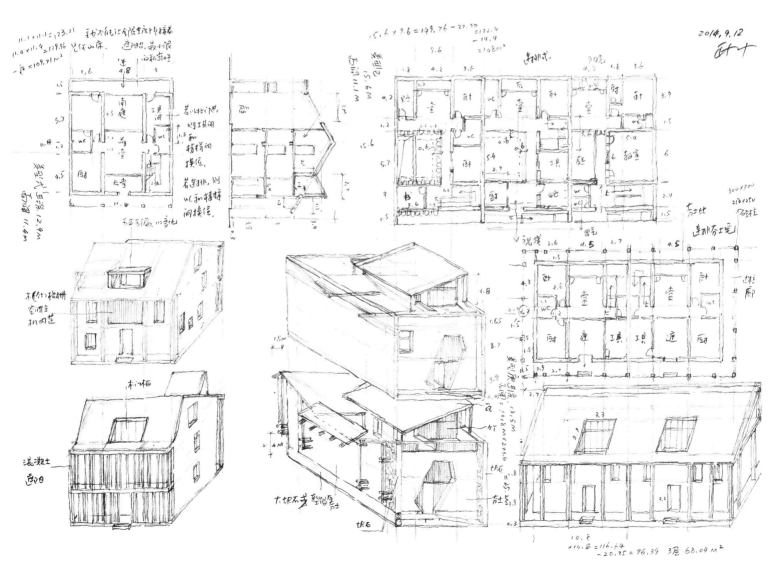

Brown sugar workshop

Xu Tiantian
DnA_Design and Architecture

Location Lishui, China
Gross building area 13,283 ft² (1234 m²)
Site area 14,090 ft² (1309 m²)
Completion 2016

Site plan

Land expropriation line
Property line

The project for this brown sugar workshop—situated in Xing village in the Zhejiang province—used a design inspired by the traditional sugar workshop industry with rich local characteristics. This workshop not only offers functions of production and exhibition, but is also a place for holding activities and has promoted the development of local tourism.

Functions

Brown sugar workshops in Xing village are production factories for brown sugar, places for village activity and cultural exhibition, and important spaces for connecting villages and fields. Near Damushan Tea Garden, brown sugar is an important industry in the village. Villagers maintain the ancient workmanship of brown sugar with over 100 years of history. Their products are widely welcomed in the laboring areas.

The project attempted to gather the industry in the village, change the disordered situation, and integrate it harmoniously into local daily life. Workshops, as a transitional extension of villages and surrounding farmland, are places where the villagers can enjoy farmland landscape while engaging in production activities. Additionally, these spaces can also be places for rest for villagers in idle times, as well as for visitors passing through, who can learn about the traditional culture of the village and experience a poetic ruralism and village life.

Ruralism

The villagers can freely participate in the creation of the workshop production environment. The buildings use construction materials seen everywhere, such as red bricks and bamboo wood as well as the most common structural form-light steel structure. As a response to, and extension of, ink and wash paintings on the walls of the village, the glass surfaces of sugar workshops in Xing village are attached with line drawings, which describe the production process of brown sugar. The line drawings, plus the production scene inside the workshop and the surrounding farming scene form a dynamic rural long scroll. This low-tech way of construction makes the architecture blend naturally in the local living environment from the origin. The materials are localized and the form simplified. The structure is not remarkable, but it effectively improves the overall appearance of the village.

Performance

The production activities in sugar workshops in Xing village are also living scenes. The control of light and dark effect in the lighting design creates a spatial atmosphere similar to that of the gallery and makes the daily production of sugar become a show activity. The spatial design with open visual lines transforms the production site into a performance theater and creates an exhibition of scenes, farmland and site for both the inside and the outside.

Some small workshops are put together in the space, which were originally scattered around the village. This underlies the value of traditional culture and can be called a museum for dynamic exhibition. The performance and exhibition characters give the workshop characteristics of stage. The workshop is not only a stage for village production activity but also a stage for village life and poetic ruralism. It can help build villagers' confidence, increase their income through village tourism, and even create a totally new experience for tourists.

Elevation 1

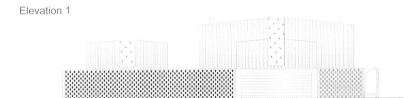

Elevation 2

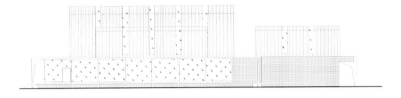

Elevation 3

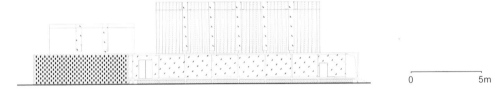

0   5m

Spatial analysis

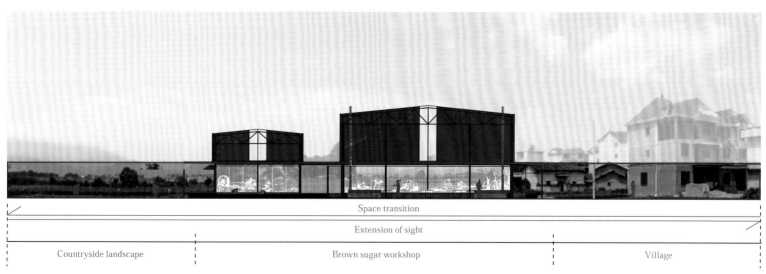

Space transition

Extension of sight

Countryside landscape   Brown sugar workshop   Village

Section 1-1

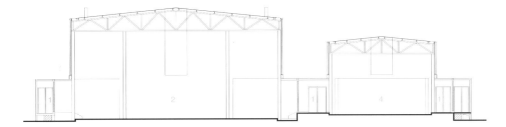

1 Corridor
2 Traditional brown sugar production area
3 Display area
4 Garden
5 Office
6 Washroom
7 Packaging room
8 Sample room

Section 2-2

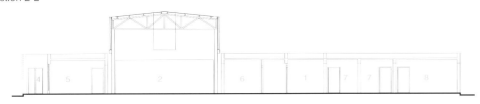

0   5m

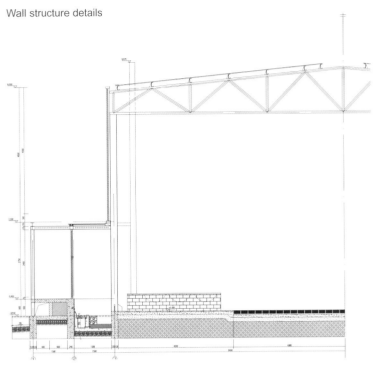

Wall structure details

First floor plan

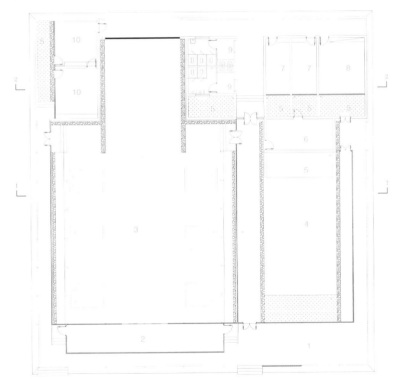

Second floor plan

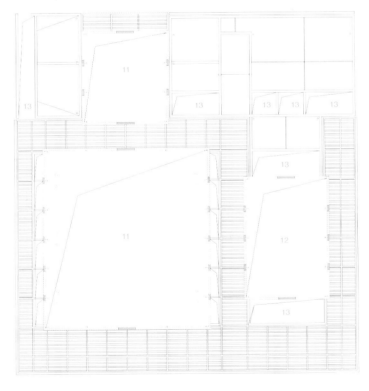

1 Corridor
2 Drying area
3 Traditional brown sugar production area
4 Display area
5 Garden
6 Tool room
7 Packaging room
8 Sample room
9 Washroom
10 Office
11 Space over traditional brown sugar production area
12 Space over display area
13 Space over garden

0   5m

Ruralation Shenaoli Library

Zhang Lei
AZL Architects

Location Tonglu, China
Gross building area 7890 ft² (733 m²)
Site area 3767 ft2 (350 m2)
Completion 2015

Village texture

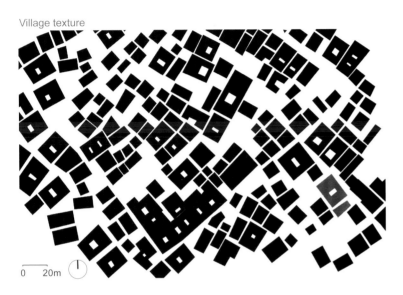

0   20m

This project, the first built product of Eshan Practice, is located at the ancient Shenao village in Hangzhou. This village has a 1900-year history with the blood of the Shentu Family. The project took the ancient house of Jingsong Hall, built in the late Qing Dynasty, as the main body with the surrounding dwellings taken into consideration during its reconstruction and renovation. It demonstrated the texture of the historical exterior surface and meanwhile kept the basic layout and beautiful wooden carvings of the traditional architecture. In this way, it created a comfortable and contemporary interior space.

Native order

The vitality and sentimental power of the rural settlement environment and its history and traditional context of 'native order' are rooted in Chinese regional reality. This living style based on the time axis and the continuation of the cultural environment is different from the concept of an historical site that faces historical urban block in the Western architectural world. Nor is it an exploration on the ecological technology that treats the village as a natural conservation area.

In this project, the understanding of, respect to, and continuation of this order was one of the keys that could integrate the new building into the local environment in a humble and appropriate posture. The architects had the responsibility of integrating the design into the setting, while also highlighting the distance between the new and the old architectures and allowing them to underline each other by giving respect to the native order.

Reconstruction of the community

The by-product of fast development of Chinese cities is the disappearance of communities. In the daily life of urban people, individuals gradually turn inward and the original neighbor relationship no longer exists. The assertion of the rural community

relationship is increasingly isolated from declining material environments and the relationship gradually turns loose due to backwardness of the spatial quality of the built environment. Therefore, the reshaping of community spirit and the reconstruction of neighboring relationship were urgent.

In this project, the strong lineage and geographical relationships of rural settlements created opportunities for working on the job. Jingsong Hall, the main body in this renovation project, was originally divided into six independent households, but during the reconstruction, some original partition boards were removed and a cut-through hall was built. This change of architectural space made the original living environment more open and attempted to promote the reshaping of neighbor relationships.

Local construction

Local construction is a way for architects to utilize the local construction tradition while learning the local craftsman tradition. The contemporary culture, which heavily relies on technical products, refuses the original relationship between the construction and people; simultaneously, the architects have to think about whether local craftsman traditions are necessary and reasonable when facing irresistible rural reality.

Local construction traditions, as crafts passed down through thousands of years, are the wisdom and skills used by residents in dealing with natural, climatic, and geographic conditions. For the architects, these crafts still have referential value in local construction. Meanwhile, as contemporary architects, there is space for improvement for the combination of traditional crafts with local styles. The last possible result is a modern structure that respects the local construction order and has contemporary characters.

Northwest elevation

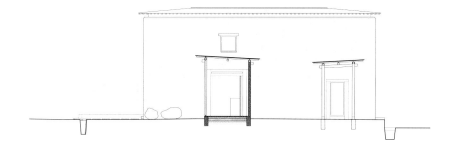

Northeast elevation

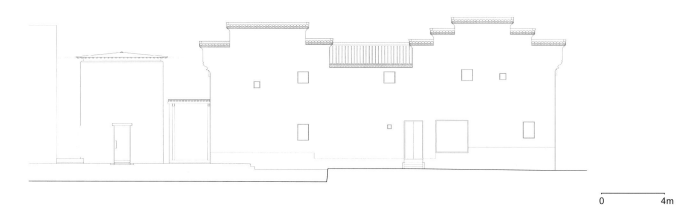

0　　　　　　4m

Section 1

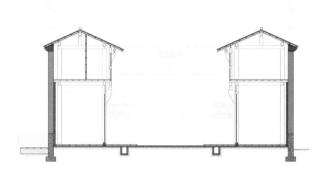

Section 2

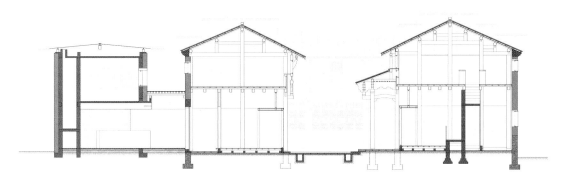

Second floor plan

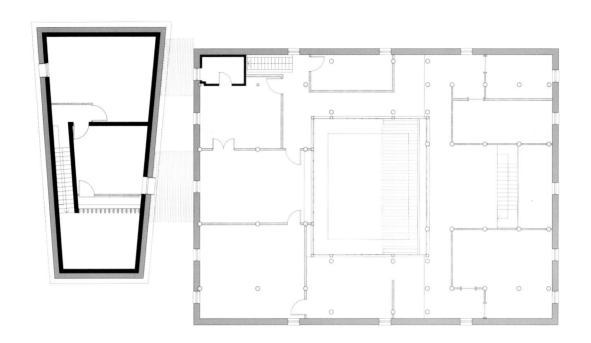

First floor plan

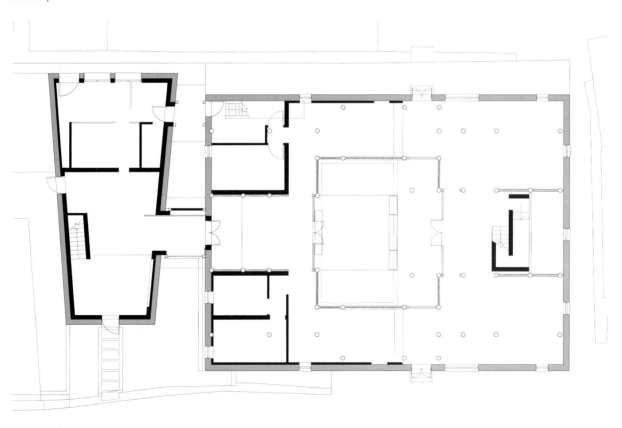

Niyang River Visitor Center

Zhao Yang
Zhaoyang Architects+ZAO+standard architecture

Location Tibet, China
Gross building area 4628 ft² (430 m²)
Site area 4628 ft² (430 m²)
Completion 2009

Site plan

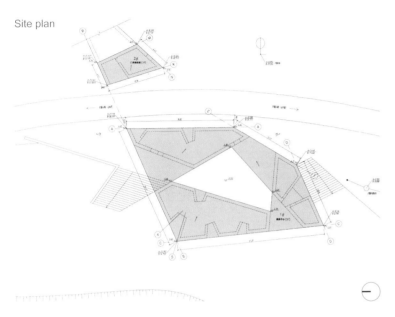

Sketch

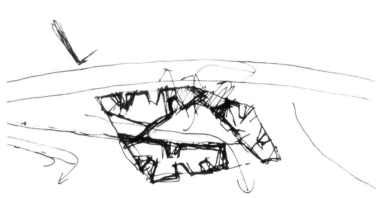

The project, located at the riverbank of Niyang River in Linzhi Tibet, is the entrance of scenic spot at Niyang River. It serves as a ticket office, a changing room for whitewater rafting, and visitor bathrooms.

Place

The Mirui highroad, where the building is located, cuts off the relationship between the river and the mountain. Therefore, how to rebuild the relationship between the isolated place and its surrounding environment was the primary problem in the design. Seen horizontally, the clear straight lines of the west and north sides of the building face the open river valley, while the continual broken line of the southeast façade corresponds to the orientation of the highroad and the turn of the mountain. The form of the interior is cut from the irregular volume wrapped by exterior outlines. The interior space is centered on an irregular square courtyard, which is connected with four openings in the architecture, corresponding to the orientation of the landscape and arrangement of movement lines. The remaining interior room after cutting contains three functions of the building: ticket office, changing room for whitewater rafting, and bathroom. This seemingly random plan, in fact, was subject to limits of movement lines, functions, and site conditions. The geometric characters of the form and space build a relationship between the architecture and the place.

Construction

The whole project used and developed traditional construction techniques of Tibetan dwellings. Above the concrete foundation are 23.6-inch (60-centimeter) thick rubble load-bearing walls. Most door and window openings were deeply cut into the walls. The walls at both sides of the openings, such as buttress walls, increase the whole rigidity of the structure and also reduce the span of the interior space.

The roof uses a wooden structure of a free beam and purlin system. The wooden beam with larger span is spliced together by 7.9 x 11.8-inch (20 x 30-centimeter) wooden strips. The waterproof membrane is covered with 5.9-inch (15-centimeter) thick aga clay. Aga clay is a common roof-waterproofing material in Tibetan architecture. The loose clay, hardened after adding water and repeated beating, forms a reliable roof waterproofing and insulation layer. The architects took advantage of the plastic property of aga clay to make eaves gutter inside the cornice. They also used channel steel rainwater outlets to build an organized drainage system.

Ambience

The architects introduced a single-color device into the public space of the building. They applied Tibetan mineral paint directly upon the rubble wall surface and highlighted the geometric changes of spaces through changes of colors. From sunrise to sunset, sunlight from different directions and elevating angles enters the building through varied openings. Walking through the building, people can experience a constantly changing color effect at different angles and hours. The interaction of sunlight and mineral pigments in the plateau creates a spatial atmosphere in the building. These colors don't have symbolic meanings in Tibetan traditional culture. They simply strengthen the spatial experience in a simple and abstract way, and shimmer with charm that is different from that of the performance of the device playing with colors in the building.

Section

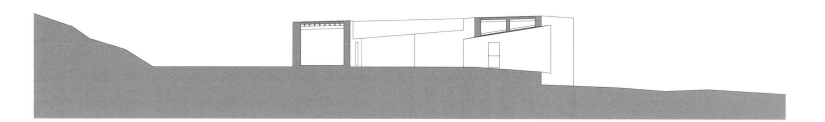

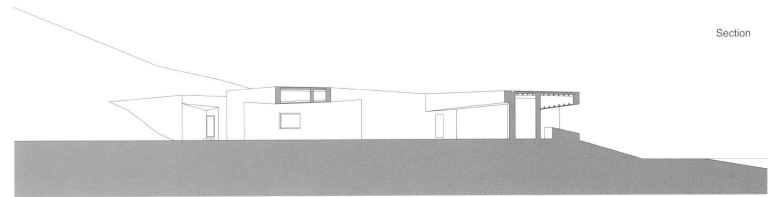

Section

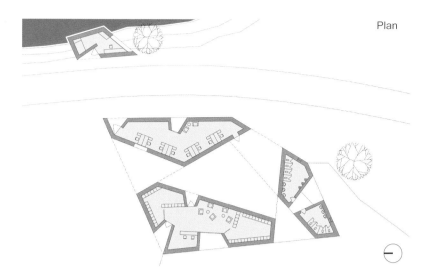

Plan

Details

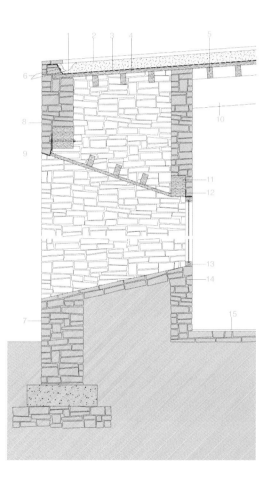

1   Gutter shaped with aga clay
2   5.9in (150mm) aga clay working as thermal insulation, waterproofing
     and protection for the SBS waterproofing underneath
3   SBS waterproofing
4   Larch board 1.97in (50mm)
5   Larch rafter 5.9in×3.15in (150mm×80mm)
6   Channel steel scupper 1.97in×3.94in (50mm×100mm)
7   Natural stone wall 17in (450mm)
8   Larch beam 12in×12in (300mm×300mm)
9   Stone holder and 0.31in (8mm) drip edge made from steel panel
10   Larch beam 15.75in×7.87in (400mm×200mm)
11   Larch beam 11.81in×7.87in (300mm×200mm)
12   Stone finishing holder made from corner steel 3.94in×3.94in (100mm×100 mm)
13   0.31in (8mm) thick security glass panel
14   14 Larch window frame 3.94in×2.96in (100mm×70mm)
15   0.79in (20mm) thick cement floor

Digital ▶

The interaction between traditional values underpinning the architectural discipline and new technological innovation has provided new opportunities for contemporary Chinese architecture firms to review their modes of practice. Innovation in digital design and building technologies, including 3D printing, kinetic architecture, BIM system, and parametric architecture, has greatly influenced the way Chinese architects conceptualize and execute their designs.

The organization of several international digital architecture workshops in China over the last three years and the parametric design features that characterize recently completed buildings come together to reflect the technological changes adopted by the profession. Recent developments in 3D-printed concrete houses in China also reveal the potential for further industrialization and mass production. Both parametric tools and BIM construction technologies will continue to impact the broader culture of Chinese architectural practices and their decisions around form-making.

Harbin Opera House

Ma Yansong,
Dang Qun, Yosuke Hayano,
MAD Architects

Location Harbin, China
Gross building area 446 acres (180 hectares)
Site area 19.5 acres (7.9 hectares)
Completion 2015

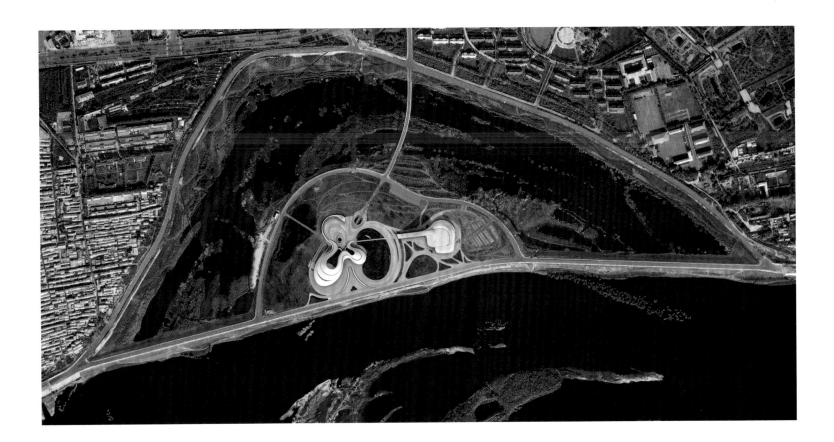

Situated in the cultural central island Songbei in Harbin at the north riverbank of Songhua River, the site includes a big theater, a small theater, an underground garage, and attached supporting houses. The building, with a steel structure envelope, features an irregular double curved surface design and is an iconic structure in Harbin.

Earth landscape

The Harbin Opera House is located at the north riverbank of Songjiang River. Its architectural design was inspired by its surrounding wetland natural views and characters of the snowing north region. Like a flowing ribbon, it grows from the natural landscape and becomes a part of the rolling white skyline of the north. In contrast to the urban skyline of south Songhua River, the beauty and uniqueness of nature make Harbin Opera House functional and an earth landscape integrated with culture, art, and nature.

Relation with nature

The glass skylight in the theater roof allows maximum natural light into the interior. Natural light shines on the ash-tree wood paneled walls of the theater atrium and highlights the ingenuity of these pure-handmade walls of local materials. Wherever people go, they can feel the transparency and emptiness brought about by pouring light. The backstage of the small theater is designed to be built with transparent soundproof glass, which makes the outdoor natural environment an extension and background of the stage and provides new possibilities for it. The interior of the big theater is mainly clad with local ash-tree wood. Its soft and warm atmosphere, natural texture, and variable organic forms allow people to feel the vitality of the space.

Interaction and participation

Different from general iconic buildings that stand lonely in cities, Harbin Opera House is a familiar structure that can be accessed in all directions. The architects intentionally underlined the interaction and participation of the residents in the design. The outdoor theater and the viewing platform at the roof of the building are open to the public and a vertical extension of the park, enjoying the views of south Songhua River and the urban skyline to the north, as well as the surrounding natural landscape. Even without entering the theater to watch performances, citizens can still walk to the roof along the ramp, encircling the building from the nearby park and square. They can personally feel the dramatic experience and artistic conception of the big theater.

Grand theater longitudinal section

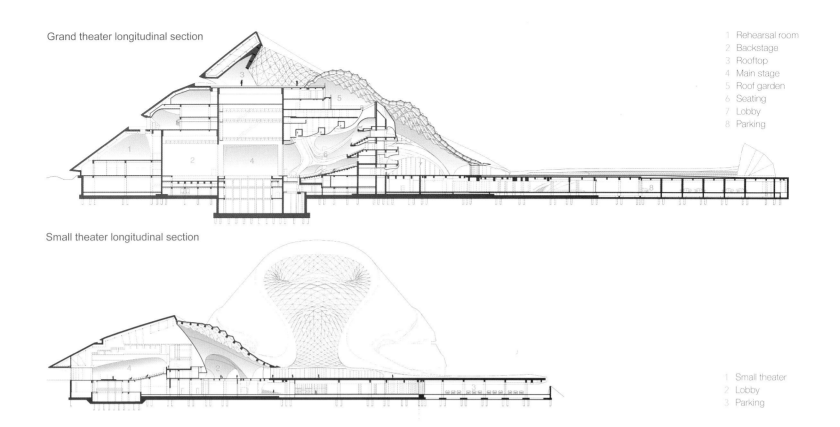

1 Rehearsal room
2 Backstage
3 Rooftop
4 Main stage
5 Roof garden
6 Seating
7 Lobby
8 Parking

Small theater longitudinal section

1 Small theater
2 Lobby
3 Parking

Grand theater transversal section

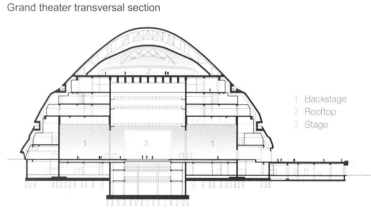

1 Backstage
2 Rooftop
3 Stage

0   20m

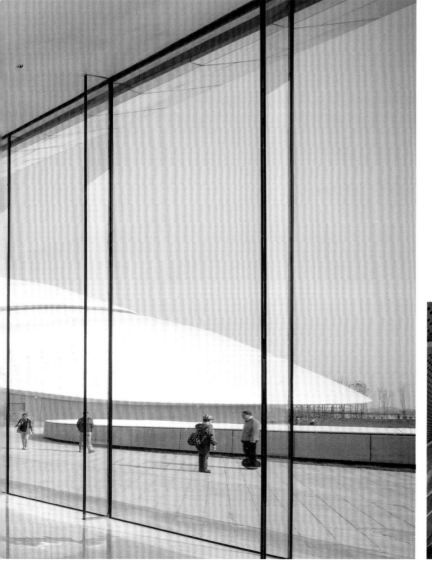

Roof plan

Second floor plan

1 Rehearsal room

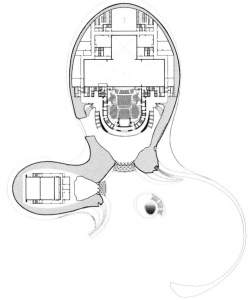

First floor plan

1 Lobby
2 Grand theater
3 Small theater
4 Rehearsal room
5 Entry to parking
6 Stair to parking
7 Plaza

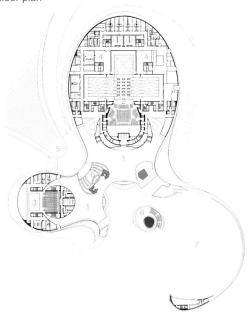

0   20m

Phoenix Center

Shao Weiping
Beijing Institute of Architectural Design
(Group) Co., Ltd

Location Beijing, China
Gross building area 780,146 ft²
(72,478 m²)
Site area 202,588 ft² (18,821 m²)
Completion 2013

Site plan

Top view of roof

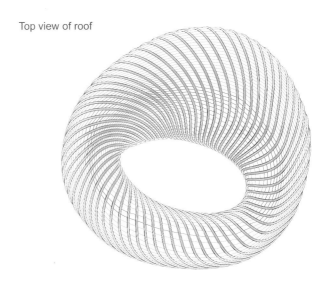

The project, which is 180 feet (55 meters) high, is located in the southwest corner in Chaoyang, Beijing with a ground area of 4.4 acres (1.8 hectare) and total building area of 699,654 square feet (72,478 square meters). Phoenix International Media Center is a comprehensive building that combines multi-functions of TV program manufacturing, office and business spaces. In this project, the architects integrated high-floor office spaces with media studios with the help of a diagram of Moebius Strip. It provides program production sites and other accessory service facilities in all respects, creating a complete space and volume. The unique architectural form and natural landscape of Chaoyang Park are organically combined into a whole.

Openness

The architects believed that a building with contemporary meanings should show open characteristics. The openness refers to openness of the environment, city, and people. A building must give consideration to its relative relationship with the environment and is also required to open to the environment and build a dialogue with it. For example, the curved skin and surrounding spaces in this design form a soft boundary, corresponding bending roads, traffic flows, and natural trees. Simultaneously, the openness is expressed in the organization of functions and spaces.

For people walking in the building, it is also very important to create a flowing and unobstructed public space. Thus, people could feel the interaction between the interior space and exterior environment. With movement lines connecting the ground and the roof, people can also experience the openness of the building in their walking.

Precision

In modern times of high science and technology, a new meaning of humanization is the accuracy of design. An accurate design, or an accurate geometric relationship that expresses a design, can turn out a beautiful result. It can make modern science and technology serve people and meet their requirements. These exquisite consumption products have already been used in the manufacturing industry and brought enormous influence to life. Phoenix Center intends to use CATIA software platform, which are usually used only in airplane, ship, and vehicle-manufacturing industries, to construct a building to industrial building precision. It creates delicate and accurate details in all accessible, touchable, and visible ranges, including many systems such as structure, skin, and decoration, to meet the requirements of a high-quality space.

Digitization

In Phoenix Center, the accurate project control based on information models and data analysis is realized and digital information technology is applied in the whole construction process for the first time in China. First, it builds highly accurate architectural information models; second, it makes adjustments of project models with parameter-preset technology through a geometric control system. Third, the non-loss information interaction of architecture models is the key link of an efficient information system and can generally adapt to and be applied in all stages of the project. The design helps to realize the digitized docking of design, manufacturing, and construction companies. With information models, construction projects with paperless detailed designs and processing can successful meet standards of accurate project control.

West elevation

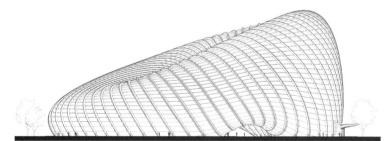

East elevation

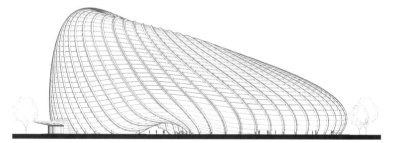

North elevation

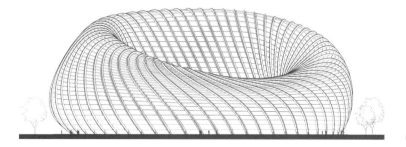

South elevation

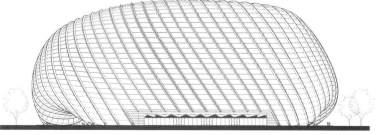

Section 1

Section 2

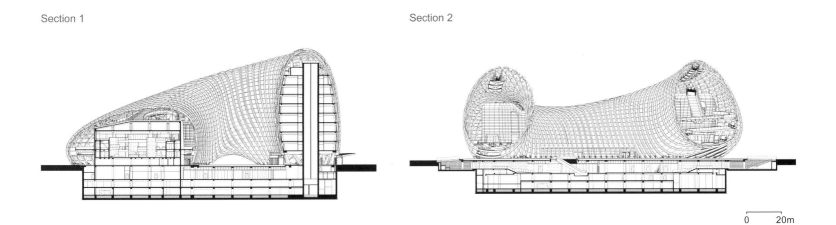

0   20m

411

Underground first floor

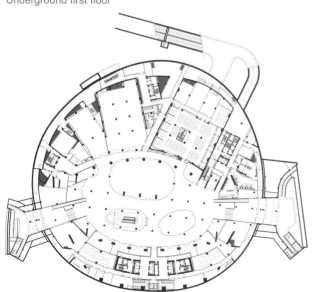

First floor plan

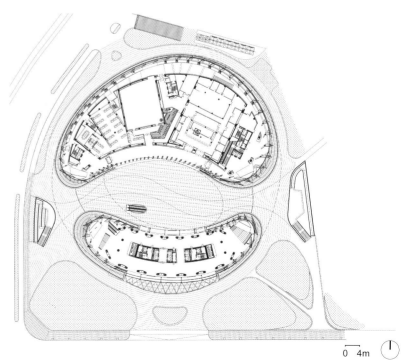

0 4m

Foshan Art Village

Song Gang, Zhong Guanqiu, Zhu Zhiyuan
Atelier cnS

Location Foshan, China
Gross building area 37,674 ft² (3500 m²)
Site area 236,806 ft² (22,000 m²)
Completion 2013

Site plan

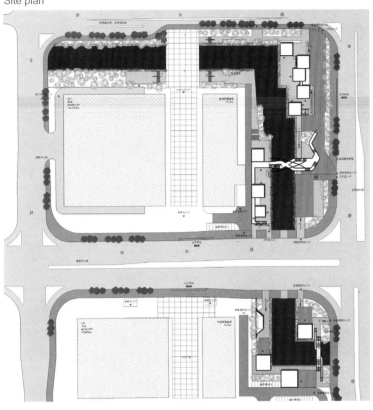

Site plan

The project, located at Foshan city Guangdong, consists of more than 10 square architectural volumes established according to the principles defined in the plan. It is situated south of Youth Palace and west of Foshan Century Lotus Stadium. The buildings were arranged along the riverbanks and function as artist workshops, galleries, art museums, art shops, art squares, and so on. They are workshops for local artists in Foshan and also provide places for people to enjoy indoor and outdoor recreation and entertainment activities. Further, these spaces with different functions can also supplement the surrounding cultural facilities. Judged from their density and spatial morphology, the project also serves was a green space for the cultural mall.

Parametric surface

The volume of the building is a square box; therefore, the key to the design was the creation of its skin. The architects drew some characteristic art symbols from some local art works in Foshan. They use parametric tools, too, for a new interpretation. Considering sunlight and uses of spaces, all patterns finally formed a variable skin, which is related with the layout and architectural functions of the interior. Ten different buildings use 10 varied skins. These skins, like the expressions of buildings, add artistic characters to the art village. At the same time, the architects paid special attention to the sense of volume formed in the skin itself. With uneven skin, it finished the transformation from 2D skin to a 3D volume.

Digital construction

The construction of skins was a key in the construction. The architects first divided the skin. It used a simple vertical and horizontal keel structure and the sizes of the members were determined according to the dimensions of the keels. The material of the skin was simplified metal or glass fiber reinforced plastic according to their positions. Taking the most complicate skin as an example, it was finally simplified into five types of standard modules. When the standard modules were decided, the manufacturing factory constructed them as per the technique requirements of the materials. By using skin modules of glass fiber reinforced plastic, the factory made corresponding wooden modules, and then made rolling-overs with these wooden modules. The modules manufactured by the factory were then classified and marked with a number, and finally transported to the construction site for assembly.

Section G

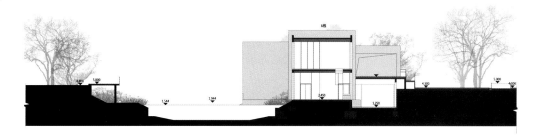

Section H

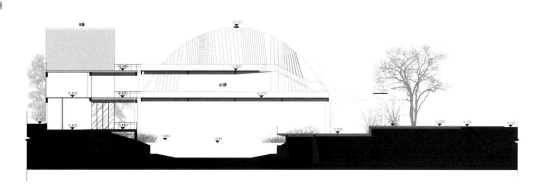

Section J

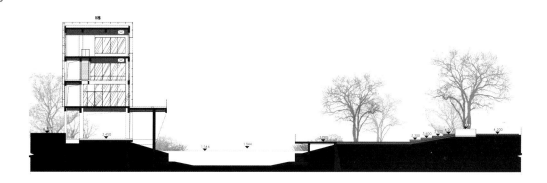

0   5m

Section 1-1

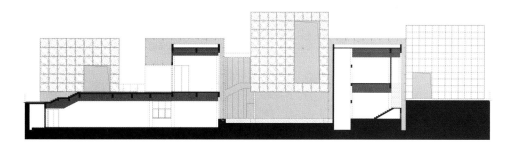

Section 2-2

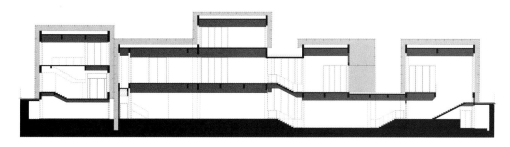

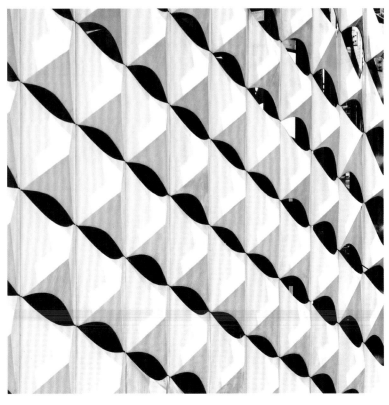

First floor plan of Building A

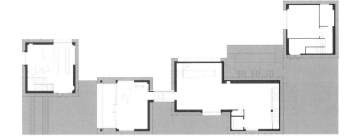

Plans

Sections

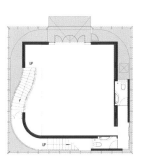

Underground first plan of Building A

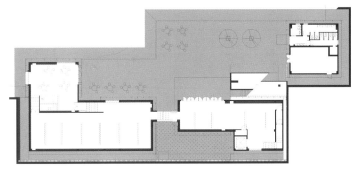

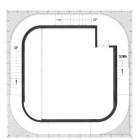

Master plan of Building A

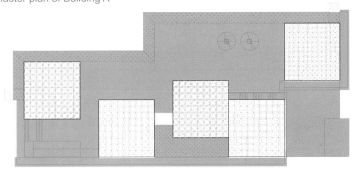

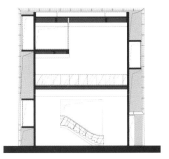

Service Center of International Horticultural Exposition 2014 Qingdao

Wang Zhenfei, Wang Luming
HHD_FUN

Location Qingdao, China
Gross building area 170,264 ft²
(15,818 m²)
Site area 655,522 ft² (60,900 m²)
Completion 2014

Site plan of Tianshui visitor center

0   50m

Site plan of Dichi visitor center

0   50m

The two service centers, located at Qingdao Shandong, are major buildings of the International Horticultural Exposition 2014. The buildings are situated at and named respectively after the two original lakes—Tianshui and Dichi—in Baiguo Mountain. They are multi-functional structures for the gathering of people, holding of activities, catering, cultural transmission, and exhibitions.

Rules

An ordered complexity was what the architects pursued in previous projects. The construction of the two buildings in this project were based on certain rules. The trigeminal node system and diamond-mesh system used by the architects are two very flexible and open geometric systems. Both allow changes in certain range, and thus allow architects, through smartly operating the system, to solve design problems and meanwhile generate complicated architectural and landscape systems.

High-tech design

In the two buildings, high-tech design becomes a major tool. The architects cleverly used a carefully selected geometric system and computerized algorithm to generate the design. Taking advantage of high-tech design, a carefully designed system could solve both architectural and constructional problems.

Low-tech construction

As most buildings are construction activities that are finished in a very short time by low-skilled workers, architectural designs must use low-tech construction tools to control construction time and cost. But even under the current conditions of China, a good construction system could make the realization of a complicate architectural volume possible.

Section of Tianshui visitor center

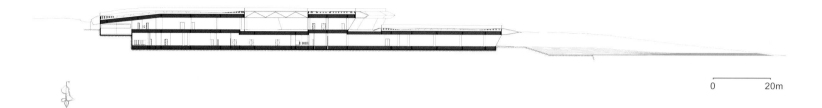

0   20m

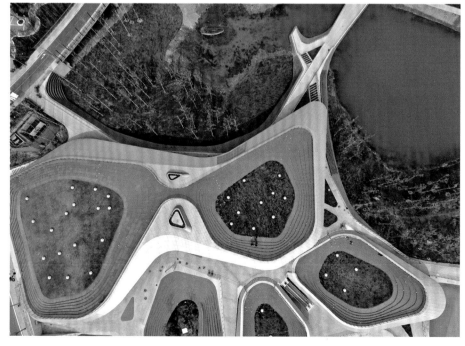

Floor plans of Tianshui Service Center

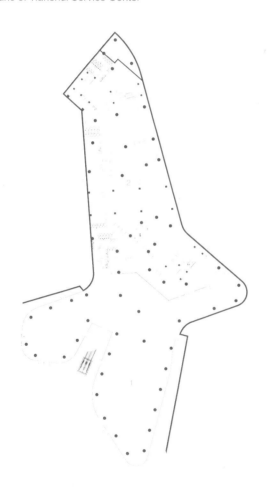

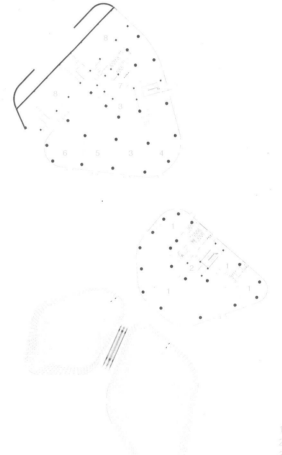

1 Restaurant
2 BOH area
3 Supermarket
4 The tourist information center
5 Shop
6 Medical treatment
7 Office
8 Equipment room

0   20m

Section of Dichi visitor center

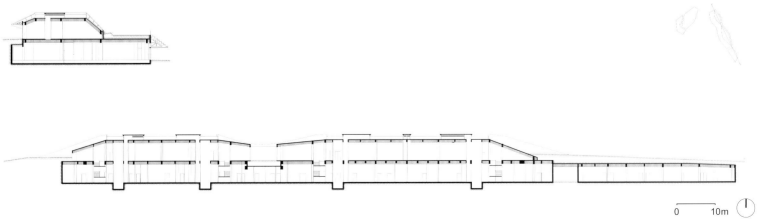

0   10m

First floor plan   Second floor plan

 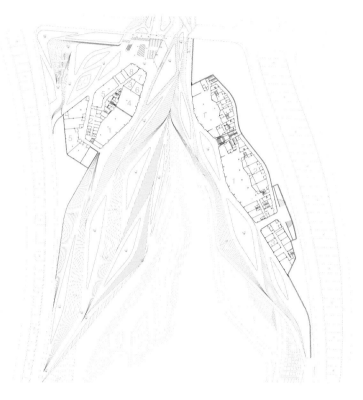

1 Restaurant   5 Shop
2 BOH area   6 Medical treatment
3 Supermarket   7 Office
4 The tourist information center   8 Equipment room

0   20m

Fab-Union Space

Philip F. Yuan
Archi-union Architects

Location Shanghai, China
Gross building area 3961 ft² (368 m²)
Site area 2045 ft² (190 m²)
Completion 2015

Site plan

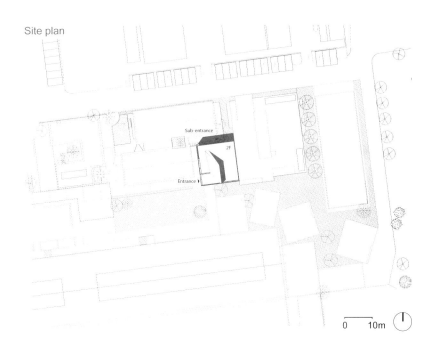

0   10m

Diagrams

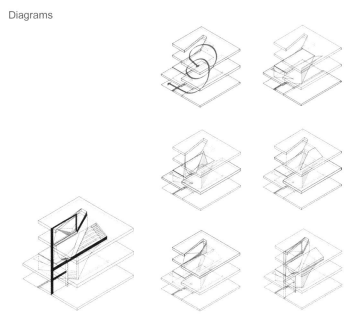

The project, a small house with an area of 3229 square feet (300 square meters), is located at the riverfront north of West Bund Arts Center in Xuhui, Shanghai. It is adjacent to some architectural design offices and art organizations. For the purposes of reducing vestment into the project and improving the efficiency of the whole space, the project was divided into two long spaces horizontally at the early stage of design. The floor slabs at different levels at both sides could provide as much possible usable area and create corresponding flexibility for possible future uses such as exhibition and office work.

Parametric regional practice

In the design of West Bund Fab-Union Space, the architects attempted to accurately define the functional meaning of geometric parameters through digitized graphic-design thinking. Meanwhile, the design made the most of traditional building materials and improved original timber footwork concrete casting techniques so as to carry out critical practice of form-shaping. The most remarkable contribution made by the design was that it underpins the important role played by digitized construction in the construction process and in innovation of workmanship. It organically combines the rough material characteristics with accurate geometric definition and expresses the basic value of architectural quality.

Functional aesthetics

Through the design and construction practice of Fab-Union Space, the architects attempted to understand the architecture–structure relationship as architectural structurology. Here, the functional value of the structure becomes a completely new aesthetic target. The 45.9-foot (14-meter) long spatial span of the building is supported

by a central vertical stair, and the 14.8-foot (4.5-meter) or 10.8-foot (3.3-meter) high spaces at both sides also need to be effectively connected with each other through it. The design was renewed and improved through bi-directional evolutionary structural optimization (BESO) and endeavored to make the structural distribution more efficient and correspond with structural logic. In such way, the whole process with improved structural performance became an important support of spatial formation. Meanwhile, the core transportation body also used a natural air-dispensation mechanism to further improve itself and meet maximum functional requirements for the ventilation system in the whole building during transition seasons.

Digitized construction

Considering that there was a four-month deadline for the design and construction of the whole building, the designers had to deal with low-tech construction companies that mainly used manual construction techniques and offered complete guidance that traditional drawings cannot supply throughout the construction process. To serve this purpose, the architects developed a new interactive-positioning method with digital and physical models as well as a measuring method to guide the construction progress.

Additionally, in viewing of the economical efficiency of putting up scaffolding for casting concrete, 75 percent of the structural surface was matched into straight grain curves and two-thirds of the straight grain formwork could be repeatedly used in concrete casting. Thus, the construction progress was efficiently accelerated and the cost decreased. Furthermore, for the remaining 25 percent double curve formwork, CNC digital construction tools were used to accurately match the surfaces.

Evolutionary structural optimization

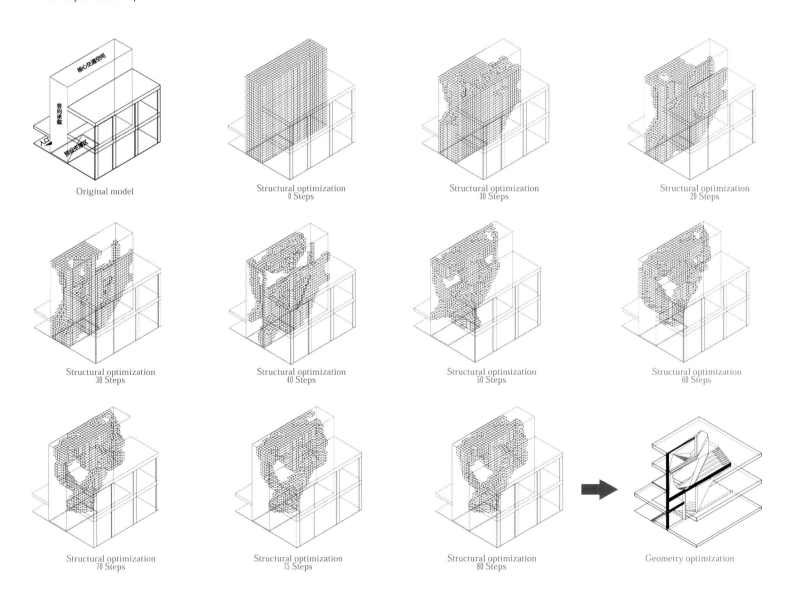

Original model

Structural optimization
0 Steps

Structural optimization
10 Steps

Structural optimization
20 Steps

Structural optimization
30 Steps

Structural optimization
40 Steps

Structural optimization
50 Steps

Structural optimization
60 Steps

Structural optimization
70 Steps

Structural optimization
75 Steps

Structural optimization
80 Steps

Geometry optimization

Initial airflow pattern at the central part

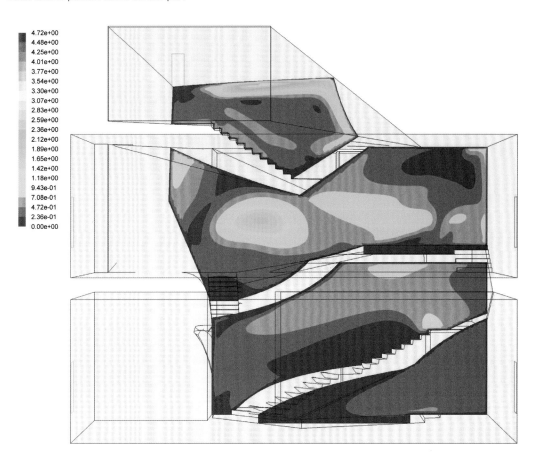

4.72e+00	
4.48e+00	
4.25e+00	
4.01e+00	
3.77e+00	
3.54e+00	
3.30e+00	
3.07e+00	
2.83e+00	
2.59e+00	
2.36e+00	
2.12e+00	
1.89e+00	
1.65e+00	
1.42e+00	
1.18e+00	
9.43e-01	
7.08e-01	
4.72e-01	
2.36e-01	
0.00e+00	

South elevation

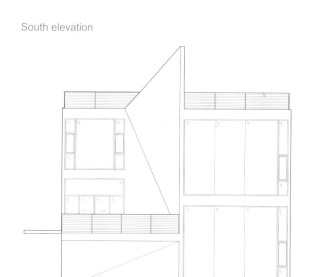

Section 3-3

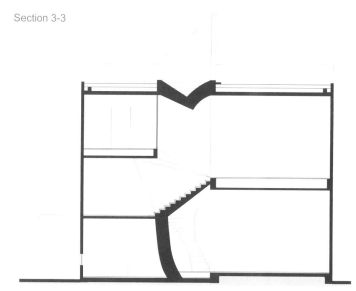

First floor plan

Second floor plan

0   5m

Chinese New Architecture Exhibition at Harvard

Wang Shu, a Pritzker winner, and Lu Wenyu, his wife and partner, were invited by the Royal College of Art as the only guest speakers of its architectural seminar in the summer of 2016. The seminar has always been seen as a grand finale of RA Summer Exhibitions. It was the first time ever that native Chinese architects are invited by this old British academy. Undoubtedly, by that time, the rapid rise of Chinese architectural culture had already caught the eye of local art festivals in Britain.

It is worthy of congratulations that Wang and Lu have gained a reputation abroad. Yet in the autumn of 2016, Wang's works were again exhibited at Harvard with much more fanfare. Other than Wang Shu, there were another 60 Chinese architects, presenting their architectural works in joint efforts. The exhibition of Towards a Critical Pragmatism: Contemporary Chinese Architecture affords, like a suddenly unrolled long scroll, the dazzling achievement of contemporary Chinese architecture in great details.

Li Xiangning, the curator of the exhibition, has such a great ambition that he introduced many young architects from all over China. On the one hand, he called together architects born in different ages after the reform and opening of China, which was an influential act almost like a comprehensive expression of Chinese contemporary history; and on the other hand, he smartly built through this exhibition seamless connections between Chinese architectural works and Western contemporary Architectural traditions. Li Xiangning, also a big name, is a professor of Tongji University's College of Architecture and Urban Planning and guest professor of Harvard University Graduate School of Design. He has such a good understanding of Oriental and Western cultures, history, languages, customs and characters that he can weave with high proficiency an enchanting new drawing of Chinese contemporary architecture.

Li Xiangning is aware that the mid-aged generation of architects (an architect is not old until he is 70 or 80 years old, as architectural projects usually take a long time to finish), has already accomplished the missions of challenging the mainstream and overturning the conservative mode in the last three to four decades. The act that they found their own studios to replace the stiff state-owned design institutes with hundreds of designers was a great breakthrough. Then young architects followed suit to create excellent works through China. He wrote in a recent issue of Time Architecture that "today, independent architects with private practices form their own communities and circles around several major cities. Most of them are backbone force at the age of 40s and 50s." That was quite true.

Presently, the most admired are architects at their golden age. They are the new growing generation of architects, among which many have studied abroad and some even worked in the Western world. The majority of them cluster in super large cities in China. They draw on the nutrients from cities and cultures and frequently appear in architectural exhibitions and media coverage. Different from the time of experimental architecture, there are a large number of young architects today whose experiments are much more diversified. They don't have a clear common program or a revolutionary slogan; they serve various clients including governments, private developers and individual owners; and they also develop a more flexible and adaptive strategy. 'Critical Pragmatism' could be a kind of description of contemporary individual architects.

The above-said certainly has already shown the aim of this exhibition at Harvard, but the exhibition of Towards a Critical Pragmatism: Contemporary Chinese Architecture has another meaning, namely, it is a tribute paid silently by Li Xiangning to Kenneth Frampton, who is a highly respected British architectural historian in the US and wrote Towards a Critical Regionalism: Six Points for an Architecture of Resistance.

Mr Frampton has taught at the University of London, Princeton University, and Columbia University. When young, he was educated at the Architecture Associate School on architecture and later became a permanent resident of the US. In the 1980s, he witnessed the decline of modern architecture of which he had had a lifelong love and the ostentation of the new-born retro postmodern architecture. Therefore, he was inspired to write Towards a Critical Regionalism, which reshaped the modern architecture in loss. Inspired by this new architectural inspiration, modern architecture was not any more monotonous but worshiped Le Corbusier's Towards a New Architecture as the Bible, becoming more diversified with consideration to the surrounding.

According to Frampton, urban and rural, traditional and scientific, handcrafted and parametric design are seemingly contrary but could coexist. They can not only make modern architecture more diversified, but also make modern life more wonderful. The curator classifies Chinese architecture into the following: cultural architecture, residential architecture, architectural reconstruction, rural architecture, and digital architecture. The classification of design can facilitate deep discussion, study, and assessment of them. Just like what Li Xiangning proposed, the true modernization journey in China has just started, but the future of new architecture in China is full of inspiring possibilities.

Chen Jiayi

Published in Asia Weekly, October 10, 2016.

Index

Photo Credits

Pavilion of Science and Technology at the International Horticultural Exposition 2014 Qingdao

Photography Hou Bowen, Yao Li

Chinese Academy of Oil Painting

Photography An Li, Han Tao, Zhou Zhiyi, He Ziming

China Pavilion for Expo Milano 2015

Photography Sergio_Grazia , Hengzhong_Lv, Roland_Halbe Phot, Hufton+Crow

Fan Zeng Art Gallery

Photography Yao Li

West Village · Basis Yard

Photography Chendu Beisen Culture Development Co.,Ltd., Li Ziqiang, Meng meng, Jiakun Architects

The Waterhouse at South Bund

Photography Derryck Menere, Pedro Pegenaute

Brown sugar workshop

Photography Wang Ziling

Ruralation Shenaoli Library

Photography Yao Li

Harbin Opera House

Photography Adam Mork, Hufton+Crow

Fab-Union Space

Photography Chen Hao, Su Shengliang

All the photos of other projects

Photography Courtesy of the corresponding architects.

Published in Australia in 2018 by

The Images Publishing Group Pty Ltd

Shanghai Office

ABN 89 059 734 431

6 Bastow Place, Mulgrave, Victoria 3170, Australia

Tel: +61 3 9561 5544 Fax: +61 3 9561 4860

books@imagespublishing.com

www.imagespublishing.com

Copyright © The Images Publishing Group Pty Ltd 2018

The Images Publishing Group Reference Number: 1464

 A catalogue record for this book is available from the National Library of Australia

For full Catalogue-in-Publication data, please see the National Library of Australia entry

Title: Towards a Critical Pragmatism: Contemporary Architecture in China

Author: Li Xiangning (Ed.)

ISBN: 9781864707793

Production manager | Group art director: Nicole Boehringer

Senior editor: Gina Tsarouhas

Assisting editor: Bree DeRoche

Printed by Toppan Leefung Packaging & Printing, in Hong Kong/China

IMAGES has included on its website a page for special notices in relation to this and its other publications. Please visit www. imagespublishing.com